The First Crash

The First Crash

LESSONS FROM THE SOUTH SEA BUBBLE

Richard Dale

PRINCETON UNIVERSITY PRESS

PRINCETON AND OXFORD

Copyright © 2004 by Princeton University Press
Published by Princeton University Press, 41 William Street,
Princeton, New Jersey 08540
In the United Kingdom: Princeton University Press,
3 Market Place, Woodstock, Oxfordshire OX20 1SY

Library of Congress Cataloging-in-Publication Data
Dale, Richard
   The first crash : lessons from the South sea bubble / Richard Dale.
      p. cm.
   Includes bibliographical references and index.
   ISBN 0-691-11971-6 (cl : alk. paper)
      1. South Sea Bubble, Great Britain, 1720. 2. Financial crises—
   Great Britain—History—18th century. 3. Capital market—Great
   Britain—History—18th century. 4. Stocks—Prices—Great
   Britain—History—18th century. 5. South Sea Company—
   History. I. Title.

HG6008.D35 2004
332.63'228—dc22   2004044319

British Library Cataloging-in-Publication Data is available

This book has been composed in Sabon

Printed on acid-free paper ∞

www.pup.princeton.edu

Printed in the United States of America

10 9 8 7 6 5 4 3 2 1

To the memory of Peter Carter (1929 to 1983),
an inspirational teacher of history

Contents

Acknowledgements

I would like to thank Professor Charles Goodhart and Professor Forrest Capie for their encouragement after reading drafts of early chapters of this study, as well as several anonymous referees who provided helpful comments and suggestions. I am also grateful to Richard Baggaley of Princeton University Press for showing such enthusiasm for the project from start to finish. I have received valuable assistance from staff at the British Library, Goldsmiths Library, the London Guildhall Library, the Bank of England Reference Library and the House of Lords Record Office. It is thanks to the Courtauld Institute that I was able to track down a portrait of Archibald Hutcheson MP who emerges as the unsung hero of the South Sea Bubble. Finally I must acknowledge a special debt to my wife Niki who acted as a tireless research assistant and without whose support this work would not have been completed.

The First Crash

Introduction

THE YEAR 1720 is a seminal date in financial history for it was in that year that stock markets in London, Paris and Amsterdam, as well as in lesser centres such as Hamburg and Lisbon, experienced a contagious collapse which brought ruin to investors and threatened the stability of governments. This was the first international financial crash and it has become the trigger for an intense debate about the rationality of investors and the very nature of financial markets. Are such markets inherently unstable? Are investors subject to periodic bouts of euphoria and despair—a kind of collective manic depression—that cannot be explained by underlying economic fundamentals? Are the Wall Street crash of 1929, the global crash of 1987, the bursting of the Japanese financial bubble in the 1990s and the subsequent international dot.com boom–bust direct lineal descendents of the 1720 crash? Or can all these episodes be explained, as some economists insist, in terms of investor rationality in the face of uncertainty and external shocks?

The South Sea Bubble has a pivotal role in this debate because it represents the extremity of investor conduct. If ever there was an example of manic herd behaviour this was surely it. By the same token, if the South Sea Bubble can be interpreted as a rational investor response to changing economic prospects and the uncertainties associated with eighteenth century financial innovation, then the rational stock market model remains intact. It is the central purpose of the present study to throw further light on this fundamental issue by focussing first on the opinions of contemporary observers and investors during and preceding the fateful Bubble year, and second on the valuations implicit in share prices and subscriptions. In the course of this exercise it will be necessary to rescue from obscurity a remarkable individual whose contemporary analysis of events leading up to the 1720 crash compares favourably with anything that has been written about it since.

Of course, there are many modern accounts of the South Sea Company and the boom–bust year of 1720. There is a very good general work by Carswell[1] who tells the story of the Bubble in terms of its political background and the personalities involved; there is a classic study by Scott[2] which examines the South Sea Company from the standpoint of corporate finance; there is a scholarly study by Dickson[3] who approaches the

subject from a public finance perspective; and there are some more specialist contributions, notably by Neal,[4] which use formal economic analysis
to explain the rise and fall of South Sea stock. On the other hand, little has
been written about investors' perspective during the Bubble, or the
various attempts by contemporary commentators to value South Sea
shares. The present study attempts to fill this gap by drawing on early
eighteenth century writings to describe and explain investor behaviour at
the time of the Bubble. And it is from such contemporary sources that the
true unsung hero of the South Sea crash emerges. The gentleman
concerned was Archibald Hutcheson, Member of Parliament for Hastings, a professional lawyer and self-taught economist, who may fairly be
described as the father of investment analysis. Hutcheson's meticulous
valuations of the South Sea Company demonstrated an alarming divergence between fundamental values and market prices in the run-up to the
Bubble, but his warnings about the inevitability of a crash were ignored
until it was much too late.

Historians of the Bubble have also ignored important clues to investors'
motivation provided by the traded prices of South Sea subscription
receipts. The new data provides conclusive evidence that in 1720 investors
did not conform to the rational model favoured by many financial economists. The analysis shows that investors lost their bearings to the point
where prices of directly substitutable financial instruments, representing
equivalent claims on the South Sea Company's dividends and assets,
became wildly out of line with each other. As described below, it was as
if the investing public were engaged in a familiar eighteenth century lottery
game, viewing each successive draw (share issue) as offering the prospect of
ever larger lottery prizes (capital gains). Finally, this study treats the
Bubble, not as a self-standing episode in English financial history, but as
one, admittedly extreme, example of the way in which investment markets
may behave anywhere, at any time. In brief, the argument here is that the
events of 1720 offer insights into the nature of financial markets that, being
independent of place and time, deserve to be considered by today's investors everywhere. The first historian of the Bubble, Adam Anderson, who
was formerly a clerk at the South Sea Company, expressed similar thoughts
nearly two hundred and fifty years ago:

> The unaccountable frenzy in stocks and projects of this year 1720 may by some
> be thought to have taken up too much room in this work: but we are persuaded
> that others of superior judgement, will approve of the perpetuating ... the
> remembrance thereof, as a warning to after ages.[5]

The question of whether financial markets are subject to periodic bouts of irrationality, as Adam Anderson implies, is a crucial issue for investors, businesses and policy makers. If the irrationality argument is accepted, investors need to be aware that prevailing market prices may not represent fair value, contrary to what efficient markets theory would suggest. Businesses may be misled into harmful investment decisions based on inflated market prices for their stock. And macro-economic policy makers may need to intervene, if only by "leaning against the wind", since bubbles, when they unwind, can lead to economic dislocation, lost output and amplified business fluctuations. The rationality/irrationality issue is therefore centre-stage at the present time and one of the main purposes of this study is to contribute to a better understanding of the subject by exploring the murky waters of early eighteenth century finance.

The story of the South Sea Bubble unfolded in a social environment very different from today's. In 1700, people's lives were overshadowed by the prospect of early death, the likelihood of serious illness and the vagaries of armed conflict both at home and abroad. Life expectation at birth was probably under 20 years for those born in the late seventeenth century, which helps to explain the youthfulness of the population—over half being under the age of 21. Smallpox, typhoid, typhus, dysentery and tuberculosis were rife and incurable, while the memory of the Great Plague was still burned into the collective consciousness. War with foreign powers was not so much the exception as the rule: from the Glorious Revolution in 1688 to the signing of the Treaty of Utrecht in 1713 England enjoyed only four years of peace, the intervening years being dominated first by the Nine Years War (1688–97) and then by the War of Spanish Succession (1702–13). Finally, there was the ever-present danger of an invasion led by the Pretender and renewed civil war between supporters of the old monarchy and the new.

The brevity and uncertainty of early eighteenth century life no doubt shaped people's attitude to money. A career committed to the laborious acquisition of wealth over time was perhaps less appealing than taking a chance on some get-rich-quick commercial venture. One manifestation of this "short-termism" was the passion for gambling displayed by all classes of society, which successive governments exploited through state-run lotteries that raised funds for the war effort. The popular addiction to gambling was also reflected in the burgeoning life insurance industry.[6] True, life policies might be taken out to reduce economic uncertainty; families could be protected in the event of a breadwinner's death and creditors could and did insure the lives of their debtors. But more often

life insurance was used to gamble on lives in which the policy holder had
no economic interest, a practice eventually prohibited by the Gambling
Act of 1774. Such third parties might be complete strangers or persons in
the public eye (e.g., Walpole, the Pretender or Admiral Byng when standing trial for dereliction of duty) in which case premium rates would
fluctuate with the fortunes of the individuals concerned.[7]

Some sought to justify gambling on the grounds that life itself was little
more than a game of chance:

> And thus by accident Events, Poverty and Riches are transplanted and shift
> their seat; and a Blast of Wind, than which nothing is more uncertain, drives
> good fortune from one hand to another. And since casualties dispose of things
> at this arbitrary rate, since the world is but a kind of lottery, why should we
> Gamesters be grudged the drawing of a Prize?[8]

The original South Sea project, a high-risk venture aimed at tapping the
riches of the New World, was designed to appeal to the gaming instincts
of the age. Furthermore, the prime initiator and executor of the project,
John Blunt, was a pioneer in the field of state lotteries and the techniques
he used to promote the South Sea Company among investors were those
he had learned in the lottery business.

Blunt and his collaborators had close connections with the new breed of
stock jobbers or "Exchange Alley men" who were often accused of engaging
in dubious financial practices. A parliamentary report of 1696 referred to the
"pernicious art of stock-jobbing" and in 1701 Defoe wrote a pamphlet
entitled *The Villainy of Stock Jobbers Detected*. Defoe subsequently accused
these gentlemen of standing ready "as occasion offers, and profit presents, to
stock-jobb the nation, cozen the Parliament, ruffle the Bank, run up and
down stocks, and put the dice upon the whole town".[9] The low public
esteem of the stock-jobbing community appears to have persisted judging
by the definition of a stock jobber given in Dr Johnson's Dictionary: "A low
wretch who gets money by buying and selling shares in the funds".[10]

The South Sea Bubble was very much a London phenomenon. In 1700,
the population of the metropolis, at well over half a million, exceeded that of
all other English towns taken together, while the second largest town,
Norwich, boasted a population of only 30,000. London had been rebuilt
after the Great Fire of 1666 and neat rows of regulation houses now replaced
the half-timbered properties with overhanging upper stories that had proved
such a fire hazard. At the same time, the main city streets had been widened
to 35–40 feet and the side streets to a minimum of 14 feet, sufficient to allow
two drays to pass. However, the central focus of London's financial district,

the Royal Exchange, retained its traditional features when rebuilt to its original specification after the Great Fire. In the sixteenth century, Lombard Street had become the venue for London's commodity, money and ship-broking markets, but the inconvenience of trading in a narrow through street exposed to the elements led to the opening of the first Royal Exchange in 1570. This magnificent building, sited between Lombard Street and Corn-hill, enabled traders to conduct their business in an open courtyard secluded from the street and surrounded by an arcaded gallery that offered protection from the weather. Above the gallery were boutiques selling luxury goods and below there were vaults for storing merchandise. Securities trading was originally conducted at the Royal Exchange but by 1700 the stock jobbers had overflowed into the neighbouring coffee houses and streets, collectively known as Exchange Alley.

London had its own highly efficient internal communications network based on newspapers and the coffee house grapevine. In contrast, road transport was poor so that a journey from London to Newcastle took nine days ("god willing", as the advertisements said), while travelling from London to Carlisle, Chester or Exeter would take the best part of a week. The relatively easy channel crossing, on the other hand, meant that Amsterdam or Paris could be reached in two days or so, weather permitting. The result was that London's business community and finan-cial market were more closely linked to the Continent and its financial centres than to the English provinces, as reflected in the prominence given to Continental news by the London press.

The political landscape of early eighteenth century England mirrored, to a large extent, divisions in society. The two major political parties, the Whigs and the Tories, were differentiated first by their respective economic inter-ests, the Tories representing the traditional landed interest while Whigs were to be found among city merchants and "moneyed men"; second by their loyalties, the Tories favouring the old Catholic monarchy and the Whigs the Hanoverian succession; and finally by their ideologies, the Tories harking back to the divine right of Kings and the Whigs supporting personal free-dom, the rights of the people and a constitutional monarchy. In the context of this political divide, the South Sea Company was sponsored by a Tory government in order to counterbalance two powerful Whig interests—the Bank of England and the East India Company—that dominated the City of London's financial markets.

The two political parties did not, however, reflect the deepest social divi-sion, that between rich and poor, because the poor were disenfranchised, only one in six adult males being entitled to vote. The annual income of poor to middling families was between £15 and £50 whereas the merchant class would typically earn between £200 and £400 and leave fortunes of £5000–15,000. The great merchant princes like Sir Theodore Janssen, a director of the South Sea Company, together with landed aristocrats, members of the peerage and holders of the great offices of state (who enjoyed perks far above their salaries) would have incomes of over £5000 and leave estates of £100,000 or more. Translating such sums into today's money is hazardous but a multiple of 100 provides a crude guide.

Clearly, the social and political conditions prevailing in London at the time of the Bubble were very different from today's. Yet Exchange Alley was blind to distinctions of social status, gender or creed and at the height of the stock market boom, Londoners of both sexes and all classes were caught up in the speculative euphoria, as depicted by Alexander Pope:

> At length corruption, like a general flood,
> Shall deluge all, and av'rice creeping on
> (So long by watchful ministers withstood)
> Spread, like a low-born mist, and blot the sun.
> Statesman and patriot ply alike the stocks,
> Peeress and butler share alike the box;
> The judge shall job, the bishops bite the town,
> And mighty Dukes pack cards for half-a-crown;
> See Britain sunk in Lucre's sordid charms.[11]

NOTES

1. See Carswell (1993).
2. Scott (1912).
3. See Dickson (1967).
4. Neal (1990).
5. Anderson (1764: 123).
6. By the end of the seventeenth century life insurance was illegal almost everywhere in Europe except England, partly because it was considered morally objectionable to put a price on an individual's life. In England, however, the business flourished during the early eighteenth century, the Royal Exchange and London Assurances offering short-term (usually one year) policies at a flat rate of 5 percent for every £100 insured, regardless of age. See Daston (1988); Clark (1999).
7. Clark (1999: 49–50).
8. Collier (1713); cited in Daston (1988: 149).
9. Defoe (1719) in Francis (1849: 377).
10. Johnson (1755).
11. Pope in Bateson (1951: 102).

CHAPTER ONE

Coffee Houses, the Press and Misinformation

THE SOUTH SEA BUBBLE coincided with the rapid development of financial markets in the late seventeenth and early eighteenth centuries. This period saw the introduction of an active secondary market in both debt and equity securities, the appearance of a new type of financial intermediary known as the "stock-jobber", and the emergency of a breed of "monied men" whose recently amassed City fortunes were viewed both with disdain and envy by the landed classes. But before considering the trading practices and techniques of the new class of financiers, it is necessary to understand the communications network on which their operations were based.

In the absence of Reuters, Bloombergs and other screen-based information services, eighteenth century traders and investors had to rely very largely on the coffee house and the press for information about investments and market movements. These two sources of information were interdependent, since journalists obtained much of their news from the coffee house, and one of the main attractions of the latter were the newspapers provided to its clientele.

COFFEE HOUSES

London's coffee houses proliferated in the sixteenth century, one pamphleteer remarking that "Coffee and the Commonwealth came in together". By 1700, there were over 2000 coffee houses in London, representing a revolution in drinking and social habits that did not, however, go unchallenged.[1] In 1673, a petition was presented arguing for the prohibition of tea and coffee in favour of beverages using home-grown barley, malt and wheat; in 1674 "The Women's Petition Against Coffee" complained that coffee made men idle and impotent; and in December 1675 a Proclamation of Charles II called for the suppression of all coffee houses (whether

selling coffee, chocolate, sherbert or tea) on the grounds that "many
tradesmen and others, do herein mis-spend much of their time, which
might and probably would be employed in and about their lawful calling
and affairs; but also for that in such houses ... divers false, malicious and
scandalous reports are devised and spread abroad to the defamation of his
Majesty's Government ...".[2] The royal proclamation was issued on 29
December but had to be recalled eleven days later (with face-saving licensing restrictions) so great was the anger of men of all parties and social
classes at the prospect of being deprived of their accustomed haunts. The
episode marks an important victory for freedom of speech, bearing in
mind that prior to 1695 there was no free press.

In time, individual coffee houses came to be associated with a particu-
lar clientele or profession. There were houses for literary "wits" (notably
Wills in Covent Garden), learned scholars and scientists (the Grecian in
Devereux Court), politicians (Whigs at the St James, Tories at the Cocoa-
Tree, near Pall Mall), lawyers (Nandos in Fleet Street) and clergy (Child's
in St Paul's). Similarly, for the commercial classes there were specialist
coffee houses catering for, inter alia, marine underwriters (Lloyds in
Lombard Street), life insurance (Tom's in Exchange Alley) regional trad-
ing interests (The Jamaica, Jerusalem and Pennsilvania in Exchange
Alley) and, as discussed in more detail below, stock-jobbers (Garraways
and Jonathan's in Exchange Alley).

The London coffee houses fulfilled several important functions. First and
foremost, they were a source of political, economic and financial information. Indeed, prior to the liberation of the press through the expiry of the
Licencing Act in 1695, they were perhaps the main source of news: several
houses made their own news sheets available to patrons, much to the
chagrin of the government which tried to suppress even this restricted
form of "publication". In the words of the seventeenth century ditty:[3]

You that delight in Wit and Mirth
And long to hear such News
As comes from all Parts of the Earth ...
Go hear it at a Coffee House
It cannot but be true.

There's nothing done in all the World
From Monarch to the Mouse
But every Day or Night 'tis hurl'd
Into the Coffee House

Plate 1 A coffee-house scene circa 1700. Copyright The Trustees of The British Museum.

So great a Universitie,
I think there ne're was any;
In which you may a Scholar be
For spending of a Penny

After 1695, the newspaper industry began to flourish and the coffee houses responded by providing an ever wider range of publications for their clientele. The coffee house then became not just a place of discourse but a library where journals could be studied by a news-hungry public. The foreign visitor Saussure observed in 1726:

> What attracts enormously in these coffee houses are the gazettes and other public papers. All Englishmen are great newsmongers. Workmen habitually begin the day by going to coffee-rooms in order to read the latest news. I have often seen shoeblacks and other persons of that class club together to purchase a farthing paper. Nothing is more entertaining than hearing men of this class discussing politics and topics of interest concerning royalty. You often see an Englishman taking a treaty of peace more to heart than he does his own affairs.[4]

The proliferation of newspapers evidently led the coffee house proprietors to agree among themselves to limit their subscriptions. A new paper called the Projector reported in 1721 that:

> ... the author of this paper being inform'd that it cou'd not, tho' given, be suffer'd to lye on the coffee-house tables had inquired, and finds that the coffee-house men have met in form, and agreed to receive no new papers. The confederates in excuse pretend expence, that papers given at first, are not always given, and that some coffee-men are at £150 per ann charge or more for papers of all kinds.[5]

Subsequently tensions between the coffee houses and the newspaper proprietors developed into a full-blown confrontation. In 1728, the coffee men complained that the cost of subscribing to newspapers was "more than the trade and profits of one half of the Coffee-Men will allow", while the newspaper proprietors took the view that the availability of news-papers was one of the chief attractions of coffee houses.[6] In the ensuing pamphlet war, the coffee men accused the newspaper men of harassing customers and eavesdropping on their private conversations:

> The same persons hang and loiter about the Public Offices, like house breakers, waiting for an interview with some little Clerk, or a Conference with a Door-keeper, in order to come at a little news, for which the fee is a shilling, or a pint of wine.[7]

The coffee house men also complained about the cost (put at £10–20 per annum) of subscribing to the growing number of newspapers which they felt obliged to take in for the benefit of their customers. Finally, they argued that in providing a readership for the newspapers, the coffee houses indirectly contributed to the papers' advertising revenues, which, in the case of the Daily Post for example, they estimated at £3 15s for a single day's notices.[8]

Based on these complaints the coffee house representatives distributed a circular to all coffee house men in London and Westminster outlining a proposal for setting up their own newspapers.[9] The paper would be published twice daily, morning and evening, at a price of $1\frac{1}{2}$d. The business would be funded by coffee house men (only) who were asked to subscribe 1 guinea for this purpose. Every subscriber would put up a notice in his coffee house desiring customers to acquaint the owner of newsworthy events. These offerings would then be written up and collected twice per day for compilation and editing at the newspaper's office. Coffee men who introduced advertising to the paper would be remunerated at a rate of 6d per advertisement. The break-even circulation of the paper was estimated at around 300 and beyond this level any profits were to be distributed to subscribers.

This unprecedented challenge to the newspaper industry elicited an immediate response from newspaper proprietors.[10] They ridiculed the idea that coffee house men, whom they characterised as illiterate and servile tradesmen of the lowest kind, were capable of producing a readable newspaper. It was also pointed out that the proposed method of gathering news from customers would destroy the privacy of coffee house conversation. Is it seriously to be understood, the pamphleteer asks, that the coffee men should become a "vehicle of Publick Intelligence, and that whatever [customers] shall think fit to talk among themselves, he will take great Care to furnish them with next Day, for their entertainment, at Second Hand, after it has passed the thick Clouds of his dull Apprehension and the Refining Fire of his Compiler's Digestion".[11]

On the substantive economics of the two businesses, the newspaper proprietors came up with detailed figures.[12] They pointed out that the coffee houses had raised their benchmark price for a dish of coffee first from 1d to $1\frac{1}{2}$d, allegedly to cover an increase in the price of imported coffee, and subsequently from $1\frac{1}{2}$d to 2d to take account of the stamp duty imposed on newspapers and the associated $\frac{1}{2}$d rise in newspaper prices. The newspapers, for their part, had to pay out $\frac{1}{2}$d on stamp duty and $\frac{1}{2}$d on distribution costs, leaving them only $\frac{1}{2}$d (excluding advertising revenues) from their $1\frac{1}{2}$d cover price to defray the costs of printing, paper, etc. The newspaper proprietors also argued persuasively that the coffee houses, far from doing them a favour by providing newspapers to customers, were depriving them of subscription revenues by allowing multiple readership of a single newspaper.

In a coup de grâce, the newspaper proprietors' response to the coffee house men culminated in a proposal to set up their own chain of coffee houses. These would undercut the established coffee men by charging only $1\frac{1}{2}$d for a dish of coffee and they would hang a sign outside stating "All the Papers taken in Here".[13] Threat had been met with counter-threat. In the event there was a stand off and neither threat appears to have been realized but the episode illustrates the pivotal role of coffee houses in news gathering and news dissemination.

In addition to their role as a source of information, the London coffee houses also formed part of the delivery and collection system for the Penny Post, which was introduced as a private venture in 1680 before being displaced by a government service two years later. The Post Office directed those who wrote letters on Holydays "to leave them at those Coffee Houses, known to be appointed by the Office, that they may be collected and delivered in due time ...".[14]

It seems that alongside the official postal service, there was an informal private post developed by the coffee houses themselves. According to Lilly, the historian of London coffee houses, bags to receive letters destined for overseas were openly hung in coffee houses where the coffee men had made arrangements for onward despatch in the care of ship-masters. For many years these private arrangements were evidently more efficient than those of the Post Office.[15]

Closely related to their role as post offices, coffee houses provided the equivalent of newspaper box numbers. Lost property advertisements, in particular, made use of this service; for instance, the Beadle at Goldsmiths Hall regularly listed lost and stolen items stating the amount of reward payable on a "no questions asked" basis for return of the items to a named coffee house.

The London coffee house was also a place of business. The great trading companies (the East India, Hudson's Bay, African, Russian and Levant Companies) all made use of coffee houses for their meetings, as did the livery companies. And at a time when few merchants had their own offices (although they might frequent the Royal Exchange), the coffee house became an informal office for transacting one-to-one business. Indeed, merchants, doctors, factors and other service providers would advertise their availability at named coffee houses where they would keep regular hours for business purposes. As one observer remarked in 1721, coffee houses were "extremely convenient. You have all Manner of News there: You have a good fire, which you may sit by as long as you please: You have a Dish of Coffee, you meet your friends for the Transaction of Business, and all for a Penny, if you don't care to spend more."[16]

The renowned story of Lloyds Coffee House shows how the provision of commercial information to a specialised clientele tended to generate business activity. After opening near the docks in 1687, Edward Lloyd moved his coffee house to Lombard Street in 1691 where, five years later, he began to publish "Lloyds List" of ship arrivals and departures. Backed by its mercantile and shipping connections, Lloyds coffee house soon became the headquarters for marine "underwriters" who wrote their names under the terms of the insurance contract to denote their acceptance as risk-takers. Ship auctions, too, were conducted with regularity at Lloyds. Such auctions, like those for a wide variety of goods held at coffee houses all over London, were typically advertised as being "by the candle", that is, while an inch of candle burned.

In summary, the coffee houses of late seventeenth and early eighteenth century London could be viewed as an amalgam of open-plan office, internet café, post office, pub and newspaper library. It was in this environment that securities trading began in a few specialised coffee houses in Exchange Alley, a development that was given further impetus when, in 1698, dealers in stock were removed from the more august surroundings of the Royal Exchange.

John Houghton, writing in 1694, tells as that "the Monied Man goes among the brokers (which are chiefly upon the Exchange, and at Jonathan's Coffee House, sometimes at Garraway's and at some other Coffee Houses), and asks how stocks go? ...".[17] Other coffee houses mentioned in connection with trading in stocks are Sam's in Exchange Alley, and Powell's and the Rainbow in Cornhill, but Jonathan's and Garroway's were evidently the main trading venues at the time of the South Sea Bubble, Jonathan's achieving more elevated status half a century later as the London Stock Exchange. Writing some forty years after the Bubble, Thomas Mortimer, author of the best-selling text "Every Man His Own Broker", describes how those wishing to deal in stocks might make use of the facilities provided by Jonathan's coffee house. "Every person who enters Jonathan's to do any business there pays 6d at the bar, for which he is entitled to firing, ink and paper, and a small cup of chocolate; and if he understands the business, is as a Broker for that day (at least for his own affairs) as the best."[18]

THE NEWSPAPER INDUSTRY

In addition to reliance on the coffee house communications network, financial markets in the early eighteenth century were dependent on the information and commentary provided by a vibrant press. The emergence of an independent newspaper industry was made possible by the expiry of the Licensing Act of 1695, which had effectively suppressed all news publication other than the government's own *London Gazette* (which has survived to this day). Thereafter, London newspapers proliferated, with a bewilderingly rapid turnover of titles and proprietors.

However, two severe constraints on press freedom persisted: Parliament refused to allow publication of its own proceedings and the laws of libel and sedition could be (and were) used against the government's opponents.[19] The judicial view was expressed by Lord Chief Justice Holt in 1704 during the trial of John Tutchin for criticising in his *Observer* the administration of naval affairs:

> ... if people should not be called to account for possessing the people with an ill opinion of government, no government can exist. For it is very necessary for all governments that the people should have a good opinion of it.[20]

The libel laws, which applied equally to authors and printers, led to several journalistic devices designed to limit the danger of prosecution. Commentary was generally anonymous, pseudonymous or written under the newspaper's name; references to individuals might be partially blanked (e.g., "Mr St-le"); and the literary style became deliberately obscure. On this last point it has been noted that "the taut phraseology of Defoe gave way to a verbosity which aimed primarily at wrapping up the meaning sufficiently to avoid the possibility of arrest."[21] Finally, Dutch newspaper reports on English affairs, being free from legal threat and therefore often more comprehensive, would sometimes be reproduced in the English press as foreign news.[22]

The demand for newspapers reflected rapid growth in nationwide literacy rates, which for adult males is estimated to have reached around 45 percent in 1675 compared with 25 percent in 1600 (with literacy rates among women perhaps 30 percent lower).[23] Furthermore, in London it may be supposed that literacy was considerably higher than in the rest of the country. The illiterate could also have access to newspaper information, thanks to the practice of reading papers aloud in public places such as coffee houses. As one observer remarked:

> ... the greatest part of the people do not read books, most of them cannot read at all, but they will gather together about one that can read, and listen to an Observator or Review (as I have seen them in the streets) ...[24]

Against this background, London could, in the early 1700s, boast of at least 18 newspapers ranging from daily to weekly, with a total of 55 separate issues per week and a combined weekly circulation of around 44,000.[25] Allowing for the fact that circulation figures considerably understated readership (by a factor of as much as 10 or 20 according to some estimates), it is clear that a significant proportion of London's 674,000 population were regular newspaper readers. This should be borne in mind when considering the large numbers of Londoners drawn into the South Sea Bubble and related speculations.

By 1720—the fateful Bubble year—there were a variety of newspapers of differing frequency, political persuasion and style. Some, like the *Flying Post* and the *Post Boy*, were orientated towards the provinces, being published at times to coincide with the mails out of London. The *Daily Courant*, England's first daily newspaper, focussed particularly on foreign news, having privileged access to official sources. The *London Gazette*, the government's own organ, was published on Thursdays and Saturdays; it consisted entirely of news and advertisements, enjoyed a reputation for caution and reliability, and had a peacetime circulation of around 2500 (much larger in times of war). There were pro-government Whig papers such as the *Flying Post*, opposition Jacobite papers such as *Mist's Weekly Journal* or *Saturday Post* and at least one independent (opposition) Whig paper, the *London Journal*. Political affiliations were particularly important in the aftermath of the South Sea scandal when some papers, such as the *London Journal* (before it was bought out by government interests) sought to fix responsibility for the financial disaster on the ministry.

By 1720, the South Sea Company had established an effective communications network, based largely on the London press, to inform the general public and make announcements to shareholders. While the Company was served by a team of salaried messengers to conduct its daily business, announcements relating to new share issues and conversion operations appeared as press advertisements and were also posted on the doors of South Sea House and at the Royal Exchange. The newspapers favoured by the Company were the *London Gazette*, the *Daily Courant*, the *Daily Post* and the *Evening Post*. From the Court minutes, it is clear that the detailed terms of each new share issue, including the price, were determined by the Court of Directors the day before issue and advertised in the press on the day of the subscription.[26] One Court meeting held in the morning even resolved to place advertisements (regarding subscribers' unpaid calls) "in all papers tonight and in tomorrow's Courant and on the Exchange and on the doors of this House ...".[27] Same day communication with the investing public was therefore possible.

London newspapers typically cost a penny—coincidentally the same price as a dish of coffee house brew and the letter post. They could be bought from news and pamphlet vendors known as "mercuries", who were often the wives or widows of printers, or from semi-destitute hawkers who sold copies on the street. Some papers such as the *Evening Post* also designated certain coffee houses as their sales outlets.

The general press gave increasing attention to financial news and commentary from the end of the seventeenth century and by 1720 stock prices were being quoted in several papers including the *Weekly Journal*, the *London Journal*, the *Daily Courant*, the *Evening Post*, the *Postman* and *Postboy*. It is also interesting to note that valuations of South Sea Company stock of varying sophistication appeared in several papers during the Bubble period, including the *Weekly Journal*, the *Theatre*, the *Flying Post* and the *Whitehall Evening Post*.

Detailed financial information was available from more specialised publications. Whiston's *The Merchants Remembrancer* contained weekly stock prices as early as 1681 and ten years later John Houghton began to publish weekly stock prices because, as he explained "altho they that live at London, may, every Noon and Night on working days, go to Garraway's Coffee House, and see what prices the Actions bear of most Companies trading in Joynt-Stocks, yet for those whose Occasions permit not there to see, they may be satisfied once a Week how it is ...."[28]

Houghton's service was soon discontinued but in 1697, "The Course of the Exchange" appeared under the name of "John Castaing, Broker, at his Office of Jonathan's Coffee-House". Castaing was a Huguenot who arrived from France in the 1680s and worked as a broker on the Royal Exchange during the 1690s. He saw the commercial need for authoritative and up-to-date price information and his twice weekly publication covering exchange rates as well as stock and commodity prices soon established a reputation for accuracy: it was cited as evidence before the courts (to determine the price of South Sea stock in 1720) and became at a later date the official price list of the London Stock Exchange. The *Course of the Exchange* gave daily prices of stocks for the past three days in each issue and was delivered every Tuesday and Friday within the City of London for an all-in subscription price of 3s per quarter. A competitor publication, Freke's *Price List*, was launched in 1714 but failed to survive beyond 1722,[29] although Freke's prices were in some respects more comprehensive than Castaing's, as noted below.

The development of both an independent press and more specialised information services complemented the opportunities for informal news gathering afforded by London's network of coffee houses. This was the communications system that supported the growth of financial markets and which, in 1720, fed the frenzied trading of speculators in South Sea stock. It did, however, differ in two important respects from the news services that support today's financial markets. First, there could be significant time lags between the occurrence of a newsworthy event and its dissemination and also between an alleged or rumoured event and its verification (or contradiction). Second, information was not received simultaneously by all market participants, so that there were "insiders" and "outsiders".

News from abroad was, of course, particularly vulnerable to long delays. The London newspapers gave surprisingly ample coverage of foreign affairs but even the reports from Continental financial centres were several days out of date. Furthermore, as the *Tatler* observed, there could be an information blackout "when a West wind blows for a fortnight, keeping news on the other side of the Channel."[30] It should also be recalled that, nearly a century after the South Sea Bubble, it took three days for an official report of the Battle of Waterloo to be reported to the Secretary of State in London, and only a few hours less for Nathan Rothschild to receive private information of the English victory.[31]

At the time of the South Sea Bubble both the "Funds" (the market in government debt) and the stock market were highly sensitive to foreign news. War with Spain was a constant threat and there was always the prospect that a successful attempt by the Jacobite Pretender to claim the throne of England could be followed by the repudiation of government debt obligations. To take but one example, a report (later discredited) of Jacobite disturbances in Scotland evidently prompted a 10 percent one-day fall in South Sea stock in February 1720.[32]

This market environment created a strong demand for news but it also presented both opportunities and incentives for rumour-mongering and false reports. Some misinformation might be harmless enough. For instance, we are told that at the height of the South Sea mania a regular service of fishing smacks brought news from London for the Amsterdam bourse whose investors were speculating in South Sea stock. Small vessels would be sent out to meet the English boats before speeding back to harbour with the latest news. But apparently some took a turn around the outside of the harbour and, having invented plausible gossip, sold it to the crowd of speculators.[33]

More sinister were the efforts of some stock-jobbers and speculators to manipulate the market through deliberately misleading reports. Joseph de la Vega, in his classic description of operations on the Amsterdam Stock exchange at the end of the seventeenth century,[34] offers many examples of such deceptions: a syndicate of "bears" might disseminate false news by having a letter dropped at the right spot;[35] and false reports might be spread of ships running aground, and shortfalls in the value of ships' freight—all this affecting the price of the East India Company's stock.[36] Daniel Defoe (no friend of Exchange Alley, it must be said) also describes a number of alleged stock market manipulations in his Anatomy of Exchange Alley written in 1719. In one case, false reports were disseminated to the effect that the Pretender had been taken captive in Milan, thereby pushing up stock prices to the advantage of the perpetrators.[37] According to Defoe sham reports, although commonplace, were generally discovered to be false by the end of the trading day; in this instance, however, the trick "held us near a fortnight in a firm persuasion of the thing".[38] In another case, a false report of an invasion from Spain (which might or might not have been deliberate) enabled those who had bought options on stock to cash in at the expense of those who had written (sold) the contracts.[39] Sir Josiah Child, "that original of stock-jobbing", is identified by Defoe as a particular culprit when it came to spreading false reports:

> There are those who tell us that letters have been ordered, by private management, to be written from the East Indies, with an account of the loss of ships which have been arrived there, and the arrival of ships lost; war with the Great Mogul, when they have been in perfect tranquility; and of peace with the Great Mogul, when he was come down against the factory of Bengal with one hundred thousand men—just as it was thought proper to calculate those rumours for the raising and falling of the stock, and when it was for this purpose to buy cheap, or to sell dear.[40]

Another story of deliberate misinformation with strong anti-semitic overtones is told by Ashton in his History of Gambling in England. During the reign of Queen Anne a man appeared, galloping from Kensington to the City, ordering the turnpike to be thrown open for him, and shouting loudly that he bore the news of Queen Anne's death. "This sad message flew far and wide, and dire was its effect in the City. The funds fell at once, but Manasseh Lopez and the Jews bought all they could, and reaped the benefit when the fraud was discovered."[41]

It may be objected that these stories are no more than unproven allegations, although de la Vega, unlike Defoe, was a stock-jobbing insider who knew the trade. Certainly, there was a widespread perception that stock-jobbing and rumour-mongering were synonymous. This view was supported by another contemporary commentator who refers to "irregular and deceitful methods of growing rich" through stock-jobbing, methods which "have been (sometimes) maintain'd and carry'd on, partly by spreading false reports concerning the public affairs, either Foreign or Domestic, in such a manner, as may influence the Buyers and Sellers of Stock".[42]

Some years later, Thomas Mortimer, in his text on stock-broking, devotes many pages to the subject of misinformation and in this connection describes the underhand activities of "servitors" (junior assistants to brokers to be found loitering around Jonathan's), one of whose functions is "to make and carry paragraphs of false intelligence to the printers of the public papers", evidently with the inducement of a bribe.[43]

The literature of the time also reflects this general perception of securities trading. For instance, Susannah Centlivre, in her play, *A Bold Stroke for a Wife*, portrays a scene in Jonathan's Coffee House in which self-serving disinformation (concerning here a Spanish seige) provides the background to trading in stocks.[44] Similarly, in the 1720 play, *Exchange Alley*, traders buy and sell stock in the Flying Ships Company, buffeted by contradictory news reports of the Russian czar, initially describing his imminent death, then his appearance at sea with a thousand warships.[45] The clear implication is that one of the traders ("Mississippi") is manipulating the news for his own benefit.

We can be fairly sure that the market abuses which contemporary opinion identified were endemic to securities trading in this period. Security prices were highly sensitive to extraneous events, especially those originating from abroad; there could be a considerable lapse of time before such events were reported (or before false reports could be discredited) in the press or through the coffee shop network; and there was no regulatory oversight of market practices. In such a regime there were ample opportunities and powerful incentives to manipulate the news, and thereby market prices. It was in this unstable and rumour-filled trading environment that the extraordinary stock market events of 1720 unfolded.

NOTES

1. See generally Robinson (1893); Lillywhite (1963).
2. Robinson (1893: 166).
3. Anon (1667).

4. Cited in Hunter (1990: 174).

5. Black (1987: 20).

6. Harris (1938: 30–31).

7. Anon (n.d.) *The Case of the Coffee House Men*, p. 7.

8. Anon (n.d.) *The Case of the Coffee House Men*, p. 16.

9. Circular dated 6 November 1728. See Anon (n.d.) *The Case of the Coffee House Men*, pp. 21–24.

10. In the pamphlet war between coffee-house men and newspaper proprietors, each side accused the other of sly business practices. It was claimed, for instance, that in some coffee houses when you called the coffee boy to pay your bill he would ask you to pay at the bar which would be tended by young girls. These alluring "gypsies" would all too frequently (it was said) tempt gentlemen customers into transactions of a different kind. Anon (n.d.) *The Case Between the Proprietors of Newspapers and the Coffee-Men of London and Westminster Fairly Stated*, p. 13.

11. Anon (1729: 5).

12. Anon (1729: 14–16).

13. Anon (1729: 18).

14. Lillywhite (1963: 19).

15. Lillywhite (1963: 21).

16. Cited in Ewald (1956: 8).

17. Houghton (13 July 1694: 1).

18. Mortimer (1762: 72, footnote).

19. Libel meant publishing anything with the malicious intent of causing a breach of the peace, while sedition involved publication of anything which would incite disaffection against the sovereign, Parliament or government, or lead people to alter Church or State by unlawful means.

20. Cited in Hanson (1936: 2).

21. Hanson (1936: 25).

22. Harris (1938: 159).

23. See Hunter (1990: 66–67, 72–73).

24. Cited in Ewald (1956: 5).

25. Circulation appears to have been checked but not substantially reduced by the $\frac{1}{2}$–1d stamp tax that Parliament imposed in August 1712 in response to a request by Queen Anne for a remedy for the prevailing "scandalous libels".

26. See Minutes of the Court of Directors of the South Sea Company, British Library.

27. Minutes of Court Meeting held September 29, 1720.

28. Houghton (6 April 1692).

29. For further details see Neal (1988: 163–178); McCusker (1986: 205–231).

30. Cited in Ewald (1956: 15).

31. News from far-off corners of the world could take weeks or even months to be reported; it is a sobering thought that it took nearly a year for Captain Cook's death in Hawaii in June 1779 to be reported in London, after the letter carrying the news had been dispatched from Kamchatka to St Petersburg and thence to Berlin and London. Hough (1995: 439).

32. *Daily Post* (16 January 1720).

33. Wilson (1941: 104).
34. Joseph de la Vega, born around 1650, dabbled in business and the stock exchange in Amsterdam while also engaging in literary pursuits. His classic work on stock exchange speculation, *Confusion de Confusiones*, was published in 1688. A modern translation, referred to here, is to be found in Fridson (1996: 147–211).
35. De la Vega (1688) in Fridson (1996: 195).
36. De la Vega (1688) in Fridson (1996: 206).
37. Defoe (1719) in Francis (1849: 360 ff.).
38. Defoe (1719) in Francis (1849: 366).
39. Defoe (1719) in Francis (1849: 382).
40. Defoe (1719) in Francis (1849: 365).
41. Ashton (1898: 247–248). Interestingly, a century later, while England was at war with France, some individuals were convicted of having spread false rumours of the death of Napoleon in order to profit from a rise in the value of government securities. Cited in Banner (1998: 52).
42. Gordon (1724: 3).
43. Mortimer (1762: 73–74).
44. Reproduced in Dickson (1967: 503–505).
45. Reproduced in Banner (1998: 50–52).

CHAPTER TWO

Exchange Alley and the Evolution of London's Securities Markets

THE SOUTH SEA BUBBLE erupted during the early development of the London stock market and could not have occurred in the absence of an active market in corporate securities issues. Furthermore, the financing activities of the South Sea Company were intimately linked with the management of government debt and the evolving market for government obligations ("the Funds"). This chapter describes the key features of both markets in order to provide a fuller understanding of the origins of the South Sea Company and the events of 1720.

THE MARKET IN GOVERNMENT DEBT

The development of the government debt market preceded the emergence of a market in corporate securities (whether debt or equity) and government issues continued to dominate trading in securities during the early part of the eighteenth century. By the time of the Bubble the national debt exceeded £50 million, holders of government debt were estimated at around 40,000, and there was a considerable secondary market turnover in government securities.[1]

In order to appreciate the various difficulties associated with funding the government's borrowing needs, it is necessary to understand that government debt was not at this time "undoubted", free of default risk, or, as we would say today, of "triple AAA" credit standing. To begin with, there were still memories of the "Stop of the Exchequer" in 1672 when Charles II defaulted on payments to Crown creditors (mostly goldsmith bankers), the subsequent debt renegotiation resulting in a 50 percent write-off of the original debt.[2] Second, there was the constant danger after the Glorious Revolution that the Jacobites might mount a successful challenge, put a Stuart King on the throne, and repudiate earlier government obligations incurred under a "usurping" monarchy. Third, the record of government debt servicing was patchy: the timing, at least, of payments both of interest and principal were often highly uncertain. Finally, throughout the late seventeenth century and early eighteenth centuries the country was either at or under threat of war, which always carried with it the possibility of a government funding crisis.

Until the 1690s, the government was largely dependent on short-term loans often involving the issuance of "tallies", that is, receipts issued against sums lent to the Exchequer in anticipation of the various tax revenues they were charged upon. The tally owner was entitled to be paid off when the relevant taxes were collected and enjoyed a stated interest rate until that time. Spending departments issued their own tallies, with little central Treasury control, and as the redemption of this debt became increasingly uncertain so the discounts on the tallies widened. By 1697, the discounts were typically in the range 20–40 percent, raising the effective cost of government funding to close to 10 percent per annum (interest allowed plus discount).[3] In a futile attempt to raise the government's credit standing and control the activities of "tally brokers" it was enacted in that year that no one was to buy a tally at a discount greater than 6 percent.

A more realistic solution to the government's funding problem was meanwhile being explored through the establishment of a market in long-term government debt. The borrowing techniques adopted, which were already employed in the Netherlands, were designed to appeal to the gambling instincts of the age. Thus long-term fund raising in the 1690s and early 1700s included a "tontine" loan, various lottery loans, and the sale of annuities, the latter involving the exchange of a sum of capital, paid from creditor to debtor, for a future income stream from debtor back to creditor.[4] All these debt issues were authorised by statute and backed by Parliament, thereby ensuring a higher credit standing than that enjoyed by earlier Crown debts.

Under the tontine loan interest (initially 10 percent) was paid to each contributor pro rata during his own life or the life of his nominees, survivors taking the interest share of those who died. The high interest rate reflected the fact that capital was not repaid. The scheme failed to attract much interest from investors and after the first experiment in 1693 the tontine was abandoned.

Under a lottery loan the government would take in money from the public by subscription. The subscribers received tickets which entitled them to a minimum interest payment over a fixed number of years plus the chance of an additional interest payment if their ticket was successful in the lottery drawings (the winning tickets were "prizes", the losing tickets "blanks"). Depending on the terms of the particular lottery loan, the principal amount subscribed might or might not be repaid after the expiry of the fixed term of interest payments, the rate of interest being adjusted accordingly; for instance, a 10 percent minimum rate was paid on the first (1694) lottery loan, but subsequent schemes, which repaid capital, offered a minimum rate of around 6 percent. Lotteries were designed for the mass market: the government printed 520,000 lottery tickets for £10 and 38,000 for £100 in the period 1711–1714, while the prize drawings which were held at the Guildhall or the Banqueting House, Whitehall, were spread over several days and attracted thousands of spectators.

A key adviser to the government on lottery loans was John Blunt, later to emerge as the chief architect of the South Sea Scheme. The hugely popular "Two Million Adventure" launched by Blunt in 1711 bore all the hallmarks of his style of financial management. The "Adventure" lottery offered a minimum 6.5 percent return to ticket holders through guaranteed prizes but the real innovation was the division of the draw into five classes or stages, with undrawn tickets carried over to the next stage. Each successive draw offered an ever-increasing maximum prize of £1000, £3000, £4000, £5000 and £20,000—investors being kept in suspense until the last draw as to whether or not they had won the jackpot (worth several million pounds in today's money). The Sword Blade Company, acting as the government's marketing and distributing agent, sold tickets amounting to £2 million in a matter of days, although the all-in borrowing cost to the government was relatively high at around 8 percent per annum.

Finally, the government sold annuities on an increasing scale from the 1690s. These took various forms: single life annuities where the income stream was paid so long as the person nominated by the annuity purchaser (who might not be the purchaser himself) continued to live; two or multiple life annuities; fixed term annuities (e.g., 99 years); and annuities that were either irredeemable (as in the case of annuities on lives) or redeemable at the option of the government. Perpetual annuities in the form of today's undated gilt-edge securities were not issued until after the Bubble.

There was a gambling element in all these investments. The tontine was an outright gamble on the life expectation of the investor (or his nominee) in relation to the life expectation of other subscribers. The lottery loans were a "protected" gamble in the sense that a minimum return was guaranteed, whether or not a prize was drawn. Some, however, developed the gaming aspect of lottery loans by hiring out their lottery tickets for a day or part of a day, the borrower then having the right to claim any prize that might be drawn on the ticket during the hiring period.[5]

Life annuities, too, represented an investment of uncertain value. In many cases infants were nominated as the life on which the annuity would be paid, but with the average life expectation at birth estimated at around 16–18 years,[6] this attempt to prolong the period of annuity payments was often defeated by the high rates of mortality among the very young.

Between 1693 and 1712 the government raised over £10 million from the sale of annuities and around £11 million from the enormously popular lottery loans. However, it continued to explore alternative methods of meeting its funding needs, given the disadvantage that attached to these forms of long-term debt finance.

The shortcomings can be seen both from the borrower's and the lender's point of view. On the borrowing side, the interest cost was relatively high, ranging between 6.25 and 8 percent from 1693 to 1711, and in addition most of the debt was irredeemable, meaning that the government was locked into high borrowing costs even when (as happened after peace with Spain in 1713) interest rates fell.

From the lender's point of view both lottery loans and annuities had one major drawback: these instruments were in principle assignable to third parties and there was as a result a rudimentary secondary market for such debt. However, the procedures for transfer were cumbersome in the extreme, which meant that investors were faced with what today would be called "liquidity risk", that is, the risk of not being able to sell an investment readily at the time of one's choosing, in addition to the credit risk associated with all government liabilities. Transferability was particularly problematic in the case of annuities for lives, where the value of the annuity depended on the life expectancy of persons whose health might be difficult for a potential buyer to assess. To reflect the lack of liquidity, investors naturally required a compensating premium on the interest yield from their loans, thereby adding to the government's cost of borrowing.

It was against this background that the authorities embarked on a policy of chartering great state-sponsored companies which, in return for loans granted by them to the government, were to be given monopoly trading or commercial privileges. An additional advantage for investors was that shares in such companies could be actively traded, thereby removing the liquidity risk associated with government debt issues. Both the East India Company and the Bank of England were given their charters in the 1690s on the above basis, in consideration for which the government received initial loans totalling £3.2 million at 8 percent, later reduced to 5–6 percent. Further loans were extracted from the two companies in 1708–1709 in return for renewal of their charters and privileges.

Once the success of these initiatives had been established, it was only one short step further for the government to propose the chartering of a new company to acquire the state's *existing* debt obligations in a large-scale debt–equity swap. This was the context in which the South Sea Company was born, as described in chapter 3. The use of private companies to fund the government had in the meantime established a close linkage between the management of the national debt and the trading of corporate securities in the emergent stock market. It is to the market in corporate stock that we now turn.

THE STOCK MARKET

The traditional investment of most households until the end of the seventeenth century was land and property. However, in the period 1690–1695, there was a boom in company flotations for general subscription which may be viewed as a precursor to the stock market mania of 1720. It has been estimated that by 1695 there were at least 140 companies with a combined capital of £4.25 million, the bulk of this sum being accounted for by three corporate heavyweights—the East India Company chartered in 1600, the New East India Company established in 1698 as a rival to the former (although the two were merged in 1709), and the Bank of England founded in 1694.

Writing at this time, John Houghton, one of the first financial journalists, explained that people "studied hard to dispose of their money, that they might command it whensoever they had occasion, which they found they could more easily do in Joint-Stock, than in laying out the same in Lands, Houses or Commodities, these [shares] being more easily shifted from Hand to Hand." He went on to say that by this development "some were encouraged to buy, others to sell, and this is it that is called Stock-Jobbing".[7]

Individuals who wished to buy shares could do so through a broker (who would charge 0.5 percent commission) or deal directly, in either case by going into one of the coffee houses where shares were traded. Having established from a broker the prices of stocks, the investor "... bids the broker buy or sell so many shares of such and such stocks if he can, at such and such prices: then he tries what he can do among those who have stocks, or power to sell them, and if he can, makes a bargain".[8]

We can describe the basis of this early system of trading in shares as "matching", that is, each share purchase was matched against a corresponding sale, the role of the broker (if a broker was used) being to match individual buyers against individual sellers. In contrast, a share trading system based on market-making would involve middlemen or "jobbers" acting as principals, taking stock into their own books and quoting both a buying and a selling price. As explained below, by the early 1700s the stock market had become a hybrid regime, with brokers increasingly acting as principals and trading on their own account.

The transfer of shares had to be recorded on the company's books to ensure a secure legal title, and for this purpose both buyer and seller would need to attend the company's offices to provide their signatures. One consequence of this method of transfer was that "spot" transactions for immediate delivery of shares could not be undertaken while the company's transfer books were closed to process dividend payments (a situation that arose at the peak of the South Sea speculation). Another consequence was that, in order to avoid the inconvenience of personally arranging transfers, buyers of shares might use nominees to hold their investments, in much the same way as they do today. The following correspondence from Richard Hoare, banker, to one of his clients, illustrates the procedure:

To

Wm. Betts.
at Kirby in Norfolk

Sir,

The method of ye Bank of Transferring stock is that the person to whom it is tsferred must make there personell apperance at ye bank to acknowledge the acceptance of the stock, therefore if you will appoint any person to have it tsferred to in trust for Mdm Culpepper I desire that you will direct them to call here as soon as may be convenient, or else I will have it transferred to one of our servants till such time as you are resolved upon the person in whose name the stock shall continue, but the charge for each transfer is about 5/-. If I can serve in any things that is in my power you may freely command him that is Sir

Your most humble Sevt.

To

Ye Hon Madam Culpepper,
at Sir Navil Catelyne's house,
att Kirby in Norfolk

Madam,

According to ye directions of yourself and Mr. Betts I have bought 300 Bank Stock for your acct, but I never had any bank stock transferred to me in my own name, but when any friend has desired the same kindness of me I have always made use of one of my servts; your stock is transferred to Mr. Arnold who has lived with me 20 yrs, and has executed a declaration of Trust which I have here enclosed and believe it will be to your satisfaction ....[9]

Investors in the stock market could undertake five types of transaction of varying sophistication: spot transactions for immediate delivery of shares; "time bargains" for future delivery and settlement ("forward" contracts in today's parlance); "refusals" or call options which allowed the purchaser to buy (but also to "refuse") stock at a stated price at some future date in return for payment of a premium; "put" options which allowed the purchaser to sell stock in a similar manner; and simultaneous buy/sell or sell/buy transactions which today we would call repurchase agreements or "repos".

In spot transactions the seller of stock gave his signed transfer form to the buyer (to be taken to the company to obtain a legal transfer on its books) only when the buyer had paid his money. In modern terminology there was "delivery versus payment" so that both parties to the transaction were protected against default. However, Thomas Mortimer in his classic text on stock broking, written in 1761, warns that if the buyer paid with a draft on a banker, rather than bank notes, the seller should go to the bank before 5 p.m. the same day to cash it or, better still, "do not part with the receipt til you have received your money at the Bankers".[10]

Investors also arranged time bargains specifying a delivery date ranging from a few days to several months in the future. Alternatively, when the company's transfer books were closed, the contract might be "for the opening of the books". Such deferred contracts, like options, were open to the risk that the counterparty might fail to fulfil their side of the bargain.

Houghton describes how an investor, after making contact with brokers in a coffee house, might buy a "refusal" or call option:

> Another time he asks what they will have for refuse of so many shares: that is, how many guineas a share he shall give for liberty to accept or refuse such shares, at such a price, at any time within six months, or another time they shall agree.[11]

Houghton explains how an investor can benefit from purchasing a refusal, namely that "for a small hazard he can have his chance for a very great gain, and he will certainly know the utmost his loss can be ...".[12] He goes on to give a detailed example of such a transaction and also provides the reader with a pro forma contract. He does the same for put contracts which he describes as follows:

> Another part relating to stock is PUTTING, that is, when they give many guineas to some to have liberty to PUT upon them, that is, to make them take, and pay the money agreed for so many shares, at such a price, in such or such a time...[13]

Finally, investors could engage in a relatively low risk transaction by buying shares for cash in the spot market and then simultaneously selling them in the forward market, where the price would typically be higher (reflecting the carrying or interest cost of holding shares). In this way the investor secured what amounted to an interest return on his money. Joseph de la Vega informs us that, in Amsterdam, this kind of transaction was typically undertaken by merchants with surplus funds:

> ... they buy shares against cash, but try to sell them immediately, for delivery at a later date, when the price will be higher [i.e. for which date a higher price is already quoted)] They ... are satisfied with the interest on their invested money ... they prefer to gain little, but to gain that little with security; to incur no risk other than the solvency of the other party in this forward contract ...[14]

Houghton, too, says that "some buy shares and sell them again for time at such advance as they can agree", thereby gaining a good return on their money.[15] The mirror image transaction involved selling stock and simultaneously buying it back at a future date, thereby allowing those who were temporarily pressed for funds to raise short-term money on their shares without disposing of their investment.[16]

The deferred contracts described above—time bargains, refusals and puts—came to be settled, in many cases, on the basis of differences in value rather than through physical delivery of shares. For instance, a time bargain might be settled on the basis of the difference between the prevailing market price on the contract's maturity date and the forward price agreed at the time the contract was entered into. Such "contracts for differences" allowed investors to speculate in the stock market without the need to transfer or, indeed, to own any shares. Contemporaries described how such mechanisms permitted even the poorest, who could not afford to own shares, to speculate for small sums.[17] De la Vega also discourses on such dealings in "imaginary stock" in some detail, although he also states that the Dutch courts were inclined to regard contracts for differences as gaming and therefore not legally enforceable.[18]

One other financial technique should be mentioned, since it was actively employed during the Bubble year. This was buying stock on margin by pledging or pawning the shares to the lender. According to de la Vega, investors were typically permitted to borrow up to four-fifths of the value of shares so pledged, thereby allowing the lender a precautionary margin to cover price fluctuations. Of course, in the event of extreme price movements, such as those that occurred in 1720, it might become necessary for creditors to sell pledged shares in order to protect themselves against loss.

The above describes the procedures and trading techniques of the emergent stock market at the time of the Bubble. It may be noted that the underlying transactions—forwards, puts, calls and repurchase transactions—were essentially the same as those that characterise today's financial markets. However, there were also important differences between the financial market regimes of 1720 and today.

Firstly, there was an absence of the institutional investors—investment funds, insurance companies and pension funds—which today dominate trading in securities. Investors were typically Londoners belonging to the expanding merchant and professional classes. Writing about the Amsterdam bourse, which had close parallels with the London market, de la Vega tells us[19] that there were three types of investor. First, the very rich tended to invest for the long term, their interest lying not in stock price fluctuations "but in the revenues secured through the dividends". Second, there were merchants who either invested for the short term or simultaneously bought and sold forward to gain "interest" thereby (as explained above). Finally, there were outright speculators who might sell for forward delivery shares they did not own or buy for forward delivery shares they had not the means to pay for, these being "bears" and "bulls", according to the precise definition provided by Thomas Mortimer.[20] Whatever the balance between these different market participants, it seems reasonable to suppose that, lacking the underpinning of long-term institutional investors, the securities markets at that time were dominated by short-term and speculative transactions, even before the frenzy of 1720.

A second key difference between the modern stock exchange and securities markets in the early 1700s is the fact that trading in the latter was neither centralised nor organised. On the contrary, the market was physically dispersed in a number of coffee houses around Exchange Alley, there was no centralised source of price information and different prices might be simultaneously quoted in different locations or, indeed, even within the same coffee house. For instance, at the time of the Bubble, the banker Thomas Martin stated that on 30 June 1720 "at one end of the Coffee House [Garraways] South Sea Stock was sold at 1,000—the other end at 920".[21]

In the early development of the stock market, transactions were mainly (although not exclusively) undertaken in the arcaded splendour of the Royal Exchange building where dealers in all kinds of merchandise were allocated their respective "walks". Dealers in stock had a walk near the centre of the building but in 1698 "the dealers and jobbers in the funds and share market, annoyed by the objections made to their remaining in the Royal Exchange, and finding their numbers seriously increase, deemed it advisable to go to Change Alley, as a large and unoccupied space, where they might carry on their extensive operations".[22]

Writing in 1719, Daniel Defoe described the layout of this new trading environment (see plate 2) as follows:

> The centre of the jobbing is in the Kingdom of Exchange Alley, and its adjacencies. The limits are easily surrounded in about a minute and a half, viz, stepping out of Jonathan's into the Alley, you turn your face full south; moving on a few paces, and then turning due east, you advance to Garraway's; from there going out at the other door, you go on still east into Birchin Lane; and then halting a little at the Sword-blade Bank ... you immediately face to the north, enter Cornhill, visit two or three petty provinces there in your way west; and thus having boxed your compass, and sailed round the whole stock-jobbing globe, you turn into Jonathan's again; and so, as most of the great follies of life oblige us to do, you end just where you begin.[23]

The main location of securities trading was the coffee house area around Exchange Alley, but trading also overflowed onto the surrounding streets—so much so that in 1710 the local inhabitants claimed in a petition that "... by the daily Resort and Standing of Brokers and Stock-Jobbers in the same Alley, not only the common passage to and from the Royal Exchange is greatly obstructed, but encouragement is given by the tumultuary Concourse of People attending the said Brokers, to Pick-Pockets, Shop-lifters, and other Idle and Disorderly People to mix among them ... to the great Damage and Detriment of all Passengers going through the said Alley about their Lawful Occasions ...".[24] The City authorities responded by trying to prohibit street trading in Exchange Alley but the practice continued for nearly 200 years.

By the time of the Bubble, therefore, trading in securities was concentrated within a particular London precinct but nevertheless fragmented among coffee houses and adjoining streets. Furthermore, ladies (significant investors in stock at this time) understandably might not wish to be exposed to the brawl of Exchange Alley, preferring instead to meet their brokers in the shops of nearby milliners and haberdashers.[25] Under these circumstances

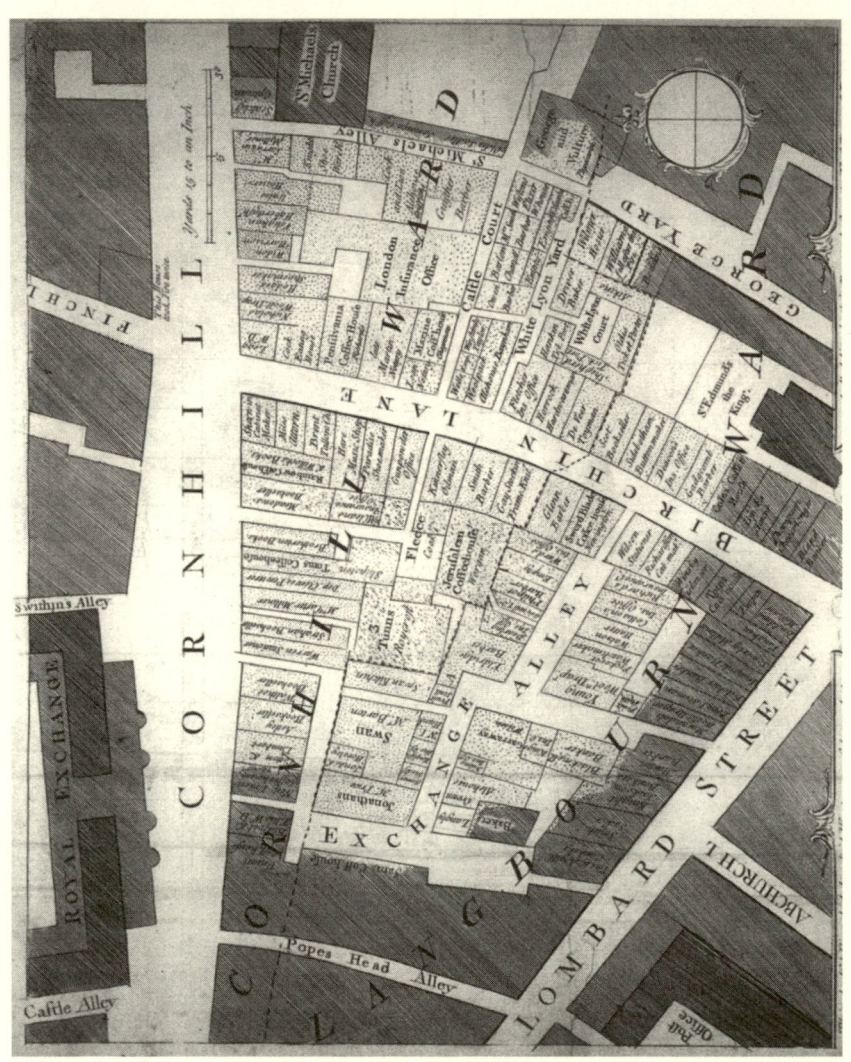

Plate 2   Plan of Exchange Alley 1748. Copyright Guildhall Library.

trading was dispersed, pricing lacked transparency and investors could by no means rely on getting the best market price at the time of purchase or sale.

Finally, a major difference between the early eighteenth century stock markets and securities trading today was the absence at that time of an effective regulatory framework, either official or self-imposed. In this context, regulation may be considered at two levels: the primary or new issue market; and the secondary market in issued stock which itself divides into regulation of professional brokers and regulation of market practices.

As far as the primary market is concerned, there were numerous complaints from the late seventeenth century onwards about the ease with which "projectors" could invite subscriptions to investment schemes that often turned out to be worthless. A commission appointed by the government reported in 1696 that "the pernicious art of stockjobbing" had "perverted the end and design of companies ... to the private profit of the first projectors" who sold worthless stock to "ignorant men, drawn in by the reputation, falsely raised and artfully spread, concerning the thriving state of their stock".[26] However, by the time of the Bubble no action had been taken to regulate new stock issues and it was only during the course of 1720, when the flotation of new companies proceeded at a frenzied pace, that the government made a determined attempt to curb the new issue market (see p. 135). Anderson provides a graphic description of the worst features of the new issue market at this time:

> Any impudent imposter, needed only to hire a room at some coffee house or other house near [Exchange] Alley, for a few hours, and open a subscription book, for somewhat relative to commerce, manufacturing, plantation, or some supposed invention, either newly hatched or out of his own brain, ... having first advertised it in the newspapers the preceding day, and he might, in a few hours, find subscribers for one or two millions ... of imaginary stock.[27]

There was a theoretical legal constraint on the establishment of joint stock companies in that the privileges of incorporation (the right of perpetual succession, the right to sue and be sued, etc.) could only be conferred by royal charter or parliamentary statute. Nevertheless, this formal requirement appears to have been largely ignored during the boom in company flotations during the 1690s and again in 1720.

Trading in the secondary market, on the other hand, was subject to periodic regulation of a rudimentary kind. Following the stock market excesses of 1690–1695, Parliament enacted the first securities statute in 1697: "An act to restrain the number and ill practice of brokers and stock jobbers". The Act limited the number of brokers to 100, required them to be licensed by the Lord Mayor of London, forbade them from trading for their own account and limited their commission to 0.5 percent of the value of shares they traded. This statute, having been renewed once, expired in 1708 although the City of London was thereafter given authority to license brokers on such terms as it saw fit and the ceiling on commission was also reimposed by statute in 1711.

From 1708, therefore, the Lord Mayor and the Aldermen of the City of London were the delegated regulatory authority for brokers, being empowered to charge an entry fee of forty shillings for licensed membership of the City broking community and an annual subscription of the same amount. Under the City's new regulations licensed brokers had to enter into a bond, inter alia forbidding them to engage in own-account trading, and a fine of £25 was to be imposed on anyone acting as a broker without being licensed. However, neither of these rules was enforced: brokers routinely engaged in own-account trading, in effect acting as both jobbers and brokers;[28] and there was a thriving community of unlicensed or "unsworn" brokers who, by 1761, were estimated by Mortimer to outnumber licensed brokers two to one. It may be noted in this context that although the City's policy was to restrict the number of licensed Jewish brokers to twelve, there appear to have been many unlicensed Jewish brokers, among whom were some of the leading brokers of the time.[29]

In addition to these half-hearted initiatives to regulate brokers, there were also a number of attempts to regulate market practices. The ineffectual attempt to separate broking from dealing has already been mentioned above. For instance, in one lawsuit arising out of the South Sea Bubble, a leading (unlicensed) broker, Matthew Wymondesold, explained that he (the defendant) "did deal very greatly in buying and selling stocks on this Defendant's own account and believes the same was publicly known to all or most persons who were considerable dealers in stocks at that time and who frequented the coffee-houses near Exchange Alley ... notwithstanding the suggestions in the Bill that a person acting by commission for others and dealing on his own account may have opportunity of imposing on his principal".[30]

There were various proposals in the 1690s to restrict forward contracts, options and contracts for differences but the only legislative step in this direction was taken in 1697 when the Act regulating brokers also required that the period between the contract date and the transfer date be three days or less, thereby effectively prohibiting forward contracts. However, even this restriction, which in any case lapsed in 1708, was circumvented through a narrow judicial interpretation of its terms.[31]

Financial regulation in the bubble period was therefore a dead letter. There were few regulatory restrictions and the few regulations that did exist were largely unenforced. Brokers were supposed to be licensed but many, if not most, were not; brokers were not supposed to deal on their own account but they typically did; joint stock companies were supposed to be formally authorised but many were not; time bargains were, for a period, prohibited but even this was circumvented; and the prohibition on street trading was largely ignored. Financial regulatory initiatives introduced during and after the Bubble year suffered the same fate, as we shall see. The so-called Bubble Act of 1720 restricting new company flotations was largely ineffective, and the attempt made in 1734 to control speculation in the aftermath of the Bubble by prohibiting all contracts "in the nature of puts and refusals"; all contracts for differences as well as short selling (disposing of securities of which the seller was not possessed) failed to eliminate these activities. Evidently, in the area of financial regulation, weak enforcement mechanisms were no match for powerful market forces.

In summary, today's securities markets are underpinned by a combination of official and self-regulation designed to protect investors by ensuring the solvency of intermediaries, price transparency, fair dealing and the suppression of insider dealing. Financial markets are further buttressed by requirements on corporate governance, corporate disclosure and accounting standards. London's stock market in the early eighteenth century lacked these basic safeguards, leaving investors exposed to many risks over and above ordinary investment risk. There remained recourse to the courts for those who felt aggrieved as a result of their dealings in Exchange Alley. Litigation was, however, prolonged and costly and, in the absence of a clear framework of securities law, offered a very uncertain prospect of success.[32] A contemporary commentator illustrates the point. Defoe's imaginary lawyer, Sir Thomas Subtle, advises his client not to take stock which he has contracted to accept at a price higher than the level to which it has now fallen (the result of selling a put option):

> After this, it is supposed they will sue you at law. Then leave it to me: I'll hang them up for a year or two in our courts; and if ever in that time the stock comes up to the price, we will tender the money in court, demand the stock, and saddle the charges of the suit upon them: let them avoid it if they can.[33]

The overall conclusion is that the stock market environment of the early 1700s differed in several important respects from today's stock exchange regime. As described in chapter 1, Exchange Alley was a

Plate 3 City of London's financial district 1746. Copyright Guildhall Library.

rumour mill that generated real and false "news" in almost equal measure; in the absence of long-term institutional investors, trading tended to be driven by speculation and the prospect of short-term gains; the market was physically fragmented (although located within a single precinct) which made pricing difficult; and there was no effective regulatory framework for either the primary or secondary markets which meant that investors were vulnerable to all manner of skullduggery on the part of company promoters, brokers and traders.

Exchange Alley was therefore a dangerous place and widely acknowledged to be so. Yet propertied men and women flocked to the market. The appetite for risk-taking on the part of investors—a reflection of the prevailing gambling culture—was matched by the entrepreneurial initiatives both of company promoters and the more established trading companies, coffee house brokers providing a necessary (albeit highly imperfect) link between capital providers and capital users.

The essential economic function of the stock market was therefore the same then as it is now. The operation of the market was also similar, with specialised intermediaries bringing sellers and buyers together in a primitive form of "floor" trading. Transactions undertaken on the market, involving forward contracts and options as well as contracts for immediate delivery, were furthermore identical to those undertaken by today's sophisticated investors. Given these parallels between the stock market of the early eighteenth century and modern stock exchanges, we can conclude that the behaviour of the former can provide useful insights into investment markets in the twenty-first century.

It remains to place the activities of Exchange Alley in the broader context of investment and savings markets. During the opening years of the eighteenth century, propertied people had a number of alternative channels for investing their surplus funds. First there were the goldsmith bankers who offered varying deposit interest rates, depending on the notice period for withdrawal, up to the legal maximum of 6 percent[34] for time deposits of one month or over.[35] At the other end of the liquidity/maturity spectrum, investments in primary land yielded around 5 percent, although higher yields were available on leaseholds, life tenancies, etc.[36] Long-term government securities in the form, for instance, of annuities yielded 6–7 percent,[37] while short-term government tallys, which could be bought at substantial discounts, yielded up to 11 percent[38] reflecting the uncertain timing of debt service payments. In technical language, the greater default risk on short-term government debt distorted the shape of the yield curve. Finally, there were a variety of corporate stocks, ranging from the East India Company, the leading equity of the period, carrying a dividend yield of 7–8 percent[39] to more speculative stocks.

Personal wealth could be held in any of the above forms, each of which had different liquidity, maturity and credit risk characteristics. The techniques available to value these different classes of asset were not dissimilar to those used by investors today.[40] Three related methods were commonly employed: interest or dividend yield; number of years' purchase (e.g., a multiple of 20 applied to a given annual rental in the case of land or dividend in the case of stock); and calculation of the "present value" of a future rental, interest or dividend stream. This last approach involved the use of discount tables, such as those published by John Castaing, to generate the relevant capital sum for a given interest or discount rate and time period.

Whatever valuation method was used, the problem for those trying to assess the value of stocks was, of course, the uncertainty relating to the prospective flow of dividends. To take account of this risk or uncertainty, it was customary to deduct, say, three years' purchase from the valuation or (which amounted to the same thing) to adopt an above market discount rate in arriving at a present value. However, investors had as much difficulty then as they do today with the quantification of risk. And, as we shall see, in the stampede for South Sea Stock in 1720 conventional valuation techniques, compound interest tables and, most importantly, common sense were all abandoned as hysteria took hold.

NOTES

1. See generally Dickson (1967: 39–75).
2. Roseveare (1991: 52).
3. Dickson (1967: 347).
4. Carruthers (1996: 75).
5. Mortimer (1762: 100).
6. Bernstein (1996: 83).
7. Houghton (15 June 1694).
8. Houghton (22 May 1694).
9. Hoare's Bank (1955: 22–23).
10. Mortimer (1762: 137).
11. Houghton (22 May 1694).
12. Houghton (22 May 1694).
13. Houghton (6 July 1694).
14. De la Vega (1688) in Fridson (1996: 151).
15. Houghton (13 July 1694).
16. Banner (1998: 37).

17. Banner (1998: 29).
18. De la Vega (1688) in Fridson (1996: 208).
19. De la Vega (1688) in Fridson (1996: 151).
20. Mortimer (1762: 48–49).
21. Chandler (1964: 105).
22. Francis (1849: 24).
23. Defoe (1719) in Francis (1849: 375).
24. Cited in Carruthers (1996: 257, note 68).
25. Anderson (1764: 44).
26. Cited in Banner (1998: 29).
27. Anderson (1764: 102).
28. Thomas Mortimer stated in 1761 that "… it is almost impossible for any Broker, who is a jobber (and there are but few that are not) to give candid impartial advice, when to buy into, or sell out of, the public funds" (Mortimer 1762: 105).
29. Dickson (1967: 498–499).
30. Dickson (1967: 499).
31. Banner (1998: 40).
32. The courts did, however, uphold the principle that a securities transaction could not be voided simply because the price had become highly unfavourable to one of the contracting parties. In *Thomson v. Harcourt* (1722) the defendant claimed that it would be unreasonable to enforce a time bargain to purchase South Sea stock at a price of 920 when the market price had since fallen to a quarter of its former value. The House of Lords determined that Harcourt had to pay the contract price of 920.
33. Defoe (1719) in Francis (1849: 364).
34. The usury laws set a maximum legal interest rate of 10 percent in 1571 which was lowered successively to 8 percent in 1623, 6 percent in 1651, and 5 percent in 1714. The Government was exempt from the legal limit as was the Bank of England after 1716. Certain loans where the principal was at risk (e.g., some ship mortgages) also fell outside the usury laws. At the time of the South Sea Bubble, borrowing at usurious rates of interest was quite common, but so long as the usury did not appear on the face of the bond (because the borrower's interest was included in the principal owed) the contract was enforceable.
35. Roseveare (1991: 20).
36. Dickson (1967: 146).
37. Dickson (1967: 470).
38. Dickson (1967: 363).
39. Dickson (1967: 363).
40. See Harrison (2001).

Origins of the South Sea Company

THE SOUTH SEA COMPANY was established on 8 September 1711 by a charter, authorised by act of Parliament, which incorporated "the Governor and Company of the merchants of Great Britain, trading to the South Seas and other parts of America, and for the encouragement of fishing".

The initial assets of the company were twofold. First, it was to have a trading monopoly covering "the kingdoms, lands etc of America, on the east side from the river Aranoca, to the most southern part of the Terra del Fuego, on the west side thereof, from the said most southern part through the South Seas to the most northern part of America, and into unto and from all countries in the same limits reputed to belong to the Crown of Spain, or which shall hereafter be discovered".[1] Second, the company was to receive an annual payment from the Exchequer of £568,279, to be secured on specific customs revenues. This represented a 6 percent return on some £9.5 million of outstanding short-term government debt whose holders were expected to convert into stock of the South Sea Company—the Company acquiring claims to the same value against the government in what amounted to a large-scale debt–equity swap.

In less than ten years the South Sea Company was to become a corporate monster with a market capitalisation of over £200 million, although, like the modern dot.com equivalent, its trading operations remained minimal and mostly loss making. The company was also destined to become the vehicle for what has been variously described as the greatest speculation, the biggest scam and the most extreme example of manic investor behaviour in English financial history.[2] To understand the nature of the calamity that befell the Company and its shareholders, it is necessary to examine the origins of the South Sea Scheme from the point of view of the three main stakeholders: the government of the day, the "projectors" or architects of the scheme, and the investors who were being asked to convert their holdings of government debt into South Sea stock.

The Government and the South Sea Company

From the glorious revolution in 1688 to the signing of the Treaty of Utrecht in 1713, England enjoyed only four years of peace, the intervening period being dominated first by the Nine Years War (1688–1697) and then by the War of the Spanish Succession (1702–1713). War made heavy demands on the public purse. It cost around £5.5 million per annum to maintain a 90,000 strong army on the Continent and a 40,000 naval force at sea and by 1710 military expenditure was absorbing 9 percent of England's national income, a sum which had to be met either from taxation or borrowing.[3]

The bulk of the government's revenue was raised from three taxes: the customs duties on international trade, the excise tax on domestic products (especially alcohol), and the land tax based on an assessment of national land values drawn up in 1692. The overall fiscal burden increased rapidly from the 1670s to the early 1700s as the percentage of national income taken by taxes rose from 3.5 percent to over 9 percent.[4] In the years immediately preceding the launch of the South Sea Company, the burden of taxation had became a serious and hotly debated political issue, particularly among the landed classes who felt they had borne a disproportionate share of increased tax rates, while the "monied men" of the City of London appeared to prosper from their involvement in the government's wartime debt management.

The extent of the government's funding difficulties was further under-lined by the fact that in the early 1700s well over one-third of its total revenues were being absorbed by interest payments alone, a figure that was to rise to over 50 percent in 1714–1717.[5] Since further taxation could be ruled out on political grounds, the government turned to borrowing. Here there were two problems. First, there was the sheer scale of new borrowing required to finance military expenditure. This was handled in the innovative ways described in chapter 2. But the government was also increasingly concerned about the *structure* of its outstanding borrowing. The long-term irredeemable debt in the form of annuities was costly and could not be repaid or refinanced, an issue that was eventually to be addressed by the South Sea scheme of 1720. The more immediate diffi-culty, however, was the volume of short-term "unfunded" debt in the form of tallies, interest arrears and other claims on government spending that would have to be rolled over if it could not be refinanced longer term. By 1711, interest arrears had built up and the short-term or "floating" debt, which then amounted to some £9 million, was being traded in the secondary market at deep discounts averaging around 32 percent.[6]

In brief, both the overall value and the unstable structure of the government's debt was undermining its credit standing and increasing its cost of borrowing. In today's terminology, the government's sovereign credit rating was being damaged by the overhang of short-term debt, thereby jeopardising its investment grade status. The proposal for a massive debt conversion scheme centring on the South Sea Company must be seen in the context of the urgent need to stabilise the structure of debt in order to strengthen the government's credit standing or "publick credit".

While debt management policy may be viewed as the primary motivation behind the government's sponsorship of the South Sea Company, there were also important political considerations, both external and internal. Externally, successive governments had been keen to extend English trading interests beyond the areas already represented by the East India Company, The Royal Africa Company, and the Hudson's Bay Company, to embrace the New World or Spanish West Indies. There were schemes as early as the mid-seventeenth century for the establishment of a West India Company but the War of the Spanish Succession provided additional strategic reasons to challenge the Spanish trading monopoly in the New World; above all, a strong English presence in the Spanish West Indies weakened French military power by depriving France of the riches it extracted from its Spanish possessions.[7]

There were, in addition, domestic political considerations that prompted the Tory government under Robert Harley to look favourably on the South Sea Company project. The two great joint-stock companies, the East India Company and the Bank of England, were both dominated by the Whig interest, as indeed were the "monied men" of the City of London. This was an uncomfortable position for a Tory government increasingly dependent on City support for its debt management policies. Shortly before the introduction of the South Sea Bill, the Tories had attempted to adjust the balance by seeking, unsuccessfully, to influence the election for directors of the two great companies. After this debacle, it was tempting to consider the creation of a third great company so constituted as to represent Tory financial interests. The South Sea Bill was in due course adapted to this purpose, the right to appoint the first board or "court" of directors being vested in the Queen rather than the shareholders, thereby opening the way for political appointments.

The Projectors

While the pressure on public finances, together with foreign and domestic political considerations, predisposed the government to favour the South Sea Company project, the businessmen behind the venture had a rather different agenda. To understand their role in the Company's evolution, it is necessary to look at the individuals involved and their previous business experience with the Sword Blade Company, an institution that had intimate links with the South Sea Company from the latter's inception and whose business operations bore a close resemblance to those ultimately followed, with such disastrous consequences, by its corporate associate.[8]

The Sword Blade Company received a charter in 1691 (making a £50,000 loan to the government for the privilege) to make French-style "hollow" or grooved sword blades, which were displacing the traditional English flat blade. A skilled group of Huguenot craftsmen was hired to manufacture the swords at mills near Shotley Bridge in Durham; the swords were then sold from the company's warehouse in New Street, Fetter Lane in London. However, by the early 1700s, the sword manufacturing business appears to have become largely defunct and a partnership of Exchange Alley men acquired control of the chartered company as a shell vehicle to be exploited for other purposes.

The Sword Blade partnership consisted of Elias Turner, Jacob Sawbridge and George Caswall. Daniel Defoe, whose venomous caricatures of Exchange Alley and its denizens were no doubt influenced by his own status as an undischarged bankrupt, provided a prophetic description of this trio, written shortly before the dramatic stock market events of 1720:

> C[aswall] a man of brass sufficient for much more business than he can be trusted with ... he rather is directed than directs, and like a certain great general, famed for more fire than flegm, is fitter to drive than to lead. S[awbridge] is as cunning as C[aswall] is bold, and the reserve of one with the openess of the other makes a complete Exchange Alley man ... T[urner], a gamester of the same board, acts in concert with C[aswall] and S[awbridge] and makes together a true triumvirate of modern theiving ....[9]

Defoe went on to predict that these men would in time ruin the jobbing trade in a generalised financial crisis:

> But 'twill be only like a general visitation where all distempers are swallowed up in the plague, like a common calamity, that makes enemies from friends and drowns lesser grievances in the general deluge.[10]

In about 1703, the partnership of Turner, Sawbridge and Caswall was joined by John Blunt who became secretary to the Sword Blade Company. Blunt was a "scrivener", a general man of business with particular skills in drawing up documents. His technical expertise, entrepreneurial drive and domineering manner were to be an important influence on the fortunes of both the Sword Blade Company and the South Sea Company of which he was to become the primary originator and chief executive.

Under its new direction, the Sword Blade Company first became involved in land speculation. The lands concerned were Irish estates which had been confiscated from Jacobites during the conquest of Ireland and were now to be sold at public auction. In 1702, the Sword Blade company agreed to pay £200,000 for estates with a rent roll of £20,000, providing a yield basis of 10 percent compared to yields on English prime property at this time of around 5 percent. Since the company did not itself have the funds to pay for the land, it undertook a financial operation that was later to become the model for the South Sea Company. The Sword Blade Company exchanged new stock for outstanding army debentures, (paper issued by the Paymaster of the Forces), the company thereby acquiring claims on the government which it used to pay for the land. Since the army debentures were then priced at around 85, equivalent to a discount of 15 percent, and the company was offering to acquire the instruments at par or 100, the holders of the debentures stood to benefit from the conversion so long as the price of Sword Blade stock itself remained above 85.

From the viewpoint of the Sword Blade promoters, the deal had an important additional attraction. They were evidently able to engage in large-scale insider trading, acquiring depreciated army debentures before the conversion offer was made in the knowledge that they would later be able to convert at par or sell on the market when the price rose in antici-pation of conversion. One estimate puts the insider profits from such transactions at around £20,000, although this may be too high.[11]

While such private profiteering seems outrageous to us today, by the standards of the time it was perhaps to be expected. After all, several directors of the Bank of England (no less) had apparently profited person-ally to a much greater extent in 1697 when the Bank purchased £800,000 of government tallies at par; since the tallies were standing at a discount of 40 percent before the announced purchase offer, those directors who, acting as insiders, bought depreciated tallies were able to make substan-tial profits—£50,000 in one case alone according to some reports.[12]

The Sword Blade Company's venture into land speculation proved to be short-lived. Problems arose over legal title to the estates concerned, a matter on which the Irish parliament was unhelpful to the company. Because of these difficulties the land was gradually resold and the business wound up, shareholders receiving a final cash distribution which was considerably less than the original value of the debentures they had subscribed to.[13]

The land business having failed, the Sword Blade partners nevertheless used the experience of their stock–debt conversion scheme to develop a much more ambitious project. The idea was to combine (1) a new trading venture in the South Seas, (2) large-scale conversion of government debt into corporate stock and (3) the establishment of a new finance-cum-trading company that would be closely linked to the Tory government, thereby offering a political counterweight to the East India Company and the Bank of England. For the promoters, the venture offered the prospect of personal enrichment, political influence and popular acclaim on the grand scale. The Sword Blade Company would meanwhile find a new role for itself as banker to the projected business.

THE INVESTORS

Investors in the early years of the eighteenth century had the same basic concerns as investors of today. They wanted to acquire assets that (1) were "liquid" or easily transferable, (2) that provided a secure income as well as return of capital (in the case of debt instruments), and (3) offered the prospect of capital gain (in the case of equities).

From the investor's point of view, the South Sea Company's initial debt conversion proposal offered advantages under each of these headings. The difficulty of transferring government debt instruments has already been referred to. South Sea stock, on the other hand, would be easily saleable in Exchange Alley. George Caswall made a particular point of this liquidity advantage when recommending the project to Prime Minister Harley in October 1710, referring to the fact that the "easy transfer of each adventurer's property" in the proposed joint-stock company would raise the price of the government debt that was to be converted into that stock.[14]

The security of investors' income returns might also be enhanced under the proposed conversion scheme. As matters stood, the payment of interest on government debt was often in arrears and the timing of repayment of principal on supposedly short-term claims was uncertain. The promoters of the South Sea Scheme were proposing to consolidate government debt obligations in the company's hands on the basis of a secure source of debt service payments charged on specific tax revenues. The interest payments from the government could then support at least a minimum dividend payment from the company to its shareholders.

Finally, the South Sea project offered the prospect of capital gains to those who were in a position to convert their holdings of government debt. This could take one of several forms. To begin with, the conversion terms might be such as to increase the market value of the debt to be converted and to enable holders of the debt to make immediate capital gains either by selling their holdings or by converting into South Sea stock and selling their newly acquired shares on the market. Those who decided to hold their stock for the time being might gain further if successive conversions and stock issues were associated with a rising stock price, while for long-term investors there was the possibility of substantial trading profits, steadily rising dividends and appreciating share values.

The potential for capital gains from new corporate ventures had already captured the investing public's imagination. In the period 1690–1695, there was a flood of company flotations embracing such exotic projects as the raising of treasure from shipwrecks, as well as more prosaic ventures involving, for example, the manufacture of drainage pumps, burglar alarms and ordinance.

Given the entrepreneurial sprit of the times, the idea of a new company with a specific remit to trade in the Spanish West Indies held a particular attraction for investors. Ever since the buccaneering days of Elizabethan England, the New World had held out the prospect of untold riches to those who were bold enough to challenge the Spanish trading monopoly in the region. All in all, the promoters of the South Sea Company would find it much easier to sell their new project to the investing public than it had been to market their earlier venture into confiscated Irish estates.

Early History of the South Sea Company

The original proposal for launching the South Sea Company came from John Blunt who wrote to Prime Minister Harley in late summer of 1710 outlining the scheme. Harley was quickly converted to the idea and when Parliament met in November the provisions for a Bill establishing the Company progressed rapidly; the necessary resolutions were passed on 3 May 1711 and the charter was finally issued in early September.

The South Sea Act provided for the conversion of the government's floating debts of £9,471,325 into South Sea stock, although, surprisingly, historians appear divided as to whether the conversion was to be compulsory or voluntary.[15] There is indeed an ambiguity here because the Act made no provision for repayment of the floating debt other than through conversion; holders of the debt may therefore have felt that they had little choice in the matter.[16]

Interest of 6 percent was payable to the Company on the debt it acquired from the conversion, secured on various duties on wine, vinegar, tobacco, etc. The Act also authorised the grant of a monopoly of trade to the east coast of South America, from the river Orinoco to the south of Terra del Fuego, and along the whole of the west coast. The new company's authorised equity capital was limited by statute to the amount of government debt that was converted; in effect, therefore, the "capital" consisted of claims against the government and any trading capital would have to be borrowed by the company on the security of its income stream from the government (in fact the South Sea Company's borrowing capacity was at the outset very considerable, given its £9 million plus holding of government debt, and it did not need to make anything like full use of this "fund of credit"). Finally, the Act vested the right to appoint the first court of directors in the Queen, and Harley, acting on behalf of the Crown, proceeded to pack the court with Tory appointees. Since the South Sea Company's charter also prohibited directors of the Bank of England and the East India Company from serving as the Company's directors, it was clear that a gauntlet had been thrown down to the Whig financial interest in the City of London.

The South Sea Company's charter was modelled on that of the Bank of England. There were standard provisions relating to the governors and directors who were required to have a minimum stockholding of £5000 and £3000, respectively, while shareholders with a minimum of £1000 in stock could vote for the governor and directors, voting rights being graduated according to the size of their investment, up to a maximum of three votes for anyone holding £10,000 of stock. There was, however, one unusual provision (evidently drafted by Blunt) which was eventually to enable the old Sword Blade partnership, as founding directors of the new company, to manipulate their colleagues and control the direction of the business. The provision in question gave committees of directors authority to act in any matter entrusted to them "as fully as the Court of Directors might do", an authority that could be used to bypass the full board when, as later occurred, the affairs of the company came to be managed by a small group of directors operating through a committee structure.

The immediate objective of the South Sea Company's management was to arrange for the conversion of floating government debt into newly issued stock of the company. This was a formidable administrative task that was to take some two years to complete. It necessitated an initial (temporary) staff of 50 cashiers, accountants and clerks to take in subscriptions, the regular staff consisting of a secretary with one head and one under clerk, a chief accountant and under accountant with four clerks, two doorkeepers, two messengers and two watchmen.[17]

In contrast to later subscriptions and conversions, this first conversion was in effect, although not in form, compulsory and the terms were fixed at the outset; namely each £100 nominal of government floating debt was to be exchanged for £100 nominal of South Sea Company stock (a straightforward "par value" exchange). Prior to the announcement of the conversion plan in May 1711, the average discount on government floating debt was around 32 percent, meaning that subscribers into stock would generally gain so long as the price of South Sea shares did not fall below 70. In the event, when the shares were first floated in October 1711 they fell to 73–76 but the price stabilised thereafter, averaging around 75 in the final quarter of the year and remaining in the 70s during 1712, before rising to 94 at the end of 1713 when subscriptions were finally closed. At this price, subscribers were enjoying an effective capital gain approaching 40 percent.

The old Sword Blade partnership, notably Blunt, Caswall and Sawbridge, converted over £65,000 of government debt, much of which, it may be assumed, had been acquired at large discounts prior to the announcement of the conversion scheme, thereby securing substantial insider trading profits along the lines of their earlier operations. It has been suggested that two leading City figures, both ex-directors of the Bank of England, who had been persuaded to join the South Sea board, were also involved in large-scale insider deals, the implication again being that such behaviour was to be expected in the business environment of the time.[18]

Having successfully completed the conversion of floating government debt into South Sea stock, the Company became a vehicle for passing through the 6 percent annual interest it received from the government on its capital. This interest was in effect redistributed to shareholders as a twice yearly 3 percent dividend, payable at Midsummer and Christmas. However, due to continuing funding problems, the government's interest payments to the Company fell into arrears in 1715. The deficiency was met by capitalising the government's interest arrears, and increasing the company's equity capital to £10 million. This arrangement interrupted the cash flow of the company which responded by distributing the Midsummer 1715 dividend in the form of bonds and paying both 1716 dividends in the form of stock.

While fulfilling its initial financial objectives, the South Sea Company also began to develop the trading side of its operations. These activities depended on commercial negotiations conducted between England and

Spain as part of the Peace of Utrecht concluded in March 1713. Under the terms of this settlement England was awarded the notorious "Asiento", the right, previously held by France, to supply Spain's American colonies with slaves. The South Sea Company in turn became the beneficiary of the Asiento concession whose provisions, listed below, today make for painful reading:[19]

1. The right to send each year a "permission" ship of 500 tons to trade at the fairs either at Cartagena or Vera Cruz. The King of Spain was to receive 28.75 percent of the profits.
2. Asientists were required to transport 4800 "piezas de Indias" annually to Spanish America for 30 years (a "pieza" was a negro with no defects at least 58 inches tall).[20]
3. Asientists were to pay $33\frac{1}{3}$ escudos on each of the first 4000 negroes and 800 entered duty free. The King of Spain was to share 10 percent of the profits.
4. Payments for the negroes could be received in money, gold, silver bullion or "fruits of the country".
5. Slaves could be carried to all Spanish American ports.
6. Unfortified "factories" (trading centres) could be established to carry on the trade, staffed by up to six Englishmen per establishment.

The South Sea Company's efforts to develop its trading business were blighted from the outset. Significantly, none of the directors had any experience of trading in the New World. An attempt to despatch two cargo vessels in 1712 with £200,000 of goods aboard failed when, due to delays, the cargo decayed in port. Subsequently the company sought to exploit the Asiento concession by delivering negroes purchased from the Royal African Company, but due to protracted and unresolved difficulties relating to competition from interlopers (including Jamaica), delayed collection of payments, and conflicts with Spain over duties payable, valuation of slaves, etc., the trade did not prosper. Indeed, during the whole period 1713–1718, the negro traffic appears to have lost money for the Company.[21] During the same period the company also despatched three merchant ships to the Spanish Indies carrying both English manufactures and foreign goods to Vera Cruz and Cartagena. The profits from this trade amounted to just over £100,000 or around £20,000 per annum for the years 1714–1718—hardly significant in relation to the Company's equity capital of £10 million and annual interest from the government of over £500,000. In any event both the Asiento and conventional trade with the New World came to an abrupt end in the summer of 1718 when war broke out between England and Spain and the Company's assets in Spanish territories were seized.

Interestingly, the stock market appears to have taken a realistic view of the South Sea Company's limited trading prospects. Just as the announcement of the award of the Asiento in June 1713 had little effect on the price of the stock, so the termination of this business in 1718 made little impact on the market, the share price remaining at around the par level, which it had reached towards the end of 1716. As one historian has put it:

> The financial community judged the value of the stock on the security of the 6% annuity which the Treasury paid to the Company for distribution in the form of dividends. Profits from trade had properly been discounted at nil.[22]

The early history of the South Sea Company was therefore unremarkable. The conversion operation went relatively smoothly and subscribers who converted their depreciated government debts made a health capital gain, as much as 50 percent by the time South Sea stock rose above par in 1716–1717, bearing in mind the 32 percent market discount previously prevailing on converted debt instruments. The South Sea trading operations contributed little if anything to the company's profits, even in time of peace, and the share valuation reflected this fact. The steady appreciation of the stock in 1713–1718 was largely attributable to the decline in market interest rates that followed the Peace of Utrecht, long-term government yields falling from 6–7 percent in 1702–1714 to about 5 percent in the immediate post-war period.[23] Neither in its stock price performance, nor in its commercial operations was there any suggestion here that the South Sea Company was soon to become the focus of feverish financial speculation and the epicentre of an international financial crash.

The 1719 Debt Conversion

Among the major stakeholders in the South Sea Scheme, the government had gone some way towards stabilising the structure of its debt, although much remained to be done, and investors were no doubt satisfied with an ample return on their (now marketable) assets. However, the soaring ambitions of the projectors had been frustrated by the failure of the South Sea trade and by the limited commercial possibilities offered by a company whose status had been relegated to that of an annuity holding company. The old Sword Blade partnership, led by Blunt, were looking to expand their horizons once more and in 1719 they were presented with the opportunity to conduct a financial experiment that was eventually to transform the South Sea Company's prospects by quadrupling its capital, multiplying its share price and, for a few months at least, placing it alongside the French Company of the Indies as one of the two great corporate entities at the leading edge of European finance.

The first indication that the South Sea Company might embark on a more ambitious programme of innovative financial activity came in early 1719. In January of that year, the Company and the Treasury agreed in principle on a debt conversion operation, later authorised by statute, that was to become the prototype for the much larger conversion scheme of 1720. The financial details of the 1719 operation are therefore important to an understanding of the dramatic events that unfolded the following year.[24]

The debt to be converted was the £1.5 million Lottery Loan of 1710 which still had 23.5 years to run, the original maturity being 32 years. The loan was costing the Treasury £135,000 per annum to service, which represented a crude interest rate of 9 percent or just over 8 percent if allowance is made for the fact that the principal amount was not repayable, that is, the so-called "loan" was, in effect, an annuity payable over 32 years.

Under the conversion scheme, the South Sea Company offered to exchange the Lottery Loan debt for its own stock, valued at par. For this purpose the Lottery Loan was priced at 11.5 years' purchase, meaning that the interest (annuity) payments were capitalised using a multiple of 11.5 times—the total annual payments of £135,000 being valued at £1,552,000. However, an additional sum of £168,750 was to be paid in South Sea Stock to the debt holders to cover debt service arrears amounting to 1.25 years' interest. Finally, the South Sea Company was to lend £778,750 to the Exchequer, bringing the total financing figure (conversion, interest arrears plus new money) to a round sum of £2.5 million. The loan to the government was to be funded through a share issue by the Company at prevailing market prices.

Assuming full conversion of the Lottery Loan (bearing in mind that conversion was voluntary), the South Sea Company's authorised capital would increase by £2.5 million, in line with its enlarged claim on the government. The interest payable on the new debt was set at 5 percent. This was consistent with the interest payable on the Company's pre-existing capital of £10 million, which had been lowered from 6 percent to 5 percent in the summer of 1718 to reflect the downward trend of market interest rates.

The South Sea Company's books were opened for the conversion in the summer of 1719 but despite active news manipulation on the Company's behalf, including false reports of the capture of the Pretender,[25] the take-up rate was only 70 percent. Under the terms of the scheme this conversion rate triggered a proportional reduction in other payments (interest arrears and loan to the government), with the result that the total financing was reduced from £2.5 million to £1.75 million. The South Sea Company's capital similarly increased by £1.75 million to £11.75 million.

How had the various interested parties benefited from this operation? Those who converted their Lottery Loans were paid out at the rate of £1150 capital for each £100 stream of annuity income, that is, 11.5 years'

Plate 4 The Royal Exchange 1729. Copyright Guildhall Library.

purchase. Based on a prevailing market interest rate of around 5 percent the present value of each £100 stream of annuity income was nearly £1400 or 14 years' purchase. This indeed was the market price quoted by John Castaing for 32 year annuities issued at about the same time as the 1710 Lottery Loan, as well as for the Lottery Loan itself if allowance is made for the 1.25 years accrued interest arrears.[26] Debt holders were therefore being given 18 percent less than full value for their annuities.

However, since a conversion involves an exchange of assets, any benefits arising depend on the valuation not only of the assets to be converted but also of the assets to be received in lieu. Here, under-valuation of the lottery loans was offset by a broadly equivalent under-valuation of the South Sea stock; conversion was to be at par but the market price of stock in the summer of 1719 was in the range 112–117 and by the year-end stood at 128. Recipients of stock could therefore sell at an immediate profit.

Finally, those who acquired South Sea Stock through the conversion substituted readily marketable shares for a relatively illiquid financial instrument (annuities). All things considered, therefore, the debt–equity exchange can be said to have provided significant benefits to those who converted.

The government also clearly benefited from the conversion which materially lowered its debt servicing costs. In terms of cash flow, the Treasury was proposing to substitute debt service payments of only £77,625 per annum (5 percent on £1,552,500) for the existing annuity payment of £135,000 per annum, although in the event these figures were scaled down by 30 percent as explained above.

On the other hand, the substituted payment was perpetual whereas the annuity had less than 24 years to run. If allowance is made for this through the use of present value tables, the capitalised value of the government's debt service saving can be shown to have amounted to around £268,000.[27] Furthermore, the government's new debt to the South Sea Company was redeemable whereas the annuity obligations were not. In effect, therefore, the government had a call option on its new debt which could be exercised (and the debt repaid) if market interest rates fell, thereby allowing it to refinance at lower cost. The value of this call option must be added to the direct interest savings in order to calculate the total benefit of the conversion scheme to the Treasury.

Finally, there was the South Sea Company itself, which had acquired additional claims on the government in exchange for its own shares. In fact the 5 percent yield on the new as well as pre-existing debt was less than the 6 percent dividend currently being paid to shareholders so it is far from obvious that the Company was improving its prospects by the conversion transaction. On the other hand, there was one aspect of the refinancing that did appear to benefit the Company.

The scheme required the South Sea Company to lend the government £544,142 (scaled down from the original figure of £778,750). The loan was funded through the issuance in July 1719 of £520,000 (nominal) of South Sea stock at the then market price of 114, realising an amount of £592,800. This left an immediate "profit" of £48,658 over and above the loan amount due to the Treasury, *plus* a surplus of £24,000 (nominal) of stock, reflecting the fact that the Company's authorised capital (and therefore issuable stock) was linked to the amount of government debt it held. In other words, the loan to the government allowed a matching increase in the South Sea Company's capital of £544,142, comprising issued stock of £520,000 and stock in hand of just over £24,000 which, at a market price of 114, could be expected to yield £27,522. Based on the immediate gain of £48,658 on the new issue of shares, plus the further £27,522 market value of yet-to-be-issued shares, the Company could be said to have generated a potential net cash flow of £76,180 from the loan segment of the conversion operation.

On the face of it, therefore, all interested parties appear to have gained from the 1719 refinancing initiative. A cautionary pointer is that both the converting debt holders and the company benefited solely because South Sea stock had risen well above par. In fact there was a fundamental flaw in the underlying investment arithmetic but this was to become evident only later when the South Sea projectors attempted to construct a massive financial edifice on the foundations of the 1719 experiment. Remarkably, the one individual who fully understood the inevitable consequences of such financing techniques was a contemporary commentator of extraordinary financial acumen who has been for too long neglected by history. But this is to get ahead of the story of the Bubble. The next episode involves a journey across the Channel to the Rue Quincampoix in Paris where local stock market developments were to have an important influence on Exchange Alley and the South Sea Company.

NOTES

1. See Sperling (1962: 1–14) for the origins of the South Sea Company.
2. The first historian of the South Sea Bubble was Adam Anderson, who was employed as a clerk by the South Sea Company during the bubble period: see Anderson (1764). Modern scholarly treatment of the subject includes: Scott

(1912); Carswell (1993); Dickson (1967); Sperling (1962). For more popular presentations of the South Sea story see Balen (2002); Cowles (1960); Erleigh (1933); Melville (1921). For a very full compendium of writings on classic bubbles, including the South Sea Bubble, see Emmett (2000).

3. Roseveare (1991: 33).
4. Brewer (1989: 91).
5. Brewer (1989: 116–117).
6. Sperling (1962: 25).
7. Sperling (1962: 8–14).
8. See Scott (1912: 434–442).
9. Defoe (1719) in Francis (1849: 376).
10. Defoe (1719) in Francis (1849: 378).
11. Carswell (1993: 30).
12. Carswell (1993: 25).
13. Scott (1912: 439).
14. Cited in Sperling (1962: 4–5). However, the liquidity advantages of tradable stock should not be exaggerated. Neal claims that "the implied difference in yields to public holders of government debt, 9% on annuities versus 4.5% on South Sea shares [when selling at a one third premium], measures in large part the advantages of liquidity that the South Sea Company shares provided ..." (Neal 1990: 92). Bearing in mind that (highly illiquid) prime real estate was yielding around 4–5 percent at this time, and that annuities were transferable, albeit with some difficulty, the suggestion that the liquidity premium on the latter could be as much as 450 basis points seems fanciful.
15. Carswell (1993: 45) states that conversion was compulsory, whereas Scott (1912: 295) states that it was voluntary.
16. See Dickson (1967: 69).
17. Sperling (1962: 17).
18. Carswell (1993: 46).
19. See Sperling (1962: 14).
20. In the chilling valuation system of the slave trade, negroes in perfect health were counted as one-half of a pieza from ages 5 to 10, two-thirds from 10 to 15, one from 15 to 30 and three-quarters above the age of 30. A negotiated adjustment to these figures would be made for smallness, deformity or sickness. Sperling (1962: 22).
21. Sperling (1962: 20).
22. Sperling (1962: 16).
23. Dickson (1967: 470).
24. See generally Scott (1912: 299–302).
25. Carswell (1993: 76).
26. Both the "Blanks" and the "Benefits" (or Prizes) were quoted at around 15.25 years' purchase, but this included 1.25 years' accrued interest. Some historians have claimed (mistakenly) that the South Sea Company's conversion offer was based on the market price of Lottery Loans; see, for example, Neal (1990: 14).
27. Neal (1990: 95).

CHAPTER FOUR

John Law and the Mississippi Bubble

By the end of the War of the Spanish Succession, France's financial plight was even more acute than England's. In 1715, the Crown's annual peacetime expenditure was nearly 150 million livres,[1] tax revenues were running at less than half this rate, and the overall national debt stood at over 2 billion livres, representing a ratio of debt to national income variously estimated at 83 percent to 167 percent. The annual interest on this debt was around 90 million livres per annum. Additional taxation, whether through "impositions" (direct taxes on individuals) or "perceptions" (indirect taxes, e.g., on salt) was hardly feasible and large-scale borrowing could also be ruled out given the poor state of the Crown's credit—the discount on both long-term debt ("rentes") and short-term or floating debt standing at around 50 percent. Finally, the machinery of finance was itself decrepit: taxes were collected through the inefficient and corrupt intermediation of the tax farms (the General Receivers of direct taxes and the General Farms of indirect taxes) while borrowing by the state was arranged through these same financiers and their shady backers. There was no national bank, as there was in England, to manage public debt issues and the debt itself was in the name of the Crown rather than the government.

When the Duc d'Orleans, as Regent, inherited this financial crisis on Louis XIV's death in September 1715, the State was effectively bankrupt in the sense that its debt-servicing obligations exceeded its capacity to raise revenue or to borrow. The Regent's new Finance Minister, the Duc de Noailles, responded in the only way open to him—by initiating what today would be termed a sovereign default on local currency debt. Under Noaille's refinancing scheme, the interest on long-term debt was unilaterally lowered to 4 percent while the short-term floating debt was reduced in value by two-thirds, from around 600 million livres to 200 million livres, and converted into a new standardised debt instrument known as the "billet d' état". At the same time the financiers who managed the two farms were arraigned before a specially constituted Chamber of Justice and charged with profiteering to the tune of 220 million livres, around half of which was eventually recovered from the assets of those concerned. Finally, Noailles devalued the national unit of account (livres) against the coinage in circulation (the louis d'or and the silver écu), thereby further reducing the effective value of the national debt. This move reversed the monetary policy of Noailles' predecessor, Nicolas Demarets, who had progressively devalued the louis d'or from 20 to 14 livres between 1713 and 1715, that is, correspondingly raising the value of the unit of account.

John Law

These radical measures still left France in a dire financial situation characterised by massive state indebtedness, deep public distrust of the state's (part-defaulted) debt instruments and an equal distrust of a monetary system in which the national unit of account could be revalued or devalued against coinage at the whim of a finance minister. Into this unpromising environment stepped a foreign interloper and financial genius who claimed to hold the solution to France's financial problems based on the restoration of public trust in money and credit.

This self-proclaimed financial messiah was John Law, a man who managed to combine in varying degrees, vision, recklessness, a pioneering understanding of the mathematics of risk and an extraordinary charm that captivated women and gave him access to courtly circles all over Europe.[2] He was born in Edinburgh in 1671, the son of a successful goldsmith whose estate he inherited at the age of 14. Shortly after he moved to London where, as "Beau Law" he lived the life of a dandy, gambler and rake until he became involved in a fateful quarrel with another beau, Edward Wilson. At an apparently prearranged meeting in Bloomsbury Square in April 1694 the two rivals drew swords whereupon Law killed Wilson with a single thrust.

The background to this incident has a direct bearing on Law's character. His supporters claimed, and still claim, that the duel was fought over a matter of honour involving Law's then mistress, a Mrs Lawrence. However, an early acquaintance, sometime employee and first biographer of Law, W. Gray, suggests a mercenary motive.[3] According to Gray, Law, short of funds after a bad run at dice, conspired with a friend of Wilson to concoct a quarrel that would force Wilson to fight or, as expected, to settle the matter with money—Wilson having the air both of a wealthy man and of one lacking the appetite for a fight (he had recently quit his commission as an ensign in Flanders). Clearly, if this was the plan it misfired badly since Wilson's courage was greater than it had appeared. Whichever version of events one chooses, the outcome was that Law was convicted on a charge of murder and while awaiting his fate in the King's Bench Prison managed to escape under mysterious circumstances.

Law, aged 23, fled across the channel and then spent nearly two decades wandering among the courts and financial centres of Continental Europe as a professional gambler. During the course of this nomadic exile he accumulated wealth in excess of £100,000 (a "plumb" in those days) while also living in princely style and in the best society. He stayed at various times in Paris, Brussels, Genoa, Venice, Florence, Rome and Amsterdam but his preference was for the Hague and it was there that he eventually established a firmer base, setting up house with his common law wife, Lady Katherine Knowles. He also made a brief return to Scotland in the hope of advising on financial policy; his proposals were rejected but by way of consolation he is reported to have won at the gaming table an estate valued at £1200 per annum from the unfortunate Sir Andrew Ramsey.

Law's success in gambling was based on a careful study of the laws of chance. A contemporary observed that "his talents and genius, which lay particularly in figures, gave him a superior and very uncommon skill in those games, which though they depend chiefly on calculation, are used by people of quality wholly ignorant of it".[4] In other words, Law was a professional among wealthy amateurs, making hay in the salons of Europe. Faro and basset were two of the most popular games of the day and he seems to have been equally successful whether playing "banker" or placing bets so large that he could not hold the money, using instead his own tokens worth 18 louis d'or. Unsurprisingly, success at the gaming table created some hostility; he was once asked to leave Paris at 24 hours' notice, and had similar experiences in Genoa and Turin; on another occasion he was advised to leave Rotterdam after helping to set up several state lotteries in Holland, from which he is alleged to have profited personally to the tune of 200,000 guilders. However, Law also made powerful friends, including the Prince de Vendome (to whom he lent a substantial sum), the Prince of Conti, Victor Amadeus, King of Sardinia and, above all, the future regent of France, the Duc d'Orleans who shared with Law an interest in backgammon, good conversation and high living.

While on his travels through Europe Law displayed a more serious side to his nature. Not content with studying the laws of chance, he began to educate himself in the field of money and finance, taking great pains to understand the financial markets and banking practices of the cities he visited, especially Amsterdam. When the Duc d'Orleans became Regent in 1715 Law, who had moved his family to Paris the previous year, was well placed to gain a hearing for his ideas. Central to his thinking was the need in France for a state bank that would issue notes to supplement the coinage, but when he failed to make headway with this proposal he sought and obtained a charter to establish a note-issuing private bank in which he, his brother William and some influential friends were shareholders. This was the first step in what was later to become a grandiose experiment with the nation's finances.

THE GENERAL BANK

The General Bank of Law and Company received its charter in May 1716 and proceeded to operate from Law's own residence in the Place de Louis le Grand (now the Place de Vendome). The Bank had an authorised capital of 6 million livres, consisting of shares with a nominal value of 5000 livres each. However, only 25 percent of the authorised capital was actually paid up, and since 75 percent of the sum paid up was subscribed in billets d'état, then trading at a discount of around 60 percent, the effective capital was only 825,000 livres. Under the terms of its charter, which was for 20 years, the General Bank could only accept demand deposits and could not borrow money at interest, but on the lending side it was able to discount bills and lend to the most creditworthy merchants, which it did at a rate of around 0.5 percent per month or 6 percent per annum (later reduced to 5 percent).[5]

The key to the success of the General Bank lay in attracting deposits, against which it would issue its own notes, since deposits represented funding at zero interest cost. Accordingly, several steps were taken to encourage the general public to exchange their holdings of coin for bank notes. First, the notes themselves were not only payable in specie but denominated in specie, meaning that customers would receive back the same amount in coins that they had deposited, regardless of any revaluations/devaluations of the livre that might occur (a convenient reminder of this benefit occurring in May 1718 when the livre, at Law's instigation, was devalued). In this way, the Bank in effect united the unit of account with the medium of exchange, thereby removing uncertainty, and providing depositors with a convenient asset (bank notes) that were equivalent to specie in value and transferability. Second, the fact that the Regent himself was patron of the Bank, and known to deposit substantial funds, gave the public confidence in the new venture. Third, Law offered customers free transaction services, such as remittances and foreign exchange facilities in order to attract business. Finally, demand for the General Bank's notes increased when a decree of April 1717 stated that bank notes could be used as legal tender in payment of taxes (payment in this form was later made mandatory in Paris), thereby developing further the Bank's links with the state.

With the General Bank attracting deposits at zero interest, and making loans at 5–6 percent per annum, its profitability would be constrained by two factors: the proportion of deposits that were backed by non-interest bearing specie reserves and the ratio of equity capital to deposits.

On the first point it seems that Law may have maintained a reserve ratio of 25–50 percent against bank notes, although there is considerable uncertainty about this since the bank's records have not survived. The fact that Law adopted a policy of complete secrecy with regard to the bank's financial operations, which were not disclosed either to share-holders or to the bank's Council,[6] suggests that he may have maintained a lower reserve ratio than would have been considered prudent. Certainly, Law could take some risks with liquidity because he had access to a lender of last resort: when an attempt was made to break the bank through the presentation of notes valued at 5 million livres for immediate conversion into cash, he was able to persuade Noailles to provide the necessary funds from the state treasury.[7]

So far as the capital ratio is concerned, it would seem that some 40 million livres of bank notes might be outstanding at any time,[8] which would suggest a ratio of equity capital to deposits of around 2 percent and a ratio of capital to loans of 3–4 percent. The basic arithmetic of the situation was highly beneficial to Law and his fellow shareholders: the 825,000 livres of equity capital in the bank was supporting earning assets of perhaps 20–30 million livres, the gross return on which was, at an average interest charge of 5 percent,[9] 1–1.5 million livres per annum before allowing for operating costs. The implication is that once the Bank was up and running, the annual return on its capital was well over 100 percent.

Indeed the General Bank was so successful that in December 1718 the Crown reverted to Law's original proposal for a state-owned Royal Bank. It bought out the private shareholders at 5000 livres per share for which the latter had paid an effective 688 livres, making a total shareholder profit of around 800 percent over 2.5 years when dividends of 615 livres per share are included.[10] Law had now established his credentials as a highly successful entrepreneur and banker while further ingratiating himself with the Regent and his circle. More to the point he had created a platform for his next move.

The transformation of the General Bank into the Royal Bank was accompanied by a shift in the scale of banking operations. This involved new branches in Lyon, La Rochelle, Tours, Orleans and Amiens; a rapid increase in the note issue (which was now redenominated in livres); and enhanced credit creation facilitated by a decline in the proportion of deposits backed by specie reserves. Law was still directing operations but by 1719 the Bank was no longer a purely commercial enterprise; it had become subservient to a much grander design to revolutionise France's finances.

THE MISSISSIPPI COMPANY

Once he had established the General Bank, Law developed the next stage of his financial experiment, which involved a debt refinancing operation along the lines already implemented in England by the South Sea Company. For this purpose Law acquired a defunct enterprise, the Mississippi Company, which held the trading rights in French Louisiana, at that time a huge geographic region extending 3000 miles North from the mouth of the Mississippi to include parts of Canada. His proposal, which received the Regent's approval, was to finance the development of Louisiana through a share issue by the newly named Company of the West that would be subscribed in state bonds. An official in the French Ministry of Foreign Affairs described the plan in terms that acknowledged the debt owed to the South Sea scheme:

> The Company that it is proposed to form, under the name of the Company of the West, has like the English South Sea Company, two objects—that of trade and that of retiring a considerable quantity of billets d'état and replacing them with shares, the credit of which it is hoped will be better sustained than those of the billets d'état.[11]

To implement his scheme Law proposed to issue 200,000 shares of 500 livres each, in order to raise 100 million livres of nominal capital. In reality, however, the capital would be less than one-third of this amount, since the billets d'état which were to be exchanged for shares were standing at a discount of 70 percent. This was a "par exchange" (500 livres nominal shares against 500 livres nominal billets d'état) similar to the South Sea Company's first share issue. The effective cost of shares to subscribers was around 150 livres, that is, the value of the depreciated billets d'état for which the shares were exchanged. In the event, subscriptions were slow and so the terms were softened to allow payment in five separate instalments. At the same time the Regent supported the flotation by taking a 40 percent shareholding on behalf of the young King, the Crown in effect acquiring its own debt. The Company initially received 4 percent per annum on the loans to the state that it had acquired (i.e., the same yield as on the billets d'état which had been subscribed for shares): the first interest payment was to be used to equip a commercial fleet, and subsequent payments passed through as dividends at the minimum rate of 20 livres per annum for each 500 livre share, exclusive of trading profits.[12]

The Company of the West, better known as the Mississippi Company, was launched in August 1717, although its capital was not fully subscribed for more than a year. The new company was given a monopoly of trade plus mineral rights for 25 years. The immediate task of Law as chief executive of the enterprise was to promote sales of land, to encourage settlers and to fit out vessels to transport colonists and their families, together with slaves, labourers, craftsmen and, of course, merchandise. There was a flurry of interest in Louisiana which was promoted as a land offering precious minerals and a fertile soil, so much so that unimproved land was sold at 30,000 livres per square league. Suitable publicity appears to have been organised by Law. The official Nouveau Mercure in September 1717 carried an article enthusing over the new colony's mild climate, its abundance of fresh game, the richness of its gold, silver and copper deposits and the prevalence of certain green rocks that "resembled emeralds".[13] According to the same publication, by 1719, the showpiece settlement of New Orleans, judiciously named after Law's illustrious patron, boasted around 800 houses, each with a holding of 120 acres. (The reality, however, seems to have been rather different: a Jesuit traveller, Fr. Charleroi, claimed that in 1723 he found in New Orleans not 800 houses, "but randomly situated huts, a large wooden store, and two or three houses unworthy of a French village".)[14] Appearances, at any rate, suggested that the Mississippi Company's trading prospects were much brighter than those of its English counterpart which by now had all but given up on the South Sea trade.

Law's commercial ambitions were not satisfied with the Louisiana concession, even though it covered an area greater than Europe. In the Summer of 1718 the Company of the West acquired the tobacco monopoly from the Crown for 2 million livres and before the year end it took over the trading activities of the Senegal Company. The geographic scope of the Company's commercial interests was then expanded dramatically in May 1719 when Law acquired the Company of the Indies (the Company of the West subsequently trading under this name*) as well

* The name "Mississippi" has persisted and hence the Company of the Indies is referred to here as the Mississippi Company.

as the China Company and, shortly after, the Company of Africa. The entire colonial trade of France, the richest country in Europe, was now vested in a single corporate monopoly under the direction of one man, and he a fugitive foreigner, former roué and convicted murderer.

The price paid for the Company of the Indies and the China Company was in the form of an agreement by the Company of the West to take on these enterprises' debts. In order to cover this obligation and to exploit the new trading opportunities, Law needed to raise more capital. Accordingly, a second share issue was planned for June 1719, this time for cash in order to meet the Company's funding needs. Fifty thousand shares were to be issued at 550 livres each to raise just over 25 million livres.

Several unusual features of this share offering are worth noting. First, the price, when it was fixed in May, represented a small premium over the shares' nominal value and a significant premium over the then market price of 450 livres. Second, Law and a small group of co-underwriters took an enormous personal gamble when, to reassure the investing public, they agreed to underwrite the share issue at their own risk, in effect committing themselves to find 25 million livres if the issue went badly. Third, the subscription terms were deliberately generous, involving a down payment of the 50 livres premium plus 10, later extended to 20, monthly instalments. Partly paid shares could be sold once the 50 livres premium and the first monthly instalment had been paid, thereby allowing highly leveraged trading in partly paid scrip.

Finally, Law arranged this second share offering in the form of what today would be called a "rights issue". Buyers of the new shares ("filles") in the primary market were required to possess four old shares ("mères") as a precondition of their purchase. However, since there was an active secondary market both in the old shares and the "rights" attaching to them (subject, as noted above, to payment of the premium), the financial consequences for the price of both classes of share were minimal. That is to say, once issued, filles as well as mères could be freely bought and sold for cash. Presumably the mère, fille, and, later, petites fille, share designations were introduced as a marketing ploy to encourage the notion that shares were in short supply and that to acquire them was a privilege (although in the final stages of the Mississippi boom Law dropped the "rights" issue approach to share issues).

Reliable share prices for this period are not available but it seems that in May, when the second share issue was being prepared, Mississippi shares stood at 450 livres, a threefold increase on their original subscription price although still below par value. By mid-June, when the new issue was formally authorised, old shares had risen to 600 and, as Law later pointed out, since the new shares, with their extended instalment terms, would certainly be worth more than the old, the underwriting gamble had paid off.[15]

An important factor in the buoyancy of Mississippi shares during this period was the rapid increase in money and credit that was occurring due to operations of the Royal Bank under the direction of Law. A further 50 million livres of bank notes were issued on 10 June, ahead of the second share offering, bringing the cumulative note issuance in the first six months of 1719 to 160 million livres. As Antoine Murphy has pointed out, Law was actively using his control of the money supply to support his share flotations, fully realizing the close connection between liquidity and the behaviour of asset prices.[16] This was something the South Sea Company could not do, given the independence of the Bank of England, although the South Sea Directors were able to expand credit by lending on the security of South Sea stock.

Law was now moving at great speed, taking full advantage of surging investor confidence and the rapidly rising Mississippi share price. On 20 July, the Mississippi Company acquired the revenues of the Mint for nine years, estimated to be worth 6 million livres per annum, at a price of 50 million livres payable over 15 months. This transaction, it may be noted, only made sense financially if Law felt he could significantly increase the Mint's profitability. On 26 July, at a general meeting of the Mississippi Company, Law declared that the dividend in 1720 would be increased from 4 percent to 12 percent, that is, to 60 livres per 500 livre share compared to 20 livres previously. On the back of this announcement, the details of a new share issue were outlined the very next day, aimed at raising 50 million livres to pay for the Mint.

The third Mississippi share offering was again for cash and on a rights basis, each purchaser of the new shares ("petites filles") having to possess four mères and one fille. Fifty thousand shares were to be issued at 1000 livres per share with payment in 20 monthly instalments of 50 livres, raising the total number of shares outstanding to 300,000 and implying a market valuation of the Company of 300 million livres. However, the announcement of the issue terms was soon overtaken by events, a wave of investor enthusiasm carrying the shares to 3000 livres during the subscription period. According to one account,[17] the Company responded by holding back some of the shares in a reserve fund and disposing of them in stages at even higher market prices, the capital raising exercise thereby yielding considerably in excess of the 50 million livres target figure. Evidently this delayed allocation allowed Law to give favours to particular individuals by allowing them to queue-jump the subscription lists. In the words of Wood, Law's nineteenth century biographer, "the names of the stockholders were not declared for some weeks, and during that interval, Mr Law's door was kept shut, while the first quality in France appeared on foot in hundreds, before his house in the Place Vendome".[18]

VALUATION OF MISSISSIPPI SHARES

At this point it is worth pausing to consider the value that was being placed on Mississippi shares. It has been suggested that the Mississippi Company was generating profits of around 18 million livres per annum, consisting of 6 million livres from the mint, 4 million livres in interest payments on the holding of 100 million livres of billets d'état, 3 million livres from the tobacco monopoly and 5 million livres or more on trading activities.[19] This would more or less justify the 60 livres per share dividend promised for 1720 which on 300,000 shares would amount to 18 million livres. Since alternative investments in state obligations were at this time yielding around 4 percent (billets d'état having risen to something like par value as a result of Law's debt conversion operations), a share price of 3000 livres, equivalent to a yield basis of around 2 percent, seems expensive but not totally out of order. Therefore, at this stage in the Mississippi boom, it would be wrong to conclude that there was an unsustainable or irrational bubble, despite a 20-fold rise in the share price since the company's flotation.

The next three months, however, witnessed a new phase in the development of the Mississippi company which would lead ultimately to disaster. Buoyed by his success to date, towards the end of August, Law proposed a massive new debt conversion operation aimed at paying off the entire outstanding state debt of 1.5 billion livres in exchange for yet another share issue, this time amounting to a startling 300,000 shares (which would double the Company's equity capital), priced at 5000 livres each. Holders of both long-term debt (rentes) and billets d'état would be offered shares at this price in exchange for their debt holdings valued at par; since by now their paper was selling for up to 20 percent more than its face value, the effective cost of shares was well in excess of 5000 livres.

The debt conversion package included two other key elements. First, the interest payable on the Crown's debts to the Company, now amounting to 1.6 billion livres (including 100 million under the original debt conversion) was lowered from 4 percent to 3 percent or 48 million livres per annum, thereby providing important savings on the Crown's debt servicing payments. Second, the Mississippi Company was awarded a 9 year lease on the tax farms for which it was to pay 52 million livres annually, or some 3.5 million livres per annum above that paid by the existing leaseholders whose contract was unilaterally terminated.

Three separate sub-issues of 100,000 shares each were made between the final week of September and the first week of October 1719, to make up the total 300,000 planned offer. These shares, known as "cinq-cents", were issued with a nominal value of 500 and a price of 5000, without the customary "rights issue" conditions. The flooding of the market with new shares might have been expected to dampen the public's enthusiasm but, once again, the share price soared to new levels, reaching monthly highs of 5900 in September, 6500 in October, 6738 in November and 10,025 in December.

Two key factors lay behind the run-away performance of Mississippi shares in the final months of 1719. First, Law made sure that monetary and credit conditions were highly favourable to asset prices. As he opened the monetary sluice gates ever wider, the Royal Bank's outstanding note issue rose from less than 200 million livres at the end of June to 1 billion livres at the end of December, a level only just short of the estimated value of the nation's coinage. At the same time, the Royal Bank began to offer very attractive borrowing terms for purchasers of Mississippi shares, namely 2 percent per annum interest subject to a borrowing limit of 2500 livres for each share deposited. The collateral terms were not out of the ordinary but the interest terms—more favourable than those available to the Crown itself—certainly were. The easy money environment meanwhile contributed to a boom in property prices, with yields on private property around Paris reportedly falling to less than 2 percent (50–60 years' purchase).

A second support for share prices was provided by the various reports that began to appear regarding the potential profitability of the Mississippi Company's operations (see table 4.1). These suggested that profits from overseas trade could amount to anything up to 44 million livres and profits from the tax farms up to 30 million livres. Revenues on this scale would support a dividend much higher than the 60 livres per share so far promised and indeed before the end of the year, on the basis of his own profit projection of 91 million livres, Law raised the prospective dividend for 1720 to 200 livres. On a yield basis of 4 percent this would justify a share price of around 5000 livres, in line with the latest

TABLE 4.1
Estimates of Profitability of the Mississippi Company 1719/1720 (livres million)

	A^a	B^b	C^c	D^d	E^e
Interest from state	48	48^f	48	48	48
Profits from tax farms	12	30	20 (38)^g	15	
Profits from mint	12	5	6	4	39
Profits from tobacco monopoly	6	4	2.5	2	
General receipts of taxes	1	–	1.5	1.5	
Foreign trade	12	19	10	10	44
Total	91	106 (131)^h	88 (106)	80.5	131
Memorandum items					
Earnings per share	152	177 (218)	147 (177)	134	218
Earnings yield (%) at share price of:					
(a) 5000 livres	3	3.5 (4.4)	2.9 (3.5)	2.7	4.4
(b) 10,000 livres	1.5	1.75 (2.2)	1.45 (1.75)	1.35	2.2

^{a} Law's estimates presented at Company's annual general meeting 30 December 1719, reproduced in Faure (1978: 304).

^{b} Anon (possibly authored by Law) (1720e: 20).

^{c} Harsin (1928: 178).

^{d} Wood (1824: 41).

^{e} Wood (1824: 42).

^{f} Divided into interest of 45 million livres and tobacco receipts of 3 million livres.

^{g} The larger figure includes an allowance of 25 million livres for miscellaneous items, for example, fisheries and bullion dealing.

^{h} According to Harsin, actual profits from the tax farms was 38 million livres in 1720. On this point, see Faure (1978: 305).

issue price, although the market price reached by year end was twice this level.

Some of the profit projections made at this time were not too far removed from reality. In particular, revenues from the tax farms were proving to be especially buoyant, due in part to economic recovery in France, and it has been suggested that realised profits from this source may have reached 38 million livres in 1720.[20] On the other hand, the Mississippi company's overall trading operations were almost certainly loss-making. Giraud, in his history of Louisiana, estimates that the cost of equipping ships, etc., exceeded revenues from the Louisiana concession and that the resulting net cash outflow was not matched by profits on other trading routes.[21] Given the negative balance on foreign trade, it seems unlikely that the Company was generating sufficient profits overall to justify a dividend of 200 livres per share.

The fact was that the largest asset of the Company consisted of 1.6 billion livres of loans to the Crown yielding a mere 3 percent which it had acquired in exchange for subscriber's debt holdings yielding 4 percent. The clear implication is that the return on the Company's major asset was well below its cost of capital. Furthermore, whereas the 3 percent return on loans to the state could not conceivably go up, it could go down, as it had once done already (on the billets d'état originally subscribed) and was shortly to do again.

One way of interpreting the market's valuation of the Company is to subtract the value of the Crown's debt, leaving an implicit valuation of all remaining activities. Taking the Company's 1.6 billion livres claim on the Crown to be worth its face value amount (which, given the reduced interest rate of 3 percent payable, is a rather generous assumption) the rest of the business, at the peak share price of around 10,000 livres, was being valued at 4.4 billion livres (i.e., 6 billion livres market capitalisation less 1.6 billion livres). Using Law's own profit projection, excluding interest payments, of 43 million livres (see column A, table 4.1), the yield basis of the resulting partial valuation is a startlingly low 1 percent. The implication is that investors had by this point lost touch with reality, especially when it is recalled that most of the Company's revenue sources, notably the tax farms, mint and tobacco monopoly, were strictly time-limited.

Be that as it may, the market remained in a state of feverish excitement throughout the second half of 1719. Mississippi shares were bought and sold in a grubby narrow street, the Rue Quincampoix, located in what is today the Les Halles district of Paris, running between the rue aux Ours to the north and the rue Aubry de Bouchor to the south. This street had long been associated with money dealing and was named after Nicolas de Kiquenpoit, a twelfth century financier. To begin with trading was conducted in apartments rented out for the purpose, but as the Mississippi boom developed, trading overflowed into the street, just as it had done in Exchange Alley. Carriages were banned in an attempt to ease the congestion and the crowds had to be driven away at nightfall with the sounding of the evening bell. Daniel Defoe provides a characteristically lurid description of the scene:

> Nothing can be more diverting than to see the hurry and clatter of the stock-jobbers in Quincampoix street; a place so scandalously dirty, as if it had been not the sink of the city only, but of the whole Kingdom .... The inconvenience of the darkest and nastiest street in Paris does not prevent the crowds of people of all qualities ... coming to buy and sell their stocks in the open place; where without distinction, they go up to the ankles in dirt, every step they take.[22]

The overcrowding eventually became too much for residents of the area and the stock market was moved briefly in June 1720, to the Place Vendome. Here the Chancellor claimed that the noise disturbed him in his neighbouring office and the market was again moved, this time to the gardens of the Hotel de Soissons where, on 1 August 1720, it re-opened as the Bourse. Trading took place in specially constructed pavillions, rented at 500 livres per month, which also housed lotteries, gaming tables and refreshments. This venue, too, was short-lived, stock-jobbing being subject to a blanket prohibition from 8 December 1720 as a result of the Mississippi crash (see chapter 7).

LAW AS FINANCIAL SUPREMO

By the end of 1719, Law was riding high. He had earned the gratitude of the Regent, as well as the Crown and its entourage by making a success of the bank and the Mississippi Company, thereby enriching himself and his royal supporters while also appearing to resolve the nation's financial crisis. He had endeared himself to the wider establishment when the Mississippi Company offered to pay all pension arrears owed by the Crown. And he had developed a strong following among the general populace through public acts of charity. More generally, the "wealth effect" from rising share and property prices, coupled with monetary expansion and lower interest rates, contributed to an economic boom and growing sense of well-being that was widely attributed to Law's financial innovations.

Law had also advertised his commitment to France. He had adopted French nationality in May 1716 in order to obtain his bank charter. Then, as he accumulated wealth, he made a point of investing nearly everything in French property; he bought no less than fourteen estates with titles annexed to them "in hopes of conciliating the confidence of the people, and precluding all accusations of having drained the kingdom of specie by sending it to foreign parts".[23] Finally, in December 1719, Law, with great pomp and ceremony, was accepted into the Catholic faith in a service presided over by the Abbé de Tencin, who later received Mississippi shares worth 200,000 livres. Coincidentally, this conversion, which at his insistence included his two children but, pointedly, not their mother, Katherine, opened the way for Law to hold public office.

On 8 January 1720, Mississippi shares reached their all-time peak of 10,100, valuing the Company at over 6 billion livres. It was fitting, therefore, that three days earlier Law had been appointed Controller General of

Finances, the highest administrative post in a country which was itself the foremost economic power in Europe. According to the letters of appointment, this high honour was conferred in recognition of "the important services that you have rendered to our state as much for the establishment of our Royal Bank, whose utility we appreciate, as for the different arrangements that have been made for the payment of our public debts, for the increase in our state revenues and for the relief of our people".[24]

Law, the outcast, had risen as high as it was possible to go. He was in effect France's First Minister, as well as presiding personally over the affairs of the largest bank in Europe and the biggest trading company in the world. Defoe, as always, had a pertinent comment on Law's meteoric career:

> The case is plain, you must put on a sword, kill a beau or two, get into Newgate, be condemned to be hanged, break prison if you can—*remember that by the way*—get over to some strange country, turn stock-jobber, set up a Mississippi stock, bubble a nation, and you may soon be a great man.[25]

There were signs, nevertheless, that Law was becoming inebriated by his own success. Backing his belief that England's commercial interests would now suffer at the hands of France, he entered into a speculative contract with Thomas Pitt, Lord Londonderry, dated 29 September 1719, under which he agreed to sell 12 months forward £100,000 of stock in the East India Company at £180,000, 11 percent below the prevailing market price.[26] This speculation, no doubt born of hubris, was to prove very costly—although not nearly as costly as Law's ultimate gamble which was to invest his entire fortune in France, mainly in the form of illiquid real estate. The professional gambler was losing his touch at the very pinnacle of his career as a statesman and financier.

As previously noted, Law's early development of the Mississippi project was modelled on the South Sea Company. It is worth considering, therefore, the similarities and differences between these two pioneering ventures. Most obviously, they shared the concept of combining a monopoly trading franchise with the conversion of state debts into corporate shares. They also used very similar marketing methods including orchestrated newspaper hype, lending on margin (i.e., using shares as security), share subscriptions on generous instalment terms, and a degree of share price manipulation involving a succession of new issues at ever higher valuations. Finally, the various investment techniques, involving forward and option contracts as well as spot transactions, were similar, which is not surprising bearing in mind that there was a common pool of investors that dealt in both South Sea and Mississippi shares. The importance of this new breed of international investor is suggested by the tens of thousands of foreigners, from Venice, Genoa, Germany, England, Holland and Spain, who were reported to have flocked to Paris in 1719 to trade in the Rue Quincampoix.

There were also some important differences between the South Sea and Mississippi enterprises. First, the South Sea Company, at an early stage, was reduced to little more than an annuity holding company when the trading side became moribund, whereas the Mississippi Company had broad commercial and trading interests to complement its debt management activities. Second, there were technical differences in the Companies' operations: Mississippi shares were freely tradable as bearer securities whereas ownership of South Sea shares had to be registered on the company's books (although partly paid scrip was in both cases assignable as a bearer instrument); and, unlike the South Sea Company, the Mississippi Company's authorised capital did not depend on the difference between the nominal value of shares and the price at which they were issued. The last point is important, because it casts doubt on the consensus view that the origins of the South Sea Bubble owed much to this feature of the South Sea Company's authorised capital.

A third point of difference is that the South Sea Company had to compete as an investment with other English share-issuing companies—both major enterprises like the East India Company as well as rival bubbles—whereas the Mississippi Company was "the only game in town". Furthermore, Law was eventually able to control *all* domestic financial assets in France, embracing state debts, bank notes, Mississippi shares and (after his appointment as Controller General) the legal status and value of coinage. Indeed, Law's jurisdiction over the entire domestic financial system was to have an important influence on the speed and extent of the Mississippi share price collapse, once the bubble had burst.

Finally, the sequencing of the two companies' expansionary initiatives was different, as was the timing of the associated share price boom and collapse. The Mississippi Company owed its origins to an attempt to replicate the successful launch of the South Sea project. However, the massive debt conversion operation carried out by Law in September/October 1719 went far beyond anything proposed up to that time by the South Sea Company and Law's apparent success became, in turn, an example for the South Sea Company to follow early on in the new year. Law's grandiose experiment therefore provided the stimulus for the South Sea Company's next spectacular move.

NOTES

1. The French monetary system was based on the livre, a unit of account used to express prices, contracts and wages, against which the value of gold and silver coins could be adjusted.
2. For biographical material on John Law, see Gray (1721); Hyde (1969); Faure (1978); Gleeson (1999); Murphy (1997); Wood (1824); McFarland Davis (1887: 289–318).
3. Gray (1721: 7–8).
4. Anon (11 November 1721b).
5. Murphy (1997: 156); Faure (1978: 117).
6. Murphy (1997: 161).
7. Hyde (1969: 82). The fact that Law had to resort to treasury funds to redeem 5 million livres of bank notes suggests that the specie reserve may have been lower than has generally been assumed.
8. At the time of its transformation into the Royal Bank at the end of 1718, the General Bank had 39.5 million livres of banknotes in circulation and a specie reserve of 9.2 million livre. Murphy (1997: 185).
9. According to Law, the interest charge, initially set at 6 percent, had by the end of 1717 been lowered to 4 percent (Murphy (1997: 161). Faure states that the interest charge was lowered from 6 percent to 5 percent. Faure (1978: 117).
10. Murphy (1997: 163).
11. Cited in Murphy (1997: 168).
12. Wood (1824: 36).
13. Cited in Murphy (1986: 91).
14. Cited in Murphy (1986: 99).
15. Murphy (1997: 189–190).
16. Murphy (1997: 191).
17. Anon (1720e: 9).
18. Wood (1824: 40).
19. Harsin (1928: 165–166).
20. Faure (1978: 305).
21. Giraud (1966: 80, 86).
22. Cited in Gleeson (1999: 127).
23. Wood (1791: 20).
24. Cited in Murphy (1997: 213–214).
25. Defoe in Lee (1869: 189).
26. Neal (2000: 659–674).

CHAPTER FIVE

The South Sea Scheme

THE SPECTACULAR progress of Law's financial experiments in France during 1719 had powerful repercussions in England. The English government became apprehensive that Law's achievements would strengthen France's national finances to an extent that could threaten England's own economic position.[1] Therefore, renewed efforts to stabilise the English national debt were called for. At the same time, investors' overwhelmingly favourable response to Law's conversion of France's debt into Mississippi stock suggested to the South Sea projectors that a similar initiative might be successfully implemented in England. Finally, the extraordinary profits reported to have been made by Mississippi investors unleashed a wave of speculative enthusiasm for stock market investments throughout Europe. Exchange Alley was therefore already primed for a major new initiative by the South Sea Company.

At this time the government was again focusing on the management of its outstanding debt, although now the particular cause for concern was not short-term debt, which had been successfully incorporated into South Sea stock in 1711, but rather the long-term debt (see table 5.1). This took the form of (a) moneys owed to the Bank of England, the East India Company and the South Sea Company, which could be redeemed on giving sufficient notice; (b) government stock at 4 percent and 5 percent which could be repaid at a year's notice; and (c) annuities for terms of years, most of which would expire between 1792 and 1807 (the "long annuities"), but some of which had an expiry date of 1742 (the "short annuities"). The annuities were viewed as especially problematical, first because they were costly to service (yields were 7–9 percent on the original capital lent) and second because they represented "irredeemable" debt that could not be repaid or refinanced at a lower interest rate without the annuitants' consent. In an era when permanent national debt was an alien concept, there was a political imperative to pay off, or at least to be seen to have a plan to pay off, outstanding government obligations. Long-term irredeemable debt was therefore incompatible with fiscal rectitude.

TABLE 5.1
Government Long-Term Debts December 1719

		£million	£million
1.	Owed to companies		
	(a) Bank of England	3.4	
	(b) East India Company	3.2	
	(c) South Sea Company	11.7	
			18.3
2.	Redeemable government stock		16.6
3.	Annuities for terms of years		
	(a) Long annuities (at 20 years' purchase)	13.3	
	(b) Short annuities (at 14 years' purchase)	1.7	
			15.0
			49.9

Source: Dickson (1967: 93).

THE SOUTH SEA SCHEME

Towards the end of 1719, the South Sea company, led by John Blunt and the Government, represented by the Chancellor of the Exchequer, John Aislabie, entered into discussions about the possibility of a massive debt conversion plan along the lines of Law's Mississippi operation. According to a contemporary account written by one of the South Sea Directors, Blunt initially proposed that all the government's outstanding debt, *including* that owed by the Bank of England and the East India Company, should be taken in by the South Sea Company, since "as Mr Law had taken his pattern from him, and improved upon what was done the year before in relation to the Lottery of 1710, he would now improve on what was done in France, and out-do Mr Law".[2] Such a move would have upset powerful City interests and the discussions therefore proceeded on the basis that the sums owed to the two great companies would be excluded from the debt conversion scheme.

John Aislabie, who was to become deeply involved in this new phase of the South Sea Company's operations, later became a political scapegoat for the scheme's collapse. History has also been unkind to Aislabie, many commentators taking their cue from a contemporary description of him as "a man of good understanding ... and very capable of business; but dark, and of a cunning that rendered him suspected and low in all men's opinion .... He was much set upon increasing his fortune and did that."[3]

Among modern writers, the verdict is much the same, Carswell, for instance, characterising him as "vain, blustering and slippery", and "one of the least attractive of eighteenth century politicians".[4] It has to be said, however, that Aislabie's undoubted character flaws—and especially his political chicanery and venality—were shared with many of his contemporaries, including Walpole. His greatest sin was to be too closely associated with the South Sea Scheme, although, paradoxically, he was one of the very few leading figures of the time to foresee the likely consequences of the market excesses of 1720.

On 21 January 1720, the great debt conversion scheme agreed in outline between the Treasury and the leading South Sea projectors was laid before the Company's Court of Directors. In essence, the proposal envisaged an offer to all holders of irredeemable and redeemable government debt to exchange their securities for South Sea stock, a privilege for which the Company would pay to the government a sum of £1.5 million outright plus a further £1.6 million maximum depending on the amount of debt actually converted. The South Sea Company would acquire claims against the government equivalent to the securities exchanged on which interest would be paid at a rate lower than that paid on the original securities.

On 22 January, the House of Commons insisted that rival tenders should be considered and in response the Bank of England submitted its own proposal on 27 January. The Bank raised the stakes by offering to pay a maximum sum of nearly £5.6 million to the government, conditional on securing the conversion of all outstanding irredeemable and redeemable debt. On the same day, the South Sea Company increased the unconditional element in its offer from £1.5 million to £3.5 million, bringing the maximum sum payable to just over £5 million; it also accepted a reduction in the interest on the whole debt owed by the government from 5 percent to 4 percent with effect from mid-1727.

The House of Commons allowed further time for the two institutions to amend their proposals and on 1 February their final offers were submitted. The Bank did not significantly adjust its proposals except to specify in advance the terms on which it was prepared to offer its stock in exchange for government securities—£1700 of Bank stock for each £100 of long annuities and a proportional amount for short annuities. The South Sea Company, on the other hand, while still declining to specify the terms on which it would offer to exchange its stock for securities, raised its unconditional payment yet again to £4 million, and the total maximum sum payable (if all the debts were converted) to just under £7.6 million.

The South Sea Company emerged as victor (if that is the right word) from this hectic competitive bidding which Aislabie later described as "setting the nation up to auction". The Company's proposals were accepted by the House of Commons on 2 February and subsequently incorporated into a Bill which received the royal assent on 7 April. The South Sea Act ran to thirty-five pages in the printed statutes, but the main elements of the final conversion scheme can be summarised as follows:[5]

1. The South Sea Company offered to buy in all outstanding long annuities, short annuities and redeemable debts, totalling approximately £31.5 million, in exchange for its own stock.

2. The Company agreed to pay £4 million unconditionally to the government plus a further conditional sum equivalent to 4.5 years' purchase on all irredeemable debts exchanged by 1 March 1722, together with a penalty equivalent to one year's purchase (up to £666,000) on all long annuities *not* exchanged by then, the maximum sum payable to the government under all headings being just under £7.6 million.

3. The government would credit the Company with an increase of £31.5 million both in its nominal capital and in the amount owed to it by the state if all the subscribable debts were exchanged. The basis on which debts were capitalised for this purpose was: 20 years' purchase for the long annuities, 14 years for the short and par value for the redeemables.

4. The government agreed to pay interest on the increased debt partly at 5 percent and partly at 4 percent until midsummer 1727 when interest on all the debt owed to the Company would be reduced to 4 percent.

5. The government could start to pay off debts subscribed into the South Sea Company from midsummer 1727, that is, the entire debt had become redeemable.

6. The government agreed to lend the Company £1 million in Exchequer Bills as an immediate source of liquidity.

The implications of the debt conversion for the government, the South Sea Company and the investing public are shown in figures 5.1 and 5.2.

How were the benefits of this conversion operation to be distributed between the various parties involved? The advantages for the government were obvious enough, since it was to (a) receive a cash payment of between £4 million and £7.6 million, (b) secure an immediate reduction in debt servicing costs which would increase from 1727 when the interest

Government	South Sea Company		Public
Liabilities	Assets	Liabilities	Assets
£11.7 million debt to South Sea Company	£11.7 million loans to government	Shares issued to public (£11.7 million nominal)	Shares in South Sea Company
£6.6 million debt to East India Co and Bank of England			
	South Sea trading franchise		Redeemable debt
Redeemable debts and annuities owed to public			Annuities

Figure 5.1   Financial structure before 1720 conversion scheme.

charge was lowered to 4 percent and (c) see its irredeemable debt converted into redeemable form. These fiscal benefits would, according to the Chancellor of the Exchequer, Aislabie, allow the government to pay off the entire national debt over 25 years.

The potential advantages of conversion to the annuitants and other holders of subscribable government debt became a matter of intense controversy between rival supporters of the Bank on the one hand, and

Government	South Sea Company		Public
Liabilities	Assets	Liabilities	Assets
£43.2 million debt to South Sea Company	£43.2 million loans to government	Shares issued to public (£43.2 million nominal)	Shares in South Sea Company
£6.6 million debt to East India Co and Bank of England	South Sea trading franchise		
less £7.6 million cash to be recovered from South Sea Company	Cash from sales of surplus stock		

Figure 5.2   Financial structure after 1720 conversion scheme.

the South Sea Company on the other.[6] The debate focused, in particular, on the terms that might be offered to the holders of long annuities, given current market values.

During February/March 1720 when the conversion proposals were being discussed in the press and the coffee houses, the long annuities were quoted in the market at a price of 24/25 years' purchase, against 20 years' purchase previously. Some attributed the strengthening of prices to a general decline in market interest rates but others took the view that the prospect of conversion on favourable terms had distorted prices and that the true or "intrinsic" value was around 20 years' purchase.[7] According-ing to the latter view, the proper benchmark against which the conversion terms should be assessed was 20 year's purchase, which was also the valuation basis used by the government to determine its debt due to the South Sea Company (above).

Neither the South Sea Company nor the Bank of England were prepared to specify in their proposals the precise terms on which the annuitants would be able to convert into their stock. A full specification would have required a fixed valuation not only of the assets to be converted (the annuities) but also of the assets to be received in lieu (company stock). In this context much was made by the Bank of England's supporters of its commitment to a conversion rate for long annuities of £1700 (nominal) of bank stock for each of £100 of annuity income; with Bank shares trading at 150 this was equivalent to 25.5 years' purchase. However, had the Bank's proposal been accepted, the actual amount received by converting annuitants would be greater or less than this, depending on fluctuations in the market price of Bank stock prior to the date of conversion.

The South Sea Company, for its part, made no reference at all to the conversion terms in its proposal to Parliament but, since conversion was to be voluntary, it would have to offer an attractive package to annui-tants, widely assumed to mean 25 years' purchase or better.[8] It was in any event quite impractical to fix the full conversion terms in advance, given the scale and complexity of the scheme, changing market conditions and the two year period (to March 1722) allowed by the government for conversion to be completed. Clearly, as in today's capital markets, the terms of the debt–equity swap could only be fixed at the time each succes-sive tranche of the swap was marketed to annuitants.

From the South Sea Company's point of view, the package deal agreed with the government involved obvious costs and risks. If the Company were unable to implement the conversion scheme, it faced penalties amounting in total to nearly £4.7 million (unconditional payment of £4 million plus £0.7 million penalty on unconverted long annuities), whereas, at the other extreme, if all the debt were converted, the cash payment due to the government would be nearly £7.6 million, representing the £4 million unconditional payment plus the variable payment on converted annuities. These vast sums were dead weight losses and the cash flow that would be necessary to meet them could only be generated through the issuance of new shares (below).

Assuming the conversion scheme was successfully implemented, the South Sea Company would in effect acquire additional claims on the government in exchange for its own shares. However, whereas the average interest payable on the Company's new and existing loans to the government would be just under 5 percent, falling to a flat rate of 4 percent from 1727, the yield on the government debt that was to be subscribed into South Sea stock was in the range of 5–8 percent. This suggests that, as with the great Mississippi debt conversion, the return on the Company's main asset was less than its cost of capital.

The South Sea projectors, however, took comfort from their experience with the pilot conversion scheme carried out the previous year. It will be recalled that on that occasion the Company was able to make additional share issues over and above those needed to fund the conversion, because the Company's authorised capital (and therefore its issuable stock) was directly linked to the amount of government debt it held. While the nominal capital was increased by the amount of debt exchanged, the pricing of South Sea stock for the purposes of that exchange was not specified. Clearly, if, as in 1719, the conversion price was above par, the quantity of stock required to satisfy the holders of government debt would be less than that which the company was authorised to create. This difference between issued and issuable stock constituted surplus shares which the Company could sell at prevailing market prices, thereby generating cash flow out of which it could pay the government.

If, in the present circumstances, the Company was able to convert the £31 million of outstanding government debt, it would be owed that additional amount by the government. But if the conversion price of South Sea Stock was, say, £200, the government debt would be bought in by issuing only £15.5 million (nominal) of stock. This would leave a further £15.5 million (nominal) of issuable stock available for sale at the market price of £200, thereby providing a potential cash flow of £31 million, some of which could be used to meet the £7.6 million payment obligation to the government. Clearly, the higher the conversion price of

South Sea stock, the greater the surplus sums that could be generated by new share issues.

This particular feature of South Sea finance has been the source of considerable confusion. It was claimed at the time and has since been restated by many commentators[9] that any surplus cash generated from new share issues was a "profit", which would be the case only if new shares could be issued at zero funding cost. In reality, of course, the new shareholders would expect a dividend on their investment which represented the Company's cost of capital. The South Sea Company was in the same position as any corporation issuing shares today; the proceeds from such sales might be invested to yield a profit but the increased equity capital arising from the share issue could not conceivably be described as a "profit" even under the most permissive accounting practices of the modern dot.com era. Furthermore, as others have pointed out, modern accounting standards require that, when new shares are issued at a premium to their nominal value, the surplus must be allocated to a non-distributable share premium account, and treated as part of the company's permanent capital.[10]

Second, much has been made then and since of the South Sea Company's refusal to fix the debt–equity swap rate, as the Bank of England had done in its proposal, on the basis of the nominal amount of stock to be exchanged for debt. Indeed, the failure of Parliament to insist on this has been described by some modern historians as "criminal".[11] Yet, as pointed out above, it was immaterial to the annuitants whether or not such terms were stated in advance, since what mattered to them was not merely the nominal amount of stock they would receive but, crucially, its market price at the date of conversion. The point was well understood by some commentators at the time and it is surprising that the misperception promoted by the Bank lobby has persisted to this day.[12]

It is true that, owing to the limitation on its issuable shares, the South Sea Company stood to benefit by not fixing the nominal amount of stock exchangeable for debt, since any appreciation of the share price above its nominal value could then become the basis for acquiring surplus cash via further share issues, as described above. It is also true that the Company had an incentive to raise the price of its shares to the point where it could, by this mechanism, be sure of having sufficient cash to pay off the government as agreed. Beyond this, however, the South Sea Company was in the same position as the Mississippi Company, or indeed any modern corporation, that is able to issue new shares as and when it chooses. For any corporation it makes sense to raise cash through new share issues only if there is a profitable use for the funds; but whereas the Mississippi Company under Law had many commercial investment opportunities, the South Sea Company had no obvious need to expand the funding of its largely redundant commercial interests.[13]

Furthermore, if the Company had fixed the (nominal) conversion terms in advance, it would still have had a powerful incentive to push up the price of its shares. Although it would not have been able to increase its issuable stock in this way, it would no doubt have wished to maximise the cash it received from the (now more limited) surplus stock it could sell. In short, a higher price might be needed on a reduced issuance of stock in order to make the £7.6 million agreed payment to the government.

Finally, the South Sea Company's ability to issue new shares was limited only because of an anomalous clause in its charter linking its (nominal) authorised capital to its holding of government debt. This clause is itself open to interpretation and it has been suggested that the Company was all along free to issue shares at its directors' discretion.[14]

Therefore, one must reject the consensus view that the origins of the South Sea Bubble are to be found in the South Sea Company's failure to fix in advance the (nominal) conversion terms of its planned debt–equity swap. The Company could not generate "profits" by raising its share price as has been widely alleged and while it had an incentive to secure sufficient funding to pay off the government, it was not a "capital hungry" enterprise that needed funds for commercial expansion. Of course, the South Sea projectors would want to see a rising share price so that they and their fellow shareholders could make capital gains. But this is an incentive shared with all company promoters and has no special relevance to the South Sea conversion scheme. However, what no one fully realised at the time was the massive scam the South Sea Company would engage in, using cash from new share issues to raise dividends in the hope that investors would not realise they were being repaid their own capital.

The real flaw in the 1720 refinancing arrangements concerns the payments the South Sea Company would have to make to the government. In order to be able to issue shares to make those payments, the Company would have to ensure that the conversion price of its stock was well above par. Yet there were no obvious means of generating sufficient profits to justify and sustain such a high share price. To take an example cited by one commentator at the time:[15] given market interest rates of around 4 percent, the Company would need to ensure a dividend yield at approximately this level, which meant that if the share price was raised to, say, £200 the actual dividend payable on the nominal capital would also have to be raised to 8 percent, equivalent to £3.2 million per annum on a capital of around £40 million. Interest from the government would be around 5 percent or £2 million per annum, South Sea trading profits might be generously included at £200,000 per annum, but the Company would then have to find an additional £1 million per annum to pay the dividend. As the author concludes, that amount could only be paid out of capital.

HUTCHESON'S FINANCIAL ANALYSIS

The full implications of the South Sea scheme and the ensuing boom in stock prices were well understood by Archibald Hutcheson, MP for Hastings, although his remarkable writings on the subject have been too often neglected by historians over the years.[16] It was Hutcheson who in March 1720 anticipated the events that were about to unfold:[17]

> ... if the truth be, as I verily believe it is, that there is no real foundation for the present, much less for the further expected, high price of South Sea stock; and that the frenzy which now reigns, can be of no long continuance in so cool a climate; and amongst a people hitherto so justly famed for wisdom and prudence; I say, if this be the case, is it not the duty of the British Senate, to take all necessary precautions, to prevent the ruin of many thousands of families ...[18]

Archibald Hutcheson, lawyer and economist, was born in County Antrim in 1659.[19] He was called to the Middle Temple and, having Jacobite sympathies, became man of business to the Jacobite Duke of Ormonde. In 1713, he was returned as MP for Hastings as a Whig although he often voted with the Tories. A close political colleague later wrote that "whenever he goes we shall lose a worthy, honest, incorruptible man which is, at this time of day, a great rarity". While respected for his probity, he appears to have been sharp-edged and difficult. It was reported that when serving on a House of Commons committee he responded angrily to the rejection of his proposals:

> [This] rejection put Mr Hutcheson somewhat out of humour, being a gentleman not a little attached to his own thoughts. He was so far provoked as to say loudly that he would never appear in that committee again, and so walked out of the House, on which some were so indecent as to hiss.[20]

Notwithstanding this episode, Hutcheson's expertise and honesty were respected enough for him to be elected subsequently to serve on the "Committee of Secrecy" that was set up by the House of Commons to investigate the South Sea scandal.

Plate 5 Archibald Hutcheson MP (1660-1740). A brilliant financial analyst whose warnings were ignored.
Private Collection. Photograph: Photographic Survey, Courtauld Institute of Art.

Hutcheson had taken a keen interest in public finance, having published in 1718 a detailed critique of the management of the national debt, "The Present State of the Public Debt and Funds". He was also a vociferous opponent of the stock-jobbing fraternity, although it is worth emphasising that as a wealthy man (he acquired a £40,000 dowry from his third wife who was the widow of a prosperous West Indian merchant) he was a substantial investor in the stock market on his own account. His views on the South Sea project were no doubt also influenced by periodic visits to Paris where his friend and patron, the Duke of Ormond, lived in exile. Here, as an interested observer of the financial scene, Hutcheson would have witnessed the Mississippi boom at first hand in the Rue Quincampoix.

Hutcheson's first major public foray into South Sea affairs came at the end of March 1720 when he published "Some calculations relating to the proposals made by the South Sea Company and the Bank of England ..." This tract establishes the basic methodology used by Hutcheson in all his writings on the South Sea project. First he sets out various assumptions, including: a current market interest rate of 4 percent, which is the basis of his discounting and present value calculations; the Company receives 5 percent interest on the whole of the debt owed by the government;[21] conversion is carried out in the summer of 1720 and the subscription proceeds received immediately; the company is wound up in 1727 and shareholders repaid the nominal value of their shares (since the government may begin to redeem its debt from this date) and the Company offers 25 years' purchase for the long annuities, as compared to the 20 years allowed for by the government. The benchmark value of the Company is taken to be the nominal value of its loans to the government plus net cash surpluses generated from share issues, any valuation above this level (i.e., "excess" valuation) having to be justified by future trading profits.

Hutcheson then assumes that both the irredeemable and redeemable debts are converted into South Sea stock, using alternative conversion prices for the shares ranging from 100 percent (par value) to 500 percent. The nominal capital of the company is increased by nearly £32 million to £43.6 million on full conversion, and there are payments to the government of £4 million (unconditional payment), plus £3.6 million (payment on full conversion of annuities) and a book loss of £3.3 million (the difference between the 20 years' purchase on long annuities allowed by the government and the assumed 25 years purchase paid by the Company), making nearly £11 million in total.

If the conversion price of South Sea stock is, say, 100 percent or par then the calculation of the loss or excess valuation that must be met by profits on South Sea trade is approximately £11 million divided by the £43.6 million nominal share capital, which works out at roughly £25 per share. Deduct from this the present value of 1 percent per annum for seven years (£6)—the difference between 5 percent payable on the Company's debt and the assumed market interest rate of 4 percent— and the "loss" per share comes out at around £19 which is equivalent to the present value of an annuity of just over £3 3s for 7 years. This is the amount per share that must be earned from South Sea trade "to make it a saving bargain to the purchasers".

Similar calculations are undertaken for conversion prices above par, but here the cash flow from the share price premium must be taken into account (see p. 79). Therefore, if the conversion price of South Sea stock is, say, 500 percent there is an additional cash flow of 400 percent × £31.8 million (the increase in nominal capital) or just over £127 million. After deducting the £11 million transfer to the government, there is a surplus of a little over £116 million or £267 per share which may be viewed as a one-off dividend or repayment of capital to shareholders. This amount, adjusted for the 1 percent interest premium payable by the government over 7 years, is deducted from the £400 premium on the share price to yield an excess valuation or loss of nearly £127 per share, which "to make it a saving bargain" will require annual trading profits of over £21 per share or £9.2 million per annum on the whole share capital. On the same basis, the annual trading profits needed to justify a share price of 300 percent, which was close to the level prevailing when Hutcheson was writing, would be £5.3 million.

The trading profits needed to cover the loss per share at alternative conversion prices for South Sea stock are shown in table 5.2. Hutcheson was in no doubt that the trading profits implied by the higher valuation of South Sea shares were wildly unrealistic:

> ... what trade can they possibly carry on to produce annually the aforesaid exorbitant sums? ... Is it not, therefore, reasonable that the South Sea Company should explain, from whence their advantages are to arise, which may be a solid foundation for the value of their stock; and that the Bill, now depending in the House of Commons, may stop till then; that thousands and thousands of unwary people may not be undone; or, which is still worse, that the Nation may not be plunged into greater difficulties than any they have hitherto had to struggle with.[22]

TABLE 5.2
Losses to be Made Good from South Sea Trade

Price of South Sea shares	"Excess" price or loss per share for new subscribers			Annual trading profits per share for seven years required to cover loss			Annual trading profit required on whole capital £million
	£	s	d	£	s	d	
100	19	0	4	3	3	4	1.4
125	25	15	0	4	5	9	1.9
150	32	9	10	5	8	3	2.4
175	39	4	9	6	10	9	2.8
200	45	19	7	7	13	2	3.3
300	72	19	2	12	3	1	5.3
400	99	18	6	16	13	0	7.3
500	126	18	1	21	2	10	9.2

Source: Hutcheson (31 March 1720b: 15).
Note: Assumes full conversion of government debts and nominal capital of £43.6 million.

TABLE 5.3
Allocation of "Excess" Price for South Sea Shares (£)

Conversion price of South Sea shares	(1) Paid to the government			(2) Transfer payment to original shareholders			(3) Loss attributable to new subscribers, ((1) + (2) = "excess" price)		
	£	s	d	£	s	d	£	s	d
100	19	0	4		–		19	0	4
125	25	15	0		–		25	15	0
150	28	4	9	4	5	1	32	9	10
175	28	4	9	11	0	0	39	4	9
200	28	4	9	17	14	10	45	19	7
300	28	4	9	44	14	5	72	19	2
400	28	4	9	71	13	9	99	18	6
500	28	4	9	98	13	4	126	18	1

Source: adapted from Hutcheson (31 March 1720b: 18).

Note: assumes full conversion of government debts and a total nominal capital of £43.6 million. In the case of subscriptions at par there is no transfer payment to the original shareholders who contribute pro rata to the government.

Finally, Hutcheson shows how the excess value placed on South Sea shares at alternative conversion prices is distributed between different parties. In table 5.3 (adapted from Hutcheson), the first column shows the amount payable to the government, the second column shows the increased share value attributable to the original shareholders (a transfer payment, in effect, from the new subscribers) and the third column, the sum of the previous two, indicates the loss per share attributable to the new subscribers, which is also the "excess" price paid for the shares.[23]

The distribution of gains and losses between interested parties is also shown by Hutcheson in terms of the premiums attaching to the conversion price for South Sea shares (table 5.4). Part of the premium is allocated as a one-off dividend or capital repayment to old and new shareholders in proportion to their respective equity stakes (roughly 3 to 1), the original shareholders again receiving what amounts to a transfer payment from new subscribers. The second column represents a payment to the government which is recaptured for the Company through the premium interest rate (5 percent against an assumed market interest rate of 4 percent) payable over the next seven years on the Company's holding of government debt.

TABLE 5.4
Allocation of Premium on South Sea Shares (£)[a]

Conversion price of South Sea shares	(1) Paid to the government			(2) Paid to the government for an equivalent advantage			(3) Capital repayment (transfer payment) to original share-holders			(4) Capital payment to new subscribers			(5) Total of columns (1) to (4) (share premium)	(6) Loss to new subscribers, (5) − (4) + (2)		
	£	s	d	£	s	d	£	s	d	£	s	d		£	s	d
150	28	4	9	6	0	0	4	5	1	11	10	2	50	32	9	10
175	28	4	9	6	0	0	11	0	0	29	15	3	75	39	4	9
200	28	4	9	6	0	0	17	14	10	48	0	5	100	45	19	7
300	28	4	9	6	0	0	44	14	5	121	0	10	200	72	19	2
400	28	4	9	6	0	0	71	13	9	194	1	6	300	99	18	6
500	28	4	9	6	0	0	98	13	4	267	1	11	400	126	18	1

Source: Adapted from Hutcheson (31 March 1720b: 18).
Note: Assumes full conversion of government debts and a total nominal capital of £43.6 million.

TABLE 5.5
Implied Valuation of South Sea Trade

Price of South Sea shares	"Excess" value of shares to be made good by profits from trade			Number of years' purchase paid for profits from trade[a]		
	£	s	d	Case 1	Case 2	Case 3
100	19	0	4	19	$9^{1}/_4$	$6^{1}/_3$
125	25	15	0	$25^{3}/_4$	$12^{7}/_8$	$8^{7}/_{12}$
150	32	9	10	$32^{1}/_2$	$16^{1}/_4$	$10^{5}/_6$
175	39	4	9	$39^{1}/_4$	$19^{5}/_8$	$13^{1}/_{12}$
200	45	19	7	46	23	$15^{1}/_3$
300	72	19	2	73	$26^{1}/_2$	$24^{1}/_3$
400	99	18	6	$99^{9}/_{10}$	$49^{19}/_{20}$	$33^{3}/_{10}$
500	126	18	1	$126^{9}/_{10}$	$63^{9}/_{20}$	$42^{3}/_{10}$

Source: adapted from Hutcheson (21 April 1720c: 31).

[a] Based on alternative assumptions regarding return on capital employed in trading (10–30 percent) as well as amount of capital employed in trading (10–30 percent on £43.6 million capital).

Here, then, is a masterly analysis of the South Sea Company's debt conversion scheme, demonstrating the profit shortfall that would arise at different conversion prices for South Sea stock, and the implications for both existing and newly subscribing shareholders, using "modern" techniques based on present values, discounted cash flow and annuity tables.

In a later addendum to the above valuation framework, Hutcheson responded to critics who claimed that his seven year time horizon did not allow for the fact that the Company's trading rights were in perpetuity, whereas its loans to the government could be redeemed after seven years. He therefore constructed a table showing the implied number of years' purchase (or price/earnings multiple in modern parlance) that investors were paying for South Sea trading profits, using different assumptions about the amount of capital employed in trade and the return on that capital to generate three different base cases for trading profits (table 5.5).

The South Sea Company and its friends presented a very different valuation basis for South Sea shares ahead of the debt conversion. In particular, an article in the *Flying Post* dated 9 April argued that the "intrinsic value" was £448 per share. The analysis ran as follows: if all debts are converted, the new (nominal) capital of the company is increased by £31 million, from £11.3 million to £42 million; assuming a 300 percent conversion price the additional capital of £31 million is acquired by issuing only £10.3 million of South Sea stock. This leaves £20.6 million of surplus issuable stock that can be sold at 300 percent, bringing in £62 million; adding this £62 million to £42 million in loans to the government and subtracting the £7.6 million payable to the government, results in a total market valuation of just over £96 million. This sum, divided by £21.6 million (original nominal capital of £11.3 million plus £10.3 million of new issued capital) yields a share value, based on assets per share, of £448 without any allowance for South Sea trade.

Hutcheson responded promptly to this grossly misleading calculation by pointing out, inter alia, that the author had divided the total asset value by only £21.6 million instead of the full nominal capital of £42 million. Making this, and other adjustments, Hutcheson demonstrated[24] that at a conversion price of 300 percent the true asset per share valuation was £221, in line with his previous calculations noted above.

The *Flying Post* was not the only newspaper to plug South Sea stock. The *Weekly Journal* of 16 April 1720 carried a calculation expressly stated to have been written by one of the Company's friends. The author purports to show that as the assumed conversion price for South Sea stock rises, the available assets per share also increase, so that at a conversion price of 300 the "intrinsic value" of stock is £448 15s and at 600 the intrinsic value is £880 8s. The absurd implication is that the underlying value of stock increases exponentially with its market price, the key flaw in this bogus argument, as in the *Flying Post* valuation, being that no account is taken of the increased capital arising from the sale of "surplus" stock (over and above that issued against converted debt) when working out the assets per share.

In reviewing contemporary valuations of South Sea stock it is worth noting that most of today's valuation techniques were used. Hutcheson calculated the present value of a future dividend stream as well as net assets per share and he used price–earnings ratios to evaluate potential profits from South Sea trade. The concept of sustainable dividends and dividend cover was also known, and used to compare unfavourably the South Sea Company's approach (paying dividends out of capital) with that of the Bank of England which allegedly never distributed as dividends more than it earned in profits.[25] One author even refers to the quality of earnings, suggesting that the South Sea trade is much riskier than banking[26] and referring in this general context to the greater volatility (including intra-day volatility) of South Sea stock as compared with Bank stock.[27]

Of course, the dividend-paying ability of a company cannot be assessed without proper accounts and since corporate accounting was at this time in its infancy investors were very much in the dark. Sir Richard Steele, writing in *The Theatre*, suggested that before annuitants converted into South Sea stock they should demand to see the accounts fairly stated, including losses on the Assiento Contract and on Spanish trade, an explanation of how the Company paid dividends of 6 percent when receiving only 5 percent from the government and details both of borrowings from the Sword Blade Company and bond issues.[28]

Another perceptive commentator suggested that the South Sea Company, as well as other corporations, should be prevented from paying out in dividends more than was earned through the introduction of an independent audit committee:

> Therefore for the preventing of any thing of this kind, it is proposed that our companies shall be obliged at least once a year to deliver in writing to twenty proprietors (exclusive of the Board of Directors) chosen by the whole proprietors sometime, suppose 14 days or more, before the call of a General Court to consider a dividend, such a state of their stock, as their accomptant shall declare upon oath, before one of the Barons of the Exchequer, to be the true state of such company's stock.[29]

This proposal for swearing to the accuracy of company accounts has resurfaced as an issue in modern times. In the summer of 2002, the US Securities and Exchange Commission, responding to numerous Wall Street scandals, required the chief executives and chief financial officers of the largest US corporations to file sworn statements certifying the accuracy of their most recent financial statements.

IMPLEMENTING A FLAWED SCHEME

It remains to consider how those most closely involved in the South Sea conversion scheme could have agreed to a final plan which seemed destined to fail. So far as the South Sea projectors are concerned, we have the benefit of John Blunt's views, evidently written some years prior to their publication in 1732, admittedly with the advantage of hindsight. According to Blunt the original plan, prior to the Bank of England's intervention, was to raise the price of South Sea stock in a series of subscriptions to around 160 percent which, on his calculations, would generate sufficient cash to remit the agreed £3 million plus to the government while paying an 8 percent dividend on the enlarged nominal capital, equivalent to a dividend yield of 5 percent at the projected price of 160. The dividend, it is true, would have to be paid partly out of capital over the ensuing twelve years "by which time gains from trade would be sufficient to perpetuate it".[30]

However, when the Bank of England intervened and the South Sea Company increased their payment to the government to £7.6 million, even this suspect arithmetic broke down. The price of South Sea stock would have to be driven higher than 160 percent to generate sufficient cash flow to meet the enlarged payments while meeting dividend expectations. In the words of Blunt:

> From the competition and opposition of the Bank may be justly dated the ruin of this scheme, and the rise of the miseries and misfortunes that have attended the execution of it ...[31]

Despite this later protestation, during negotiations with the government Blunt had refused even to consider undertaking the conversion scheme jointly with the Bank (below). Carried away by the successful conversion operation of 1719, the giddying success of John Law's parallel operations in France, and the sheer scale of the new project in which he would be the pivotal figure, Blunt seems to have entertained few doubts about the feasibility of the South Sea scheme as it finally evolved.

On the government side, John Aislabie played the lead role. He was in close contact with the South Sea Company from August 1719 to January 1720 when he first proposed the conversion scheme to the Company's General Court and he was subsequently responsible for piloting the South Sea Bill through Parliament. Aislabie later claimed in his defence[32] that when the Bank of England intervened and the project was opened to competitive bidding, he had tried to persuade the Company to undertake the scheme jointly with the Bank rather than be forced to offer terms that would threaten it successful implementation. John Blunt, however, was adamant, responding memorably: "No sir, we will never divide the child". According to his own account, Aislabie was appalled that the House of Commons had "set up the nation to auction" and when he heard that the South Sea Company was determined to outbid the Bank he immediately sold out his South Sea stock.[33]

The fact remains that, despite any doubts he may have harboured, Aislabie took responsibility on the government side for implementing the South Sea scheme once it had been approved by the House of Commons. Indeed, as an ambitious politician he had little choice. Given the popular clamour he was bound to give the scheme its best chance. Had he intervened "and the stock had tumbled upon it ... would not every man concerned in stock or subscriptions have looked upon him as the author of their destruction, and the directors be justified in the opinion of mankind, who would have declared that they could have executed their scheme with success, and supported their stock at that high price, and paid the seven millions, if he had not interposed and ruined the undertaking?"[34] Aislabie's political career would be finished if he tried to contain the South Sea boom just as it would be if the scheme went ahead unchecked and miscarried. His only chance was to provide whatever help he could in the hope that the South Sea Company would muddle through.

However, Aislabie had one other reason for supporting the South Sea scheme. Along with key members of the government—the first Lord of the Treasury, the junior Treasury Secretary and the Postmaster General— Aislabie had been credited with fictitious South Sea stock at a favourable price which could be "sold" at a (hopefully) higher market price on a later date, the recipient of the stock being paid the difference between the "strike" price and the market price on the date of "sale". In effect these were call options distributed gratis by the Company to those in a position to support it while the South Sea Bill was passing through Parliament. The modern equivalent is the stock option given to a corporate executive to incentivise his performance.

The South Sea Company had, in this sense, bought the government's support and in a similar manner it had secured the backing of the Crown by giving stock options to the King's mistresses, the Duchess of Kendall, the Countess of Platen, and possibly even the King himself. Finally, the votes of some 40–50 members of Parliament were sought through the distribution of options of varying amounts, although the details will never be known since the notorious "Green Book" in which the entries were made disappeared along with the South Sea Company's cashier, Edward Knight, when the latter fled abroad in 1721.

It later transpired that a total of £574,500 fictitious stock had been given out in this way, at an average strike price of just over £200, the total consideration due from the "buyers" being £1,213,575 (an amount that was, of course, never received by the Company). By the time the South Sea Bill received the royal assent in early April, the stock price was well over 300 and the profit on these call options—representing a cash claim on the Company—stood at more than £600,000.

Looking at the evolution of the South Sea scheme it is possible to identify parallels with more recent stock market developments. First, the competition between the Bank of England and the South Sea Company for the privilege of converting government debts resulted in massive over-bidding and, in the final outcome, ruinous terms for the "winner". Similarly, in the late 1990s competition between telecoms companies to secure European licences produced wildly inflated terms that contributed to the bursting of the telecoms bubble in 2001/2002.

Second, the (undisclosed) use of stock options to secure the support of those who were in a position to help the South Sea Company has its modern counterpart in executive stock options which are not shown as expenses in corporate accounts.

Third, as was recognised at the time, the absence of any proper accounting or disclosure framework made it virtually impossible for investors to know what they were buying when they acquired South Sea shares, a situation that has obvious parallels with modern accounting failures in cases such as Enron and WorldCom.

Fourth, the South Sea Company's affairs were managed by a single dominant chief executive and an inner cabal, with no effective oversight by the rest of the Court of directors. The resulting breakdown in corporate governance bears close comparison to failings in this area which have surfaced in the aftermath of the 1990s stock market bubble.

Fifth, while there was no precise equivalent in 1720 to the modern stock market analyst, the plugging of the South Sea Company's shares through planted newspaper articles, bogus valuations and coffee house rumour-mongering is not far removed from some of the more tendentious buy recommendations circulated by brokerage houses during the dot.com boom.

Finally, in 1720, as in the late 1990s, investment markets were driven by great popular excitement over financial and commercial innovation. Then it was the marriage between government finance, private finance and commercial enterprise. In the 1990s, it was the "new economic paradigm" associated with the internet revolution. In both episodes there was a general perception that the world was on the threshold of a new era of wealth creation in which all could participate. John Blunt, looking back at the upheavals of 1720, painted a picture of the popular mood that evokes more recent stock market events and, more particularly, the emergence of the day trader:

> The distemper of the times, which captivated the reason of mankind in general, no only in England but in all the neighbouring countries; who leaving the usual methods of labour and industry to gain estates, were all tainted with the fond opinion of being rich at once, which caused many persons to engage much beyond their fortunes, not only in South Sea stock, but in every pernicious bubble that could be devised.[35]

This, then, was the prevailing mood in the early months of 1720, a year in which the South Sea scheme would claim responsibility for the first international stock market Bubble, the world's first financial crash and the first state orchestrated bailout of investors, the forerunner of today's lender of last resort operations.

NOTES

1. The Earl of Stair, Ambassador to France, in the Autumn of 1719, argued that Britain should as a matter of great urgency formulate a scheme for discharging the national debt if Law was not to "raise the trade of France on the ruins of our trade". Cited in Carswell (1993: 79).
2. Toland (1726: 406–407).
3. Darwin (1950: 319).
4. Carswell (1993: 189).
5. Carswell (1993: 230–231); Dickson (1967: 176).
6. See, for instance, Trenchard (1720a).
7. For contrary views on this point, see Anon (8 March 1720c: 38); Anon (1720a: 10–11).
8. Hutcheson (31 March 1720a: 12).
9. Scott (1912: 307), for instance, commenting on potential sales by the South Sea Company of surplus stock, states that "it was plain there would be a very considerable profit in stock, and this became more valuable as the price rose". For other examples of this misconception, see Dickson (1967: 101); Carswell (1993: 89); Morgan and Thomas (1962: 32).
10. Chancellor (1999: 62).
11. Clapham (1944: 83–84) refers to the failure to fix the conversion terms in advance as an "astonishing parliamentary oversight, or criminal omission". Plumb (1956: 299) refers to this omission as a "deliberate and criminal neglect". A leading modern financial historian states that "the fatal attraction and duplicity [sic] of the scheme lay in the fact that the South Sea Company could set whatever conversion price it wished for the shares given to the debtholders in exchange for the old annuities ..." Neal (1990: 99).
12. See Anon (1720i: 38–40). Interestingly, Anderson (1764: 94) states that the "grand fallacy" of the South Sea Scheme was the failure of the Company to put a price on their stock for the purposes of the conversion. For the reasons stated in the text this would have been impractical which was why the Bank declined to fix a conversion price in its proposal.
13. Hutcheson (21 April 1720c: 35) argued that the South Sea Company had no conceivable need for the money it was raising to finance its trading interests.
14. See Heckscher (1930–1931: 321).
15. Anon (8 March 1720c: 15 ff.).
16. See generally Hutcheson, *Collection of Calculations and Remarks*, all tracts in volume.
17. Hutcheson was not the only publicist to challenge the market's valuation of

South Sea stock. For instance James Milner, merchant and MP, wrote that he "could not for my life find out how of £31mn at 5 and 4% and the long annuities to be purchased in at above par, by only being transferred from the Exchequer to the South Sea, should be worth three times the money they were worth in the hands of the government" (Milner 1720: 17). The journalist Sir Richard Steele, writing under the pseudonym of Sir John Edgar, published several critical articles on the South Sea Company, including a valuation purporting to show that at a conversion price of 150 percent South Sea shares were worth only £113 and at 200 percent only £149 (*The Theatre*, 19–22 March 1720). John Trenchard, the author of *An Examination and Explanation of the South Sea Company's Scheme for Taking in the Publick Debts* (who quotes Hutcheson with approval) has already been referred to. However, none of these commentators provided a fully specified valuation framework of the kind developed by Hutcheson. In this sense his critical evaluation of the South Sea project is unique.

18. Hutcheson (31 March 1720b: 8).
19. See Cruickshanks et al. (2002: 449–452) and Sedgwick (1970: 163–164).
20. Cobbett (1806–1820: 163).
21. In fact the average interest payable was slightly less than this at around 4.9 percent.
22. Hutcheson (31 March 1720b: 16).
23. The redistributive effect of increases in the South Sea share price as between new and old shareholders was "rediscovered" by Eli Heckscher. In his analysis of South Sea finance, published more than 200 years after Hutcheson's writings on the subject, Heckscher demonstrates the validity of Hutcheson's approach but makes no reference to Hutcheson, presumably because he was not aware of the latter's work. See Heckscher (1930–1931: 321–328).
24. Hutcheson (21 April 1720c: 28).
25. Trenchard (17 February 1720b: 25); Anon (8 March 1720c: 10, 22).
26. Anon (8 March 1720c: 22).
27. Anon (8 March 1720c: 10).
28. Steele, alias Sir John Edgar (5–8 March 1720).
29. Trenchard (17 February 1720b: 25–26).
30. Blunt (1732: 21).
31. Blunt (1732: 31).
32. Cobbett (1806–1820: 884).
33. Aislabie (1721: 12).
34. Anon (1721a: 22).
35. Blunt (1732: 76).

CHAPTER SIX

The Bubble

THE LEADING ROLE played by John Blunt both in the establishment of the
South Sea Company and the formulation of the debt conversion scheme
has already been described. When the time came to implement the
conversion scheme, Blunt took control of the Company's affairs, the
Court of Directors becoming little more than a rubber stamp. Given
this central direction by a single domineering managing director, it is
necessary to say something more about the individual concerned and
his method of operation.

JOHN BLUNT AND SHARE PRICE MANIPULATION

Early in 1720, Blunt set out to establish personal control over the South
Sea Company. He sought to by-pass the Court of Directors and the
formal committee structure by setting up an informal cabinet council
or inner cabal, consisting of himself and half a dozen trusted colleagues,
assisted by the chief accountant (a relation) and the chief cashier, Knight.

According to Toland's *Secret History of the South Sea Scheme*,[1] the
cabinet council at first met secretly but "being grown warm in the saddle"
they would gather regularly at Knight's house on those days when the
Court of Directors was convened, delaying the Court's proceedings, turning up late to the Court room in South Sea House and rushing through
business late in the afternoon.[2]

Key financial matters came before the Treasury Committee and,
although Blunt was not a member of this body, he succeeded in control-
ling its activities. This he did through the sub and deputy governors,
ineffectual men who were under his thumb, and the chief cashier or
Treasurer. When anything important was coming up before the Committee, Blunt made sure that he and his cabal were invited to attend as
"advisers" and they proceeded to debate and vote as if they were full
Committee members. Furthermore, the Committee minutes were written
on loose sheets which could later be altered by the Treasurer to suit the

circumstances. In this way actions that were allegedly Blunt's alone appear to have been "approved" by the Committee.[3]

As the price of South Sea stock rose, Blunt enjoyed increasing popular acclaim, his manner became more overbearing and colleagues became less inclined to oppose his views. After the third money subscription in mid-June, when at the height of his powers, he took his family in a grand equipage to take the waters at Tunbridge Wells where he praised the merits of "our" South Sea Scheme before cheering onlookers. But he cut short his trip when he heard that some directors had misgivings about his plans, returning to London in a rage and declaring to his chastened colleagues that "he did not know but it might cost him his life to have left off drinking the waters so abruptly".[4]

Blunt's imperious manner at this time has been captured by the *Secret History* which reports that when his co-directors showed signs of dissension, he would "put himself into a commanding posture, adopt a prophetic style" and deliver the following words (or something very similar) "with an emphasis and extraordinary vehemence":

> Gentlemen, don't be dismayed: you must act with firmness, with resolution, with courage. I tell you 'tis not a common matter you have before you. The greatest thing in the world is referred to you. All the money of Europe will center amongst you. All the nations of the earth will bring you tribute.[5]

Blunt was clearly in the same mould as his modern counterparts—the chief executives of Enron, WorldCom, Tyco et al.—who became corporate heroes as their businesses expanded on the back of rising share prices. But just as they fell from grace when their stock prices collapsed, so did Blunt's powers diminish as South Sea stock declined from the late summer of 1720:

> But when the tide turned, when stock began to fall, and consequently that his power was at an end; then this poor man (forsooth) was but one in 31 [directors], as he was wont to express it himself.[6]

Blunt's management of the South Sea Company's affairs cannot be divorced from his own account dealings in South Sea stock. He justified his self-enrichment to colleagues on the grounds that "… in any other nation but this, they would have given him a reward of £500,000 for the service he had done to his country" but since no such gift was in prospect "he thought he might take the opportunities to reward himself".[7] Such opportunities were numerous: he evidently bought government debt as well as South Sea stock ahead of the announcement of the conversion scheme; he allocated to himself and his circle excess stock issued during the money subscriptions when the price was advancing; after the third money subscription he sold stock forward "for the opening of the books" in order to take his profits; and he even bought call options on the midsummer dividend knowing that this would be raised from 3 percent to 10 percent.[8] Some of Blunt's largest deals were evidently conducted while taking the waters at Tunbridge Wells, where he is said to have written every post to his brokers. Allegedly "his journey to Tunbridge was a blind ... to cover the projected sale of his own stock".[9]

Blunt appears to have had a very large long position in South Sea stock during the spring and early summer of 1720. It is hardly surprising, there-fore, that during this period his constant refrain was "that the advancing by all means of the price of the stock was the only way to promote the good of the Company".[10] Once again, a close parallel can be drawn between the managing director of the South Sea Company and today's business tycoons who are powerfully motivated to maximise their company's share price in the short run so that they can exercise their call options at great profit. Like so many company directors during the dot.com boom, Blunt also managed to sell out close to the top of the market, leaving ordinary investors to bear the cost of the subsequent collapse. When the dust had settled, it was found in 1721 that Blunt had amassed a fortune of £187,000, equivalent to many millions of pounds in today's money and far beyond anything to be expected of a man on a salary of a few hundred pounds.

Blunt's powerful personality, his dominant position in the South Sea Company and his large-scale self-dealing in company stock constitute an essential backdrop to the events that were to unfold from the spring of 1720. For it was now that the Company had to consider how to implement the debt conversion scheme that had been accepted by Parliament. In the absence of a predetermined strategy, it is clear that the timing, sequencing and scale of the various conversion offers and share sales made between April and August 1720 were dictated largely by market conditions. Never-theless, Blunt and his immediate circle sought at the outset to borrow tactics from the Mississippi Company and to engage in what Hutcheson described as the "artful management of the spirit of gaming".[11]

The decision was made to phase new subscriptions in a way that was calculated to maximise the South Sea share price. In a later defence of his actions, Blunt explained the approach as follows:

> ... by taking [the debts] in at different times, prices, and proportions, the proprietors thereof, (through apprehension of being either left entirely out, or coming in afterwards at a higher price) would be quickened to make their

Plate 6   Royal Exchange Scene 1788. Copyright Guildhall Library.

subscriptions, whereby the execution of the scheme would be rendered more easy and certain.[12]

If the market was to be fed with new South Sea stock at ever higher prices, it would be necessary to use the press and the coffee house rumour mill to maximum advantage. The planting of bogus valuations in friendly journals has already been mentioned and no doubt suitable stories were put about in Exchange Alley; for example, that, following peace with Spain, the South Sea Company would receive £1.5 million compensation for assets seized in the Spanish territories,[13] or that the South Sea trade would be renewed by England ceding Gibraltar to Spain.[14]

Beyond this public relations exercise, a number of financial techniques familiarised by Law were introduced to attract investors. First, where new stock was issued for cash, generous subscription terms were allowed, ranging from a 20 percent down payment and eight two-monthly payments of 10 percent (first money subscription) to a 10 percent down payment and nine six-monthly payments of 10 percent (third money subscription). Since the subscription receipts, unlike shares, could be transferred through a simple legal assignment, there was a ready market for speculators in this partly paid (and therefore highly leveraged) scrip.[15]

Second, the South Sea Company encouraged investors to borrow against the security of its shares. As part of its package deal with the government, the Company was allowed to borrow £1 million in Exchequer bills (these were equivalent to cash) which it subsequently lent out to purchasers of South Sea shares at 4 percent. But the Company lent far larger sums at 5 percent (later reduced to 4 percent) from its own cash resources against the security of both shares and subscription receipts, total lending under this heading eventually exceeding £11 million. Blunt later claimed that the Company had acted prudently by limiting advances to only half the prevailing market value of the security. He also argued that if the Company had not returned money to the market in this way, there would have been a severe credit squeeze:

> There would be great sums from subscriptions and other money remaining in hand, which if kept dead, till the same could be applied to pay off the annuities and debts, might prove very prejudicial to, and stagnate the Public Credit, and be likewise prejudicial to the further execution of the Act. Therefore, it was thought proper, that money should be used, in lending on the stock of the Company ....[16]

Unlike Law, John Blunt could not pump up the money supply because he did not control the national bank but at least he could recycle funds that would otherwise lie dormant within the Company.

The South Sea cabal went one stage further and used its powers over the Company's cash to buy stock in Exchange Alley. This was consistent with the total discretion given to the Treasury Committee "to lend or imploy the Company's money that is or shall be in cash ... in such manner as they shall judge for the Company's interest".[17]

Blunt, following Law's example, made maximum use of dividend announcements to raise investors' expectations and the price of stock. On 14 April, the day of the first money subscription, the Company revealed that the midsummer dividend would be increased from 3 percent to 10 percent, a move which, according to Toland's account, "perhaps contributed more to intoxicate the minds of the people than anything done besides".[18] However, this policy eventually backfired when, later in the year, the Company attempted to maintain the price of its stock by making absurdly unrealistic dividend promises which the market rightly interpreted as a sign of desperation (see p. 137).

Finally, Blunt and his colleagues sought to "lock up" stock by delaying the issuance of shares and preventing converting annuitants from taking an immediate profit by selling out and thereby depressing prices. Those annuitants who converted into South Sea stock in April/May were not credited with stock in the books of the Company until the end of December.[19] Similarly, the Company failed to issue receipts for the third and fourth money subscriptions, evidently with a view to restricting the supply of partly paid scrip.

To what extent did these manipulations boost the price of South Sea stock and help to explain the blowing up of the Bubble? The direct effects may have been less important than some have suggested. Lending on the security of stock was an established practice and such loans were available from goldsmiths; the real question is why so many investors were prepared to incur debt to buy South Sea shares. Restricting the supply of shares and subscription receipts may have deferred some sales of stock but determined investors could and did transact in the forward market to circumvent this problem.

However, the indirect effects of the Company's attempt to ramp the share price may have been significant. As early as March there were press reports to the effect that the South Sea Company was buying its own stock and employing other stock-jobbing devices to push up its share price.[20] Given public access to the press via coffee houses, it seems likely that there would have been a general awareness among investors from March onwards that devious methods were being used to boost the market for South Sea stock. Far from discouraging investors, this knowledge, coupled with the South Sea Company's known close connections with the government and the Crown, may have encouraged the view that there was a powerful conspiracy to "fix" the stock price to the advantage of all.[21]

THE IMPLEMENTATION OF THE SOUTH SEA SCHEME

The South Sea Scheme was implemented in six stages between mid-April and mid-October 1720, comprising two conversion offers and four money subscriptions (see table 6.1). The really striking aspect of this schedule is that the money subscriptions, which involved a staggering sum of over £75 million when fully paid up, far outweighed the £31 million of convertible debt. The implication is that the South Sea Company, an enterprise with no obvious need or use for additional funds, was seeking to take advantage of the conversion scheme to raise huge amounts of cash. In order to understand how this came about, it is necessary to describe the chronology of events that followed passage of the South Sea Act.

By announcing on 14 April a £2 million share issue to be subscribed in cash or eligible bonds, the South Sea Company reversed the logical sequence of its funding operations. Technically, it should have begun by offering to convert government debt, thereby increasing its authorised capital and paving the way for further share issues against cash. However, Blunt was keen to secure the best possible conversion price and evidently intended that the proceeds of the money subscription should be used to push the stock price still higher.

TABLE 6.1
South Sea Company's Share Issues 1720

1. 14 April: First money subscription, £2.25 million stock at 300
2. 28 April: Registration of annuities for first conversion
3. 29 April: Second money subscription, £1.5 million stock at 400
4. 19 May: Terms of exchange announced for first conversion, stock priced at 375
5. 17 June: Third money subscription, £5 million stock at 1000
6. 14 July: Registration of redeemable debts for second conversion
7. 6 August: Registration of redeemable debts and annuities for second conversion
8. 12 August: Terms of exchange announced for second conversion, stock priced at 800
9. 24 August: Fourth money subscription, £1.25 million stock at 1000

South Sea shares were already on an upward trend, having risen from around 130 at the beginning of February to just over 300 in early April as the conversion scheme found its way onto the statute books. The first money subscription appeared to be quite tightly priced at 300, but after allowing for the generous subscription terms—20 percent down payment and the balance at two-monthly intervals—the effective price was approximately 290 which was in line with the prevailing stock price. The subscription lists were filled almost immediately and the partly paid scrip quickly traded at a premium, assisted by the Company's announcement on 14 April that the midsummer dividend would be raised to 10 percent (although paid in stock). The subscription receipts representing an initial down payment of £60, were a highly leveraged investment and while the underlying stock price virtually doubled to 600 by the end of May, the quoted value of the subscriptions rose almost sevenfold to £400.[22]

There was an "oversubscription" on this first offering of stock of £250,000, bringing the total (nominal) amount of the issue to £2.25 million, for which investors would over time have to pay £6.75 million at a price of £300. The question for the South Sea Company was what to do with this cash (only 20 percent of which was received immediately) given its financial obligations to the government, its commitment to pay off holders of redeemable debt either in cash or stock and the options it had gifted to its friends which were now heavily "in the money".

In fact, the Company had another and more immediate use for the money it had raised. On 21 April, the General Court had given the directors a general power to lend money on the security of South Sea stock with the specific objective of sustaining market prices, the Sub-Governor informing the General Court that "the profit of the Company ... does chiefly depend on the price of the stock at the times of the execution of the Act".[23] Accordingly the directors agreed to lend up to £500,000 for four months at 5 percent subject to a maximum of £3000 per individual and on terms that £250 could be lent against the security of £100 of stock, allowing a precautionary margin of around 30 percent on the prevailing market price of 350. As it transpired, nearly £1 million was lent in this way in the month from 21 April to 19 May.[24]

The success of this first money subscription encouraged Blunt to follow up with a second barely two weeks later. The new subscription, which was opened on 30 April, was for £1 million of South Sea stock at a price of 400, with even more generous instalment terms, namely a 10 percent down payment and nine calls at three- or four-month intervals. The pricing of the issue was bold, given a prevailing market quotation of

340, but the extended payment terms meant that the "true" subscription price was just over 370. Again, investor interest was intense and by the end of May the quoted price for receipts from the second subscription, which had initially cost £40, had risen to £400, a tenfold increase in one month. As with the first share issue, there was a large oversubscription, this time amounting to £500,000. Therefore, the Company, which would eventually expect to receive £6 million from the £1.5 million (nominal) of stock sold, secured an immediate cash inflow of £600,000.

The first two money subscriptions, taken together, raised just under £2 million immediately and would over two years or so bring in a total of £12.75 million assuming all instalments were paid by subscribers. Such a sum would more than cover all the Company's commitments, including payments to the government, repayment of bonds, and bribes. Hutcheson pointed out towards the end of April, that the Company did not need large sums for the expansion of its trade, his conclusion being that the cash surpluses being raised would in due course be returned to shareholders in the form of dividends. But in that case, he asked, "may not every purchaser [of South Sea stock] manage that money to his own particular advantage, as well as the Company can do for him?".[25] It was clear to him that the recycling of investors' funds via a non-trading corporate entity made little financial sense.

Against a strong market background, the third phase of the South Sea Scheme addressed one of its core objectives: the conversion of the long and short annuities. Annuitants who wished to convert had to register their interests on 28 April and agree to subscribe their debts into South Sea stock "at such times and upon such terms and conditions as the said Company shall appoint".[26] This form of words meant that annuitants who registered were signing a blank cheque, yet such was the enthusiasm for South Sea stock that two-thirds of the long and short annuitants agreed to convert on terms yet to be decided by the Company. In the event, those who had registered were given an opt-out, for when the terms were announced on 19 May they were allowed until 25 May to withdraw (which evidently none did). To acquire shares at an exorbitant price is one thing, but to agree to acquire shares at an unknown price to be determined unilaterally by the issuer at some future date is quite another.

Anderson interpreted the annuitants' willingness to bind themselves to conversion on terms as yet unknown as a sign of increasing irrationality among investors:

> ... so that in this, and most of the other transactions relating to this great and
> unparalleled affair, the subscribing parties, especially in the former part of the

madness, were equally accessory to their own future losses with the conductors of the scheme; all ranks and classes of people eagerly forwarding their own ruin, through an excessive thirst for gain.[27]

The terms announced on 19 May fixed the conversion price of South Sea stock at 375 and valued the long annuities at 32 years purchase and the short at 17 years' purchase. As it turned out, these terms were attractive to the annuitants, so long as they were free to sell the stock they received at prevailing prices. The conversion price of 375 was in line with the current market value but the attractive feature lay in the valuation of the annuities. As already indicated, the long annuities were traded in the early months of 1720 at 24/25 years' purchase, a valuation that no doubt reflected the expectation of favourable conversion terms but also the declining trend of market interest rates. The example below, taken from Scott,[28] shows how the conversion calculation worked for long annuities, taking account of the fact that a proportion of the conversion price was paid not in stock but in bonds and cash:

Conversion of £100 long annuity into South Sea stock
£100 annuity capitalised at 32 years' purchase = £3200

£3200 payable as to : £2625 in stock at £375 = 700 nominal of stock

£575 in bonds and cash

Given a market value of, say, 24 years' purchase or £2400 for a £100 annuity, it can be seen that annuitants were getting a good deal—an excess valuation of one-third assuming they could sell their South Sea stock at the conversion price of 375.[29] Put another way, converting long annuitants stood to gain so long as the price of South Sea stock did not fall below 260.[30] The subscription terms for short annuities were similarly attractive, 17 years purchase being offered as against a recent market price of 14 years.

As matters turned out, however, there were two problems confronting those who converted. First, the South Sea Company, alert to the possibility that subscribers might wish to realise their gains by selling stock, thereby depressing the market, withheld the issuance of shares until the end of December. Converting annuitants were therefore locked into their share holdings unless they were prepared to sell in the forward market, which some did.

Second, from the Company's perspective there was a loss on the conversion arising from the difference between the Company's and the government's valuation of the annuities. Specifically, the conversion terms allowed 32 years' purchase for the longs and 17 years for the shorts, whereas the government credited the South Sea Company at the rate of 20 years purchase for the longs and 14 years for the shorts. This implied a hefty book loss which had to be added to the cash sums due to the government. If one "sees through" the Company to the underlying transactions, those who converted were acquiring (indirect) claims on the government significantly less valuable than those they were giving up. The fact that this transformation appeared to be the other way round and to the benefit of subscribers was due entirely to the high price of South Sea stock which far exceeded assets per share, as Hutcheson's analysis had already shown.

The successful conversion of the great majority of annuities marked the beginning of the final stages of the South Sea Bubble, as speculation in Exchange Alley reached fever pitch. In the first three months of the year, the price of South Sea stock had more than doubled, from 128 to around 300. In April the market paused as it digested the first two money subscriptions, dipping below 280 in the middle of the month before bouncing back to just under 340. It remained at around this level until the third week of May when, following the announcement of the annuitants' conversion terms, it rose rapidly, first to 400 (20 May), then to 500 (29 May) before touching 600 on 31 May. This vertical ascent continued into the following month, the stock price breaching 700 on 2 June, and 800 on 4 June, at which point it had risen by around 125 percent in six weeks. There was then a further pause until 22 June when the Company closed its books for two months in order to process the midsummer dividend. The closure of the books disrupted trading and therefore makes it difficult to identify the high-water mark of the Bubble but, as discussed below, there appears to have been a final speculative surge in late June which did not abate until after the third week of July.

FINANCIAL MARKET ENVIRONMENT

At this point it is necessary to interrupt the chronology of the Bubble to consider the broader financial environment in which events were unfolding. This is because the stock market boom extended well beyond the South Sea Company to other established corporations as well as start-up enterprises. It also embraced other financial centres in Continental Europe.

During the period 1 January to 22 June 1720, when the South Sea books were closed, the share prices of other leading companies also

TABLE 6.2
Stock Market Prices 1 January to 22 June 1720

	1 January 1720	23 June 1720	Percentage increase
South Sea Company	128	765	498
Bank of England	150	240	60
East India Company	200	340	70
Million Bank	127	440	246
Royal African Company	24	140	483
Stock Market Index[a]	100	306	206

[a] *Data source*: Castaing (1720) (lowest daily prices). Memorandum item: increase in stock market index, excluding South Sea Company = 132 percent.

[a] Unweighted composite of share prices in the above companies.

soared (see table 6.2) with the Royal African Company, in particular, registering an increase similar to that of South Sea shares. A crude index of the stock market rose by 206 percent during this period, or 132 percent excluding the South Sea Company.

There was also an extraordinary boom in new investment projects or lesser "bubbles" as would-be entrepreneurs and, it has to be said, swindlers climbed onto the speculative bandwagon. Towards the end of 1719 there had been a handful of new flotations, including York Buildings (a property company), two marine insurance companies and several annuity or pension companies. The pace of new flotations picked up in January/February when companies with a total nominal capital of £37 million were launched, the majority in insurance or other financial services. Flotation activity intensified in May/June when a total of 50 projects were announced and in the frantic week ending 11 June flotations totalling no less than £224 million in nominal capital were advertised in the press.[31] Remarkably, of the two hundred plus flotations that Anderson identifies, only four were to survive to become viable businesses.

Great play has been made by popular historians of the Bubble with the more absurd projects advertised, such as a machine gun with square bullets, an air pump for the brain, a scheme for extracting gold and silver from lead, trading in hair for wigs, etc. Some of these were no doubt hoaxes and others may have been inserted by the newspaper publishers themselves to generate public interest in their journals (letters to the editor were frequently editor-authored). However, the great majority of projects were in "sensible" areas such as fisheries, mining, insurance, manufacturing, building and property development, agriculture, health, household goods and overseas trade, representing more-or-less the full range of today's *Financial Times* industrial classification excluding modern technology.

The common characteristic of these lesser bubbles was that they typically involved big headline capital sums of £1 million, £2 million or more, designed to convey the importance and potential scale of the enterprise, while requiring only very small initial contributions from investors. According to Anderson[32] some of the down payments were set as low as 6 d per £100 share (0.025 percent), others at 1 s per £1000 share (0.005 percent), but more typically the subscriptions ranged from 0.125 to 1 percent of the nominal share value. The receipts for these subscriptions were traded in Exchange Alley and, since they represented such a small proportion of the fully paid-up nominal value of the shares, they were even more highly leveraged than South Sea partly paid scrip. Accordingly, prices were highly volatile and at their peak some of these bubbles were showing capital gains equivalent to twenty or even thirty-five times their original purchase price (the record seems to have been held by General Insurance with a 65-fold capital gain). The low initial subscription also opened up the market to the humbler sort of investor, in effect creating a poor man's bubble.

Anderson has described the frenzied trading in these lesser bubbles at the peak of the South Sea boom. His account provides a perfect example of what today would be called the "greater fool theory" of stock market speculation:

> Yet many of those very subscribers were far from believing these projects feasible: it was enough for their purpose that there would very soon be a premium on the receipts for those subscriptions, when they generally got rid of them in the crowded Alley to others more credulous than themselves. The first purchasers of these receipts soon found second purchasers, and so on, at still higher prices coming from all parts of the town ....[33]

It was easy enough to launch a new project in this over-heated investment environment. All one had to do was to find a person of known substance to act as a named sponsor, advertise the project in a paper, naming a coffee house where subscriptions would be taken, and turn up at the appointed place and time to issue receipts against investors' down payments. No business plan, authorisation procedure or prospectus was necessary and funds were entrusted to unknown persons who might (and sometimes did) abscond with the day's takings.

From the investors' point of view, it was simpler still. They would queue at the named coffee house to make their down payment, receive signed receipts from the keeper of the books, and then more often than not hurry out into the maelstrom of Exchange Alley to seek purchasers who were prepared to pay a premium for their subscriptions. Few seem to have intended to pay future calls on the partly paid shares.

The investment psychology behind the proliferation of small company flotations at this time brings to mind the launch of internet start-up companies during the peak of the dot.com boom in 1999. The experience of one dot.com fund raiser makes the point:

> You would walk into the offices [of a venture capitalist] in New York and people would immediately offer money to you if they thought you looked smart. We didn't have any data on the market; we didn't have a product demo; we didn't have anything. We had a business plan, but that was it.[34]

The South Sea boom was remarkable in its own right but it has to be seen as one key element in a speculative wave that engulfed Europe during 1720. The fever had begun in Paris and then moved to London; Amsterdam and Geneva were closely involved in both the Mississippi and South Sea schemes; over 40 new investment projects were advertised in the Netherlands in the four months to mid-October; in Hamburg there were dealings in projected insurance companies; the court of Madrid was reported to have turned down a number of proposed projects; and receipts were taken in Lisbon for "the Brasil Bubble".[35]

In Exchange Alley itself a picture of the intensity of speculation in the spring and early summer of 1720 emerges from the London press. Profits from speculation led to a boom in coach-building, with 200 new coaches in London and many more on the stocks,[36] there was an acute shortage of hackney cabs due to the demands of Exchange Alley;[37] pickpockets took £8000 in less than two weeks from the huge crowds,[38] the Court of St James was deserted in favour of Exchange Alley and one could more readily gain access to the King himself than to South Sea directors.[39] Rags to riches stories abounded and there were reports that property prices in and around London were soaring, with yields falling from 5 percent to 2 percent.[40] However, one must bear in mind that newspapers were prone to wild exaggeration, as in one report to the effect that a South Sea Director had amassed a fortune of £3 million in three months[41] (this turned out to be a large multiple of any fortune made from South Sea speculation).

The London attorney of a Dutch investor, having decided to visit the Alley at this time, wrote back to his principal:

Plate 7   Street scene in Change Alley in front of Garraway's Coffee House at the time of the South Sea Bubble. Copyright Guildhall Library.

I had a fancy to go and take a look at the throngs … and this is how it struck me yesterday: it is like nothing so much as if all the lunatics had escaped out of the madhouse at once.[42]

Of course, the huge crowds around Exchange Alley meant that some people were taking time off work. It was reported from the Hague that preoccupation with the South Sea boom meant that "trade has completely slowed down, that more than one hundred ships moored along the river Thames are for sale, and that the owners of capital prefer to speculate on shares than to work at their normal business".[43] The intensity of financial activity is also conveyed by the following description of transfers of Lottery Annuities at the Bank of England for later subscription into South Sea stock:

There was on Monday [July 4] a great crowd at the Bank of England … and the hurry was so great, that they could not keep to the usual method of transferring, but conveyed the books, by a ladder, up and down from the office windows, which is up one pair of stairs; and ranges of tables were set in the courtyard, where the people had more air and room to breath in, and to subscribe their names in the transfer book, the like of which was never known before.[44]

The feverish state of financial markets in the summer of 1720 helps to explain the South Sea Company's next breathtaking move in its implementation of the conversion scheme. On 17 June a third money subscription was taken, this time for £5 million (nominal) of stock at an issue price of 1000, the terms being a 10 percent down payment with the balance payable in nine six-monthly calls, the first of which was not until July 1721. The extended payments were intended to compensate in part for the premium pricing, one-third above the prevailing level of 750. Even so, the true subscription price was only just below 900, assuming a discount rate of 5 percent, so that the success of the issue again underlines the prevailing irrationality of investors. It was reported that the Company "had money enough paid in for near eight millions, and had to abate each subscription proportionately".[45]

The sense of unreality pervading Exchange Alley seems by now to have affected Blunt and his circle. The £5 million share issue at 1000 implied a £50 million cash inflow over the next five years, a sum that Scott correctly describes as "utterly ridiculous".[46] It is also impossible to imagine for what purpose the Company would need permanent funding on such a scale, even if it were obtainable. However, the South Sea Company did need an immediate injection of short-term liquidity, given the extraordinary sums that it was lending on stock and on subscription receipts.

We know from the subsequent House of Commons investigation that, from mid-April to the end of September, the Company lent approximately £9 million on stock and nearly £2.25 million on subscription receipts, although there is some uncertainty about the distribution of loans over the six months.[47] A reasonable estimate would be that around £4.5 million was lent to mid-June, knowing as we do that at least £3 million was lent out towards the end of the month and that there was little lending in July. In addition to this claim on the Company's resources there were the option bribes to be paid out (around £1 million) and the cash element of annuitants' conversion terms to be met (over £2.6 million). All this was in addition to the cash sum of £7.6 million that would eventually be due to the government on final implementation of the conversion scheme.

Against these commitments the Company had generated cash flow of £2.02 million from the first money subscription (20 percent down payment plus first 10 percent instalment payment) and £600,000 down payment from the second. It had also received in June the £1 million of Exchequer Bills (effectively cash) lent by the government. A statement of the Company's sources and uses of funds during the period would therefore look something like table 6.3.

Clearly, the Company was having to borrow heavily to fund its commitments. Faced with short-term liquidity pressures and the desire to make further loans against its stock, it would find an immediate use for the £5 million down payment it was due to receive from the third money subscription. Indeed £3 million of the funds raised in this manner were lent out straight away in the last few days of June. The subscription itself

TABLE 6.3
South Sea Company: Sources and Uses of Funds mid-April to mid-June 1720

	£million
Sources	
First money subscription (2 payments)	2.02
Second money subscription	0.60
Exchequer Bills from government	1.00
[borrowings and bond issues	4.48]
Total	8.10
Uses	
Lending on stock and subscription receipts	4.50
Payment of bribes (options)	1.00
Cash element of conversion	2.60
Total	8.10

was filled in the customary manner, with lists of prospective buyers collected by the South Sea directors, although one-fifth of the issue was opened to the general public who filled their allocation in a matter of hours. John Martin, of Martin's Bank, subscribed for £500 with the explanation that "when the rest of the world are mad we must imitate them in some measure".[48]

Blunt and his inner cabal did not wish to see a large volume of subscription receipts coming onto the market at a time when they were seeking to off-load their own positions in South Sea stock.[49] Accordingly receipts were not given out—an omission which was to become a source of intense controversy later on. Even so, a contemporary estimate suggests that one-sixth of the third subscription was at once sold for cash, the contracts providing for delivery of receipts "as soon as the Receipts shall be delivered out by the said Company".[50] Clearly, the financial markets were sufficiently adaptable to enable determined traders in stock or scrip to circumvent bureaucratic restrictions on transfers.

The third money subscription in mid-June is widely viewed as the high water mark of the South Sea boom. And at this critical juncture, when the excitement in Exchange Alley had reached fever pitch, it is interesting to observe the conduct of three key figures in the South Sea drama: Walpole, Aislabie and Hutcheson.

Robert Walpole was soon to become Prime Minister after establishing his reputation in the South Sea affair. Yet, having adopted a sceptical view of the company's financial prospects, and, refrained from buying or holding South Sea stock during the three month boom period to mid-June, he climbed belatedly onto the bandwagon. Reversing his previous judgement, he sought to buy at the top of the market by entering the lists for the third money subscription both on his own behalf and that of his friends and relations.[51]

John Aislabie, who lost his reputation in the South Sea affair, pursued the opposite course. He had made substantial profits by trading in South Sea stock but now realised that matters had got out of hand. Having disposed of his own shares, he took it upon himself, as the Crown's financial adviser, to warn the King against investing in the third money subscription since "the stock was carried up to an exorbitant height by the madness of the people and that it was impossible it should stand."[52]

Archibald Hutcheson, whose reputation in the South Sea affair has not survived into modern times, continued doggedly to warn all who would listen to him of the inevitability of a financial crash, based on his own impeccable financial analysis. On 11 June, he delivered to members of the House of Commons a summary update of his valuation of the South Sea

Company,[53] taking account of the first two money subscriptions and the partial conversion of the annuities. He concluded that the shares were worth at most £200, exclusive of profits from trade, as compared with a market price of 740 and predicted a dreadful reckoning when "the present reigning madness should happen to cease".[54]

HUTCHESON'S CALCULATIONS

Following the successful completion of the third money subscription, Hutcheson undertook a new analysis of the South Sea Company.[55] This included a current valuation of the shares together with a projected valuation based on the assumption that the remaining irredeemable plus redeemable debts were converted, using three alternative conversion prices for this purpose, namely 1000, 1500 and 2000. The methodology can be illustrated by showing his calculations on the assumption that all the remaining unconverted government debts were converted at a price of 1000 per share.[56] It should be noted, however, that Hutcheson was working on the basis that the third money subscription was for £6 million, rather than the £5 million achieved, due to an over subscription.

Hutcheson calculated the total nominal capital of the Company at £26.6 million after the third money subscription as against the £42 million that would be realised once all government debts had been converted. He then showed that up to the end of June the original shareholders and later subscribers had paid in cash or subscribed government debts with a total value of £96 million (he assumes throughout that subscriptions are fully paid up). However, the total value of the Company's assets (cash plus loans to the government) was only £80 million, the £16 million difference reflecting the £7.7 million due to the government on full conversion plus the £8.3 million difference between the government's valuation of annuities (20 years' purchase for the longs, 14 years for the shorts) and the Company's conversion terms (32 years for the longs and 17 years for the shorts). Accordingly the value of the shares was put at £300 (£80 million/£26.6 million × £100 nominal value) excluding profits from trade.

However, if the Company's nominal capital were increased to the maximum £42 million through the addition of £15.4 million capital at a subscription price of 1000, the net assets rose by £154 million to £234 million, which yielded a share valuation of £557 (£234 million/£42 million × £100 nominal value). Hutcheson then calculated the loss or gain for the various classes of shareholder, based on their proportionate share of the nominal capital and therefore net assets, as shown in table

TABLE 6.4
Shareholder Losses and Gains

Subscribers	(1) Subscription price (£)	(2) Attributable nominal capital (£million)[a]	(3) Value of (2) (£million)	(4) Amount paid for (3) (£million)	(5) Gain (+)/loss (−) (3)–(4) (£million)
Original shareholders	100	12.33	68.64	11.20	+57.44
First money subscription	300	2.47	13.79	6.75	+7.04
Second money subscription	400	1.54	8.58	5.60	+2.98
First conversion offer	375	3.66	20.42	12.49	+7.92
Third money subscription	1000	6.60	36.77	60.00	−23.23
Projected subscription	1000	15.40	85.80	154.00	−68.20
Totals		42.00	234.00	250.04	−16.04

Source: Adapted from Hutcheson (14 July 1720d: 52).
[a] Allows for 10 percent stock dividend summer 1720. NB: Sums may not add up due to rounding.

TABLE 6.5
Shareholder Losses and Gains (£)

Subscribers	Cost per share[a]	Net assets per share	Gain/loss per share
Original shareholders at 100	90.9	557.1	+466.2
First money subscription at 300	272.7	557.1	+284.4
Second money subscription at 400	363.6	557.1	+193.5
First conversion offer at 375	340.9	557.1	+216.2
Third money subscription at 1000	909.1	557.1	−351.9
Projected subscription at 1000	1000	557.1	−442.9

Source: Adapted from Hutcheson (14 July 1720d: 52).
[a] Allows for 10 percent stock dividend summer 1720.

6.4. The losses and gains for different classes of shareholder were also expressed in terms of the share price, as indicated in table 6.5.

Having demonstrated in this way the redistributive effects of the soaring price of South Sea shares, Hutcheson pointed out that, at a share price of 1000, the Company would be valued at £420 million, which, based on the yearly land taxes, was twice the value of all the land in Britain. He concluded that investors would not be able to meet their commitments on partly paid subscriptions unless the Company repaid their share of the capital in the form of dividends. This, he says, would do little harm *except* for the fact that, as his figures show, there were big losers and gainers "which, in my opinion, must make it absolutely impossible for those who subscribe at the highest prices, to comply with their engagements".[57] Since his calculations assume that all subscriptions are fully paid up and the cash received and reinvested by the Company, the implication is that the value of South Sea shares is significantly lower than he suggests.

Hutcheson completed his analysis by calculating the maximum dividend sustainable by the South Sea Company on the basis that the present value of that dividend, discounted at an appropriate market interest rate, should not exceed the company's true or intrinsic value. He undertook a series of calculations, using different valuations, discount rates and annuity periods, ranging from 7 years to perpetuity. Based on this approach, he concluded that, on a post-conversion valuation of £234 million (see column 3 of table 6.4), the maximum affordable perpetual dividend at an interest rate of 4 percent would be under £22 6s per annum. He pointed out that those who had bought stock at £400 or below would then enjoy a satisfactory return of over 5 percent on their original outlay, but "it is ruin and destruction to those who come in at 1000 ... for they must pay the Company, or to some others, £40 or £30 per annum [the cost of borrowing] for the money subscribed for £100 stock, and which, yet, will afford them a dividend only of £22 6s per annum".[58]

In his final observations Hutcheson noted that "the managers of the South Sea Scheme appear to me to have copied exactly from the French Mississippi, in all the steps which have been taken"[59] and predicted the same doleful consequences which by then (mid-July 1720) had overtaken John Law. He concluded with some vigorous comments on the iniquities of unbridled speculation, the moral state of the nation, and the urgent need for legislative action "to put a hook in the nose of this great Leviathan of the South Sea".[60]

PEAK OF THE BOOM

Hutcheson was not to know that the valuations he made in July were calculated at the turning point of the South Sea boom. There is some confusion here about the precise timing of the market peak because the South Sea Company's books were closed for two months on 22 June while the midsummer dividend was being prepared. The prices quoted during this period are therefore not spot prices but rather forward prices "for the opening of the transfer books".

Larry Neal, noting that this forward price was quoted at a high of 950 on 1 July (Castaing) or 1050 on 24 June (Freke),[61] states correctly that the difference between the two-month forward price and the spot price should reflect the implicit market interest rate as well as the dividend rate on the stock. He argues that the underlying spot rate was probably roughly constant while the books were closed, since the last spot price of 765 on 22 June (Castaing's data) was not very different from the opening 740 spot price on 23 August. His suggestion is that the jump in the quoted forward price to approximately 1000 around the turn of the month was due to a sharp rise in the implicit interest rate: "So it is likely that one of the most dramatic parts of the bubble, the final leap upward after 22 June, was in large part illusory and reflected not so much a buying mania as a desparate crunch in the London money market".[62]

This interpretation cannot, however, be accepted as it stands. For one thing, it is a well-established proposition of finance theory that, subject to a risk premium, the forward price should be an unbiased predictor of the future spot price, meaning in this case that the market's expectation at around the end of June was that the spot price would open at approximately 1000 on 22 August. Second, if there were a sudden credit squeeze, it is more likely that the spot and forward prices would diverge through an absolute decline in the former rather than a rise in the latter. Third, the Bank of England at this time joined the South Sea Company by lending freely on its own stock, first at 5 percent and then, from 14 July, at 4 percent (the South Sea Company having made a similar reduction on 20 May).[63] Declining interest rates for borrowing against stock hardly suggests a severe squeeze. More importantly, Neal's interpretation does not take account of direct evidence from the market, particularly the market for subscription receipts which, being transferable by simple legal assignment, continued to trade while the transfer books were closed.

In reality, there was a big surge in the stock market on 23 June, the day after the South Sea books were closed. Receipts for the first two money subscriptions rose by 8–10 percent, the third money subscription jumped by one-third, Bank stock rose by 10 percent, East India stock by 12 percent and the Royal African Company by no less than 25 percent. It is therefore safe to assume that the spot price for South Sea stock would also have risen sharply, so helping to explain the 1000 price for the opening of the books recorded by Freke for 24 June (no price was given for 23 June).

The boom in South Sea paper was, furthermore, sustained well into July, judging by the performance of subscription receipts (see table 6.6). These dipped in early July but reached new peaks in the week beginning

TABLE 6.6
Prices of South Sea Subscriptions:[a] weekly highs taken from "Freke's prices of stocks"

Week beginning:	First subscription (£90 paid)	Second subscription (£40 paid)	Third subscription (£100 paid)
20 June	665	630	340
[22 June	550	565	250[c]]
27 June	660	630	340
4 July	675	570	310
11 July	720	625	350
18 July	**720**	**630**	**400**
25 July	710	600	420
1 August	700	570	400
8 August	670	550	380
15 August	670[b]	560	390
22 August	**650**[b]	**515**	**350**

[a] Highest daily prices.
[b] After deducting third instalment payment of £30 due 14 August.
[c] 150 nil paid premium plus £100 down payment.

18 July. Also, Castaing's highest ex-dividend quote of 900 for South Sea stock was reached on 12 July and again on 20 July, equivalent to nearly 1000 in cum-dividend terms.[64] The implication is that the South Sea Bubble was most fully inflated in the second and third weeks of July.

Blunt and his inner cabal decided to take advantage of the summer bull market to carry on with the debt conversion scheme. This involved taking in the redeemable and the remaining unconverted annuities. The operation was conducted in two stages, the redeemable debt managed by the Bank of England being registered for conversion on 14 July and the remaining debts (annuities plus redeemables managed by the Exchequer) registered on 4 August. Once again the terms were to be set at the discretion of the Company. These were announced on 12 August, but on this occasion there was no opt-out for those who had registered. As with the earlier conversion, the issuance of stock was delayed in order to discourage selling.

The terms were again favourable to annuitants, assuming (critically) that the stock they received could be sold at around prevailing market levels. The conversion price of South Sea stock was set at 800, or roughly 10 percent below the market level, while the long annuities were valued at 36 years' purchase and the short at 17.5 years (compared with prevailing market prices of 35 years and 17 years, respectively), with nearly 10 percent payable in cash and bonds. A long annuitant therefore stood to receive £3200 in stock at 800 (i.e., £400 nominal in stock) plus £400 in cash for every £100 of annuity income. However, the actual market value of the package was £4000 given a current share price of around 900. If the benchmark valuation for a £100 long annuity is again taken to be 24 years' purchase or £2400 (see p. 105), the excess valuation was about 60 percent. Stated differently, converting annuitants would gain so long as the price of South Sea stock did not fall below 500.[65] Of course, some might prefer to sell their annuities for cash in the rudimentary secondary market at a price that reflected the potential conversion value, rather than take a risk on being able to sell South Sea stock.

Holders of redeemable debt were offered a much smaller safety cushion, since they required less inducement to convert. Their debts could, after all, be repaid by the government at par at any time. Accordingly, the Company valued the redeemable debt at par plus 5 percent, which meant that investors would gain on conversion so long as South Sea shares did not fall below 763.[66]

The conversion offer was once more a great success. When the subscriptions had been processed, it emerged that to date 80 percent of the annuities and 85 percent of the redeemables had been taken in, and that £26 million of the £31 million subscribable debts had been exchanged for South Sea stock. The Company could claim to have gone a long way towards implementing the conversion scheme.

The cost of the support operations necessary to achieve this conversion level was, however, reflected in continuing liquidity pressures. Towards the end of July, the Company had decided to waive the third payment (due 15 August) on the first money subscription and the second payment (due 14 September) on the second money subscription, by treating the payments as lent to the subscribers. At the same time, the Company was continuing to lend on stock and also buying shares for its own account: a total of over £2 million was spent on stock purchases, mostly in August and September.[67] The £5 million received from the third money subscription would not have been sufficient to cover stock purchases (perhaps £1.5 million) and lending against stock (around £4.5 million) between mid-June and the end of September.

One commentator portrayed the South Sea Company's profligate use of its funds during the boom period as follows:

> Tiz amazing that a company at first erected upon pretence of trade should take so little care to begin, fix, or improve any Trade, and that when at last they had got into their possession a great deal of ready money, they should employ their genius in stock-jobbing, or so to speak plain, in gaming away their own Treasure, and encouraging others in the same frenzy.[68]

Against the background of growing liquidity problems, the Company opened a fourth money subscription for £1 million on 24 August at a price of 1000, an over subscription of £0.25 million bringing the total to £1.25 million. The success of this issue again points to irrational investment behaviour since the terms (20 percent down, balance in four calls at six-month intervals),[69] would indicate a true price of about £950 for the subscription against a prevailing share price of 820. Not only were the share and subscription prices far in excess of any realistic valuation, but the relationship between the two was anomalous. Significantly, the great South Sea insider, Blunt, staked only £500 in the fourth money subscription, despite a directors' undertaking to subscribe £3000 each.

Towards the end of August, Hutcheson revalued South Sea shares, taking account of the latest conversion terms (36 years' purchase for long annuities against 20 years allowed by the government) that gave rise to an even larger book loss for the Company. He calculated the asset value per share at £342 and demonstrated that only if the chain letter continued and the remaining issuable shares were sold at a staggering

Plate 8 The South Sea Bubble by Hogarth. Speculators ride on a roundabout, Honour is broken on a wheel by Self-interest and the Pope plays pitch-and-toss with two priests. Copyright Guildhall Library.

1625 would the asset value per share be brought up to the £1000 level at which so many had bought.

However, the chain letter was already going into reverse. By the end of August, South Sea shares were trading in the range 770–820, compared with 880–900 in the middle of the month and 980–1000 in mid-July. Of course, when a speculative bubble bursts it is not always necessary to explain the timing in terms of specific events: if a balloon is blown up hard enough it will burst of its own accord without being pricked. Nevertheless, there were several worries affecting South Sea investors in the late summer of 1720, not least of which was the shattering outcome of John Law's precursor Mississippi experiment.

NOTES

1. John Toland's "Secret History" was first printed in *A Collection of Several Pieces of Mr Toland: with Some Memoirs of his Life and Writing* (London, 1726). It is evidently not the work of Toland himself but was possibly written by his friend, Sir Theodore Janssen, a South Sea Director who was no doubt keen to clear his name by demonstrating Blunt's dictatorial management style (see Chancellor 1999: note 66). Blunt's own version of events, written by himself or a close collaborator, appeared in *A True State of the South Sea Scheme as it was First Form'd...* (London: 1722/1732). Aislabie (or a close friend) also pitched into this pamphleteering war with *The Case of the Right Honourable John Aislabie Esq* (London: 1721).
2. Toland (1726: 419).
3. Toland (1726: 422).
4. Toland (1726: 433).
5. Toland (1726: 443).
6. Toland (1726: 443).
7. Toland (1726: 437).
8. Although he appears to have been frustrated in this attempt when the Court of Directors, in his absence, refused to issue tradable dividend "warrants" and instead credited shareholders directly with additional dividend stock. See Minutes of Court Meeting held on 29 August 1720.
9. Toland (1726: 432).
10. Toland (1726: 423).
11. Hutcheson (14 July 1720d: 64).
12. Blunt (1732: 15).
13. Steele, alias Sir John Edgar (12–15 March 1720: 1).
14. Boys (1825: 15).
15. Subscription receipts were assignable by endorsement. Accordingly "it was almost universally stipulated in every contract [for subscription receipts] that the seller, whether for ready money or time, should deliver the company's receipt to the buyer, which endorsed, would entitle him to the subscription" (Anon 1720b: 7).

16. Blunt, (1732: 44).
17. Dickson (1967: 142).
18. Toland (1726: 425).
19. Dickson (1967: 131).
20. Steele, alias Sir John Edgar (5–8 March 1720).
21. Scott (1912: 303–304) argues the opposite case. He suggests that investors were unaware until much later of the Company's manipulation of its stock price and that in the absence of this information they behaved rationally if optimistically.
22. Castaing (1720), relevant dates.
23. Cited Dickson (1967: 141).
24. Scott (1912: 318).
25. Hutcheson (21 April 1720c: 35).
26. Dickson (1967: 131).
27. Anderson (1764: 96).
28. Scott (1912: 309).
29. Scott (1912: 310) suggests that the comparison should be made not with the prevailing market price of annuities but with the more "realistic" price obtaining in 1715 (16 years' purchase maximum). But this historic price does not reflect the choice facing annuitants in the spring of 1720.
30. £100 annuity cost at 24 years' purchase   £2400
Paid by South Sea Company in bonds and cash   £ 575
Remainder payable in South Sea stock   £1825
£700 of South Sea stock given for sum of £1825, yielding "break-even" share price of £261.
31. Scott (1912: 415).
32. Anderson (1764: 102).
33. Anderson (1764: 102–103).
34. Cassidy (2002: 237).
35. Dickson 1967: 153).
36. John Applebee's *Weekly Journal* (7 July 1720).
37. *London Journal* (18–25 June 1720).
38. *London Journal* (9 July 1720).
39. *London Journal* (18–25 June 1720).
40. *London Journal* (25 June 1720).
41. John Applebee's *Weekly Journal* (11 June 1720).
42. Cited in Wilson (1941: 122).
43. Cited in Murphy (1986: 171).
44. *London Journal* (9 July 1720: 3).
45. Cobbett (1806–1820: 434).
46. Scott (1912: 320).
47. See Scott (1912: 321) and Dickson (1967: 143) re conflicting views on timing of loans.
48. Cited in Carswell (1993: 133).
49. Toland (1726: 441).
50. Cited in Dickson (1967: 129).
51. Plumb (1956: 308).

52. Cited in Carswell (1993: 132).
53. Hutcheson, "An Estimate of the Intrinsick Value of South Sea Stock" (11 June 1720) within Introduction to Hutcheson (1720d: 41).
54. Hutcheson, "An Estimate of the Intrinsick Value of South Sea Stock" (11 June 1720) within Introduction to Hutcheson (1720d: 42).
55. Hutcheson (14 July 1720d: 42 ff.).
56. Hutcheson's meticulous, even pedantic, approach is reflected in calculations involving up to ten decimal places. Something of the character of the man is suggested by the following qualification to his calculations: "Note, that ... I have stated the debts, to be taken in [£31, 664, 554-18s-3d] at 2d more than the same really are, and which increases the whole capital the same sum. This trifling error was observed after finishing the "Calculations" ... but the amendment thereof would have occasioned some small alterations in several of the other sums ... which I thought a very needless trouble, since the reader without it will have sufficient light in this matter." Hutcheson (14 July 1720d: 49).
57. Hutcheson (14 July 1720d: 48).
58. Hutcheson (14 July 1720d: 63).
59. Hutcheson (14 July 1720d: 65).
60. Hutcheson (14 July 1720d: 68).
61. This should be 25 June.
62. Neal (1990: 101).
63. The Bank of England lent over £1 million in this way (Dickson 1967: 193).
64. Throughout this period, Freke's quoted prices include and Castaing's exclude, the 10 percent midsummer stock dividend (although, confusingly, Castaing's highest price of 950 on 1 July is cum-dividend). The result is that Freke's prices are consistently 10 percent or so above Castaing's. However, since the stock dividend was equivalent to a bonus issue, it should not have raised the market value of South Sea shares, other than through the effect on investor psychology. Freke's cum-dividend prices at this time therefore provide the most appropriate benchmark for comparison with earlier price series.

    Intriguingly, Castaing's initial forward prices for the opening of the books include the phrase "and deposit" suggesting that there was a requirement for a margin deposit of the kind demanded in present-day futures and forward markets to protect the seller of stock against default on settlement day.
65. (2400 − 400)/400. See also note 30.
66. Scott (1912: 323).
67. Carswell (1993: note 140).
68. Anon (1720f).
69. The original schedule of calls relating to the fourth subscription is the subject of some confusion. Dickson (1967: 125) indicates that four calls of £200 were to be made every nine months over 3 years. Carswell (1993: 146) states that the calls were to be over 2 years. Freke's published schedule also shows four six-month calls over 2 years, although this is adjusted from 16 September (8 calls of £100 over four years) when the Company was considering relief for subscribers. Castaing does not publish a schedule for the fourth subscription until the beginning of October by which time the original schedule had been extended and the calls reduced.

CHAPTER SEVEN

The Crash

IN THE FIRST few days of 1720, both John Law and the Mississippi Company appeared to be unassailable, with Law's appointment as Controller-General of Finances coinciding with the high point of the Mississippi boom. Yet by the end of the year, Law had fled France in disgrace, the stock market had been shut down and the Mississippi Company effectively dismantled. Between the apogee of the Mississippi Bubble and the final denouement, France witnessed a bewildering sequence of contradictory financial measures whose cumulative impact was to destroy the French public's confidence in paper money for more than three generations.

The development of financial policy in France during this annus horribilis can be conveniently divided into two sub-periods: until the end of May the objective was to reduce the role of specie in favour of bank notes, with the ultimate aim of demonetising the former; thereafter the policy went into reverse as bank notes were phased out and finally demonetised in favour of traditional coinage. The extent of Law's personal responsibility for the policy confusion associated with this massive U-turn is a matter of debate,[1] but it is impossible to avoid the conclusion that the master gambler and entrepreneur lost his bearings from January 1720, most of all by failing to foresee the market consequences of his actions.

REDUCING THE ROLE OF SPECIE

Law started the year by adopting an aggressively interventionist approach aimed at regulating the price of Mississippi shares and limiting the public's use of specie. At the end of 1719, the Mississippi Company had opened an office in the Rue Quincampoix to buy and sell its own shares, at a bid-offer spread of around 1 percent,[2] with a view both to displacing professional stock-jobbers and supporting the share price. Then on 9 January, the Company began to issue what were in effect call options on its shares, or "primes", a 1000 livre down payment entitling the purchaser to acquire

Mississippi shares at a strike price of 10,000 livres during the next six months. Law later explained that the purpose was to dampen speculation in the forward market where prices for future delivery had reached 12,000–14,000 livres. However, the options were initially under priced so that shareholders dumped shares in favour of primes.[3] Subsequently, as the market was flooded with primes, and the spot share price also fell away, the options moved "out-of-the-money" and became virtually worthless; Law's response was to convert 300 million livres of primes into shares at the rate of 10 primes to one Mississippi share.

This fiasco was quickly followed by another when on 22 February the Company's share dealing office was closed, resulting in a share price collapse of 26 percent in one week. Popular resentment at this decline forced Law's hand and on 5 March the office was reopened, under a face-saving change of name,[4] with an explicit mandate to convert Mississippi shares into bank notes and vice versa at a fixed price of 9000 livres per share. This move effectively monetised Mississippi shares by equating them with bank notes, but it also caused the bank note issue to balloon as shares were converted into notes.[5]

Concern over monetary inflation prompted yet another bizarre financial shift. A decree of 21 May imposed a phased reduction in the price of Mississippi shares to 5000 livres over the ensuing six months, alongside a parallel reduction in the value of bank notes (see p. 127). In the face of outraged public opinion, the decree was revoked on 28 May, but by then confidence had been fatally undermined and the share price, having fallen by 17 percent between 21 May and 27 May, fell by a further 44 percent to 4200 livres between 28 May and 31 May. The Mississippi Bubble had burst.

During this period, Law was also trying to discourage the hoarding of specie by an increasingly distrustful populace. The public's preference for traditional coinage was undermining the policy of displacing metallic money with bank notes while also threatening to exhaust the specie resources of the Royal Bank. In order to encourage conversions of specie into bank notes, Law used both financial incentives and direct controls on the ownership and use of gold and silver coinage.

On 22 January, the internal exchange rate of the louis d'or was raised from 34 to 36 livres and on 28 January lowered again to 34 livres, with the intention of persuading the public to switch into bank notes during the grace period allowed for conversion at the higher price. The operation was repeated on 25 February in a more dramatic manner when the price of the louis d'or was raised by no less than a third to 48 livres before being lowered once more to 36 livres on 5 March, the idea again being to encourage conversions from specie into notes at a temporarily favourable price. Although some dishoarding of specie occurred, one can imagine that such manipulations in the price of monetary assets would severely damage confidence in the financial system and those responsible for its operation.

Alongside changes in the internal exchange rate, Law introduced a series of regulations penalising the use, holding and exportation of metallic money. In successive decrees between the end of January and the middle of March, he (i) prohibited the export of specie and gold bullion;[6] (ii) prohibited the wearing of diamonds and precious jewellry;[7] (iii) prohibited the production of gold and silver artefacts;[8] (iv) limited holdings of specie to 500 livres per individual or institution;[9] (v) mandated that payments of over 100 livres be made in bank notes;[10] and, finally, (vi) announced that gold was to be demonetised and silver progressively reduced in value.[11] These dictatorial measures were accompanied by an inquisition under which individuals were encouraged to inform on one another and suspected offenders were subject to house searches, confiscations and severe financial penalties.

Law's increasingly desperate experiment came to an end when policy shifted yet again in response to an exploding money supply, itself the result of pegging the price of Mississippi shares. The public's holdings of bank notes had virtually doubled in the four months to late May in the context of growing inflationary pressures. With some 2.6 billion livres of notes outstanding against specie amounting to some 1.3 billion livres, the decision was taken (whether or not initiated by Law) to halve the price of bank notes over a six month period so as to bring the value of the note issue into line with that of specie.[12] Just as important, the move was designed to protect the Royal Bank's specie reserve which had fallen to around 15 percent of the value of publicly held bank notes.[13] The decision to devalue the note issue was announced on 21 May, along with the planned lowering of the price of Mississippi shares to 5000 livres (see p. 126).

Unsurprisingly, the public felt betrayed by the devaluation of a new monetary asset (bank notes) which it had been encouraged and then forced to use as a replacement for traditional metallic money. Daniel Pulteney, the British Representative in Paris, observed that:

> It is in everyone's mouth that they are robbed of half of what they were worth, that it is the most notorious cheat that ever was committed and that it is very plain now that Mr Law has as little capacity as integrity.[14]

The popular outcry led to a rapid policy reversal. The measures of 21 May were revoked on 28 May but by then confidence in shares and bank notes had been irreversibly damaged, there was the prospect of a run on the Bank as people sought to convert to specie and the whole financial edifice founded on paper money was in imminent danger of toppling over. On 29 May, with his "system" unravelling, Law was dismissed and placed under house arrest, ostensibly for his own protection.

END OF LAW'S EXPERIMENT

Despite the apparent ruination of his grand scheme, Law was recalled by the Regent on 2 June to direct the Bank and the Mississippi Company, as "Intendant Générale du Commerce". It seems that Law was to be given the chance to help clear up a mess that was mainly of his own making, and to take the blame if things continued to go badly. However, from this point on he was no longer fully in charge of financial policy.

There was no let up in the flood of monetary decrees although now they were all directed towards the restoration of specie and the phased demonetization of bank notes. Between June and October there was a rapid succession of measures involving: (i) partial suspension of the convertibility of bank notes into specie;[15] (ii) five successive changes in the internal exchange rate;[16] (iii) the abolition of the 500 livre limit on specie holdings;[17] (iv) a progressive withdrawal of the number of bank notes in circulation for public burning;[18] (v) the announcement of a planned demonetization of high denomination bank notes;[19] (vi) a requirement that 10,000 and 1000 livre notes could only be used for payments if half the sum to be settled was paid in specie;[20] (vii) an arbitrary 75 percent reduction in the value of bank accounts, which merchants had been encouraged to use in lieu of bank notes; and, finally[21] (viii) the announcement in October that bank notes were no longer to be legal tender, with immediate effect for the payment of taxes and from 1 November for all other transactions.[22] Deprived of its raison d'être, the Royal Bank closed its doors on 27 November. Law's experiment with paper money had come full circle, although large numbers of people had been ruined along the way.

The Mississippi Company submitted to a similar although less determinate fate. There were further bewildering impositions on shareholders, including a 3000 livre per share supplementary call in early June,[23] a reduction in the nominal share value to 2000 livres in mid-September,[24] and a requirement in late October that all shares be lodged with the company and that any "profiteering" original subscribers who were found to have sold, must restore their original subscription by purchasing shares at a penal price

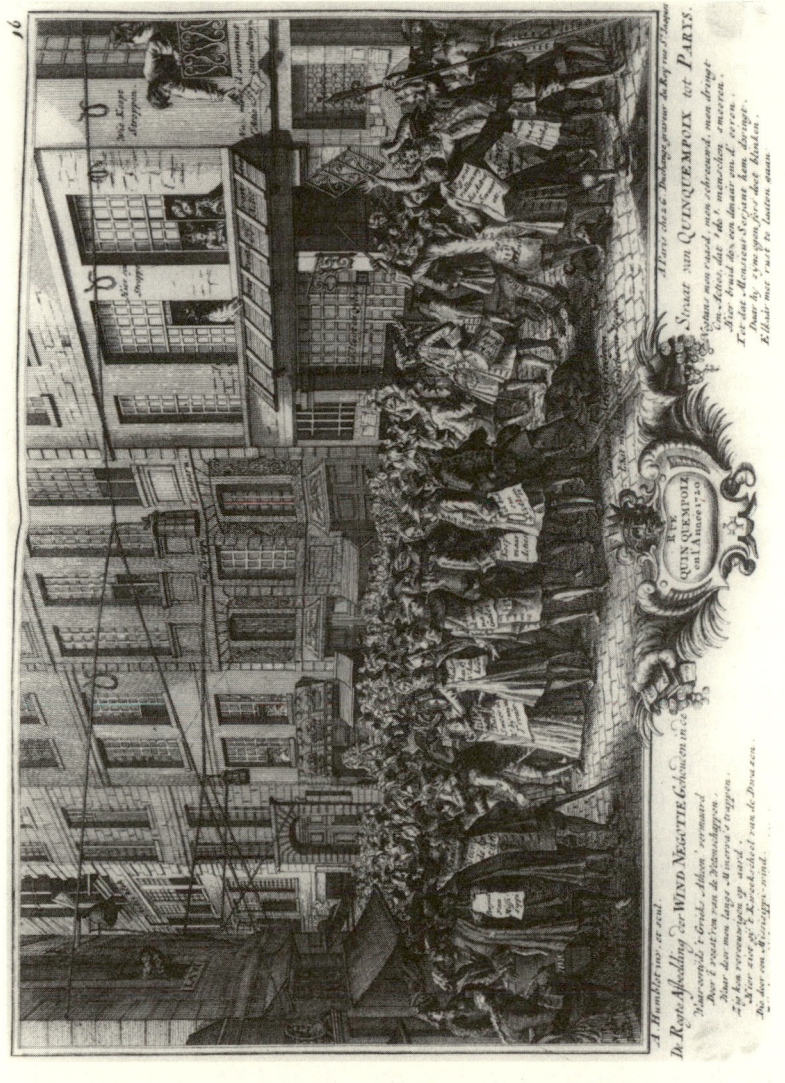

Plate 9 Rue Quincampoix in 1720 during the Mississippi boom. From Het Groote Tofereel der Dwaasheid, Amsterdam, 1720. Copyright Guildhall Library.

of 13,500 livres.[25] Shortly after this last confiscatory measure, the mint, tax reforms and administration of the royal revenues were taken away from the Mississippi Company, which was to continue in truncated form as a trading business until late in the century. Finally, on 8 December trading in shares and stock-jobbing were prohibited.

Law, transformed from popular hero to villain in the space of six months, became a fugitive once more, fleeing France on 17 December with the connivance of the Regent who also provided him with a small pension. However, Law's wife, Katherine, was detained in France, he had no access to his landed wealth which was later confiscated, and he was severely embarrassed financially because his long-standing forward contract with Lord Londonderry for the sale of East India stock was showing a loss of £600,000. After further wanderings in Europe, includ-ing a return to England (made possible by a royal pardon conferred in 1717), Law settled in Venice where he gambled, formed a unique collec-tion of paintings by the great masters, and held court to curious visitors. He died on 21 March 1729 aged 57.

Law was a brilliant mathematician and gambler, a considerable entre-preneur and an original thinker on financial issues but he could also lay claim to be the worst minister of finance the world has ever known. His regime was characterised by almost daily changes in the rules governing the pricing, convertibility and permissible use of financial assets embra-cing bank notes, specie and shares. The frequency, complexity and incon-sistency of these edicts (totalling 44 in less than nine months) made it impossible even for sophisticated observers like Daniel Pulteney, let alone ordinary citizens, to understand what was going on or how best to manage their financial affairs. The inevitable consequence was a general-ised collapse of confidence.

Matters might have gone differently if Law had kept separate his two great innovations: the Mississippi Company and the Royal Bank. By floating the former on a tide of money created by the latter he eventually destroyed public confidence in both. Hutcheson, too, believed that the Mississippi project would have been less vulnerable "had not the Royal Bank been incorporated with that Company, by lending, at first, money on that stock, at a high valuation, and, afterwards, by making Mississippi stock and bank notes convertible, at the rate of [900] per cent." The consequence, as he pointed out, was an explosion of paper money and "a mortal stab to the French credit".[26]

However, being spread across both shares and bank notes, the loss of financial confidence was not fully reflected in the Mississippi share price which declined by approximately two-thirds from peak to trough. After all, French investors in the summer of 1720 were faced with an unenviable choice between the market risk of Mississippi shares, the convertibility risk of bank notes and the regulatory risk (devaluations, restrictions on use, etc.) associated with specie. Those investors who were determined to realise their profits from the Mississippi Bubble were therefore inclined to convert into silver and gold and export the proceeds (some 500 million livres left the country in this way in 1720 according to some estimates) thereby depressing the external exchange rate which fell from 39 livres to the pound in May to 92 livres by September. A better indication of the collapse of the Mississippi Bubble is therefore provided by the share price expressed in sterling, which fell from a peak of around £325 in January to below £50 in September.[27] The decline of over 80 percent was comparable to that of South Sea shares in July–December (see below).

We have already seen that the Mississippi Bubble had a direct influence on the South Sea project by prompting a copycat debt conversion scheme in 1720 as well as share price manipulation based on tried and tested Mississippi techniques. The bursting of the Mississippi Bubble in the early summer of 1720 had a double-edged impact on the South Sea boom. The initial effect in May/June was to accentuate the rise in South Sea shares as speculators deserted the Rue Quincampoix in favour of Exchange Alley. However, as events unfolded in France, comparisons began to be made between the fate of Mississippi investors and the likely prospects for South Sea shareholders. By the late summer, there can be little doubt that the Mississippi experience was a factor in the reversal of investor psychology among stock market investors in England.

Hutcheson, as a close observer of the French financial scene, was quick to see the connection between the Mississippi and South Sea experiments. Writing in mid-July he observed that "the managers of the South Sea scheme appear to me to have copied exactly after the French Mississippi in all the steps which have been hitherto taken" and concluded that the eventual outcome of the English venture would be equally disastrous.[28]

BURSTING OF THE SOUTH SEA BUBBLE

The collapse of the Mississippi Bubble was the prelude to a more dramatic deflation of asset prices across the channel. By mid-summer, South Sea shares were trading in the range 900–1000 which translated into a market capitalisation, assuming shares to be fully paid up, of £340–380 million or £210–£230 million if the company's holdings of its own shares are excluded.[29] At the same time, the collective capitalisation of all the speculative projects or lesser bubbles that had been launched in and around Exchange Alley was estimated to be around £300 million.[30] The combined capitalisation of shares traded in Exchange Alley was now a multiple of the total value of all lands in England.

As previously indicated, a stock market collapse does not necessarily have to be "explained" by outside events; it is sufficient that market valuations have become too stretched to be sustained. And, as Hutcheson had repeatedly warned, the mid-summer market valuation of South Sea shares made a crash inevitable. To underline the point, in early September he published a review of South Sea share valuations he had made at each successive subscription. These are summarised below:[31]

1. If the South Sea Company had made no new share issues in pursuance of the conversion scheme, but simply taken in all the outstanding government debts in exchange for cash and bonds, the Company would be £26 million worse off than before and the shares would be worth £37. This reflected the dead weight loss of the amounts to be paid to the government and the premium terms (i.e., years' purchase) offered to annuitants.
2. After the first money subscription and the first conversion of debts—undertaken at prices of 300 to 400—the stock was worth around £100.
3. After the third money subscription, taken at a price of 1000, the stock was worth some £300.
4. After the second conversion of debts (redeemables plus remaining irredeemables) at a conversion price of 800 the share value was £340.
5. After the fourth and final money subscription at 1000 the shares were worth about £360.

These estimates excluded any contribution from South Sea trade but they erred on the generous side by assuming that all subscription moneys were paid up front rather than phased, that there were no defaults on payments due from subscribers, and that all money received by the Company was immediately lent out at the prevailing market interest rate (which was put at 4 percent). Hutcheson pointed out that the true financial position of the Company was considerably worse than his valuations might suggest because if the stock price weakened, many subscribers at 1000, of which only £100 had been paid up, would choose to default on their remaining calls. In addition, the Company had, of course, lent freely on the security of its own stock and subscription receipts, loans which could well prove irrecoverable if the stock price fell.

These last considerations underline an important feature of the South Sea boom. Not only did the share price reach a level far in excess of any realistic valuation, but the dynamics of the situation created the potential for a self-feeding financial collapse. First, there were the loans on stock and subscription receipts: the Company itself had lent a staggering £11 million plus in this way and goldsmith-bankers had also lent large although unquantifiable sums, much of it reportedly involving stock pledged to cover loans of £600 per share.[32] In the event that the share price fell below the value of the security (e.g., 600) there would be forced sales of pledged stock, thereby driving the price still lower.[33]

Second, any share price fall to a level below the price at which investors had subscribed would provide an incentive to default on remaining calls; although shares might be cancelled as a result, the Company would nevertheless be deprived of expected cash flow. Finally, a declining share price would jeopardise future money subscriptions aimed at exploiting any difference between the Company's issued and issuable share capital. In other words, just as a rising share price created the opportunity for cash generation, a falling share price had damaging implications for future cash flow.

Beyond the unsustainable market valuation of its shares and the inherent fragility of the South Sea Company's finances, there were a number of "trigger" factors that help to explain the timing of the South Sea crash. Market psychology was undoubtedly affected by developments in Paris and the unravelling of John Law's experiment; commentators, such as James Milner, were warning from the spring onwards that the South Sea Company was heading for the same fate as the Mississippi Company and these comparisons may have begun to weigh on investors in the summer months.[34] Hutcheson's dire predictions, disseminated in pamphlets and summarised in newspaper reports, also began to make an impact. According to Adamson the "fair and candid calculations" of "that ingenious gentleman Archibald Hutcheson" were having an influence in Exchange Alley as "some began to have their eyes opened by [his] judicious calculations".[35]

It has been stated by several financial historians that tightening credit conditions in the summer months played a major part in the timing of the crash, Larry Neal going so far as to suggest that there was a "desparate credit crunch in the London money market" from late June onwards.[36] Certainly, there are numerous contemporary anecdotal reports attesting to the near impossibility of securing credit in the *late* summer of 1720 but great caution is needed here. In the first place, there is little direct evidence of rising short term interest rates. Prime fixed rate instruments such as East India's 5 percent bonds, which were typically issued with six month maturities, showed little price change between mid-June and the end of August. Indeed, the average quarterly yield on these bonds actually fell slightly from 4.99 percent in January–March 1720 to 4.94 percent in July–September 1720![37] Of course, there was a heavy demand for funds to pay for subscriptions to South Sea stock but these remittances were recycled back to the market as soon as they were received and it is important to note that the South Sea Company was not a net taker of funds during 1720.

It is true that extraordinarily high interest rates were paid by some individual borrowers but it is unwise to draw general conclusions from such cases. Dickson, for example, supports his assertion that interest rates "soared" in the summer of 1720 by citing the case of a Mr Colin Campbell who borrowed £16,000 for two months on 22 August (i.e., after the Bubble had begun to deflate) at 5 percent per month.[38] However, the same individual borrowed at 2.5 percent per month five days later; indeed he borrowed from a variety of different sources at widely differing rates, suggesting that his credit standing was not the highest (he appears eventually to have fled abroad to avoid his creditors).[39]

The fact is that the market for personal credit was highly imperfect, allowing very big differences in borrowing costs at any point in time, depending on the source of the loan, the credit standing of the borrower and the security offered. Hutcheson, for instance, states that some investors were borrowing at rates of up to 10 percent per month or even 1 percent per day as early as April 1720.[40] Yet we can find a Mr Thomas Harrison borrowing £40,000 at only 5 percent per annum in mid-June 1720, near the peak of the South Sea boom.[41] There is no firm evidence here to justify the view that a spectacular credit crunch brought the boom to an end.

On the other hand, once stock prices had begun to weaken, collateral values (of pledged securities) became uncertain, the credit standing of some over extended individuals came into question, and a number of goldsmith-bankers defaulted because the security on which they had lent proved insufficient. These developments in turn led to what today would be called "credit rationing", meaning that many would-be borrowers were shut out of the markets, not because credit was tight, but because perceived default risk had increased to the point where lenders were only prepared to advance funds to undoubted borrowers or against the highest quality collateral.[42] The Bank of England's credit policies are, for instance, consistent with this interpretation. It did not raise the 5 percent interest it typically charged for discounting promissory notes and bills of exchange when credit markets deteriorated in late September/early October. Instead, it restricted such lending to very short maturity instruments (e.g., 15 days for domestic bills, 7 days for foreign bills) before temporarily suspending such lending altogether.[43]

There was another episode of credit rationing during the global stock market crash of 2000–2002 when many companies were shut out of the short-term commercial paper market, despite falling interest rates, because of fears of rising default risk.[44] At the same time those who were able to issue debt instruments had to pay a higher risk premium to investors. But the important point to note is that this type of credit squeeze is typically the *consequence* and not the *cause* of financial shocks and asset price collapses.

While the 1720 crisis in credit markets is best viewed as a knock-on effect rather than as a primary cause of the stock market crash, there was one important government initiative that undoubtedly helps to explain why the South Sea Bubble burst when it did. This was the so-called Bubble Act which received the Royal Assent on 11 June. The Act is a remarkable instance of special interest legislation that was pushed through by friends of the South Sea Company in order to stamp out competition from the rival bubbles that were being advertised daily in the London press. The South Sea Directors evidently feared that unless the proliferation of the other bubbles were halted "it might take off abundance of their Bubbles, and by lessening the number of their buyers, lessen, if not spoil, their market".[45] Accordingly, the Act made it an offence after midsummer 1720 to "presume to act as a corporate body or to direct an existing charter to unauthorised ends", thereby effectively prohibiting the flotation of any new companies without the specific authorisation of Parliament.

Archibald Hutcheson was a member of the House of Commons Committee that drafted the legislation. He found himself in opposition to the South Sea interest since what he wanted was not new legislation to control company flotations (he felt existing laws were adequate for this purpose) but rather a new regulatory framework designed to eliminate stock-jobbing malpractices that he believed were responsible for the prevailing market excesses.[46] In today's terms, Hutcheson was arguing for a Securities Exchange Commission to regulate the securities market rather than draconian restrictions on the new issue market that would inevitably stifle commercial enterprise.

The South Sea interest prevailed but its victory was short-lived. Enforcement action under the new legislation was delayed for over two months but on 17/18 August writs of "scire facias" were served on four companies (English Copper, Royal Lustreing, York Buildings and Welsh Copper) for contravening the Act by misapplying their charters. The shares of these undertakings promptly collapsed (York Buildings, for instance, falling by 90 percent within a month) and shares of other companies that were perceived to be vulnerable to enforcement action suffered a similar fate.

What the South Sea directors had failed to foresee was that the collapse of fringe enterprises would have devastating knock-on effects on core Exchange Alley stocks, including in particular shares of the South Sea Company. First, many investors had borrowed to fund their subscriptions to the smaller bubbles targeted by the new Act. When prices collapsed, they became forced sellers of other stocks in their portfolios in order to repay their borrowings.[47] Second, the collapse of some companies was so sudden that goldsmith-bankers who had lent on the security of shares were unable to sell pledged stock quickly enough to protect their loans.[48] As in so many modern financial crises, rapidly falling collateral values exposed lenders to default, accentuated concerns about credit risk and gave further impetus to the "flight to quality", that is, away from stocks and debt instruments in favour of cash. Finally, the heavy losses suffered by investors in the smaller bubbles contributed to a shift in market sentiment from greed to fear.

In the six weeks following enforcement of the Bubble Act South Sea shares, which had already fallen more than 10 percent from their mid-July level, declined at an accelerating pace, to 775 at the end of August, 520 in mid-September, 290 on 1 October and 170 on 14 October. Over a period of three months, the South Sea Bubble had burst, carrying the rest of the stock market with it (table 7.1).

The South Sea directors' initial response to the collapse was to try to stabilise the share price. The Company spent the best part of £2 million in August/September buying its own stock through its official broker, Matthew Wymondesold.[49] Even this massive support operation could not offset the weight of selling. In a further act of desperation the directors tried to reverse market sentiment by resolving at the end of August to declare a 30 percent Christmas cash dividend and to guarantee a 50 percent annual cash dividend for the next twelve years, a proposal subsequently endorsed by the General Court held on 8 September.

The last initiative proved to be counterproductive, as investors realised that the Company was in no position to deliver on its increasingly

TABLE 7.1
Stock Market Prices August–October 1720

	24 August[1]	14 October	Percentage decrease (%)
South Sea Company[2]	820	170	79
Bank of England	224	135	40
East India Company	315	145	54
Million Bank	400	180	55
Royal African Company	122	40	67
Stock Market Index	100	36	64

Source: Caistaing (1720) (lowest daily prices).
Notes: (1) After re-opening of the books of the South Sea Company. (2) Cum dividend prices.

extravagant promises. Hutcheson calculated on the basis of annuity tables that, even if the proposed dividends were paid, the present value of the prospective cash flow would be no more than £489.[50] However, he also calculated that the Company's resources would not permit it to pay a dividend at this rate for more than nine years, even if all subscriptions were fully paid up, which looked increasingly improbable.[51] The clear implication was that the directors were offering to repay shareholders not only the capital they had subscribed but also capital that the Company did not possess.

The stock market crash, which had begun in Paris, now engulfed not only London but also Amsterdam where, in November, it was reported that "The Fall of their [Dutch] Stocks has ruined many of their Famous Merchants; and stopping of Payment there hath been almost as much in Fashion as with us".[52] The Dutch banking system was nevertheless able to withstand the shock. Capital held by Dutch and French investors was withdrawn from London and Paris to the relative safety of the Bank of Amsterdam; gold placed with the English East India Custom House for export to Holland from London rose from under 3000 ounces in the last two weeks of October to over 20,000 ounces in the first two weeks of November; and the pound fell against the Dutch schelling to a level that was to be the lowest recorded during the eighteenth century.[53]

The emergent financial markets of Europe were witnessing the first international crash, as investors sought refuge in safe haven assets. Exchange rates, international capital flows, and share prices reflected a growing sense of panic, the fear of default threatened a seizure in credit markets and there was an ominous search for scapegoats, evidenced in its most extreme form by anti-semitic rioting in Amsterdam.[54]

NOTES

1. A full analysis of Law's role in policy making is to be found in Murphy (1997). In view of the policy confusion during 1720, it is worth noting, too, that Law appears to have shown symptoms of acute nervous stress on occasion, as reported in Wood (1824: 113–114).
2. Letter by Thomas Crawford, British representative in Paris, cited in Murphy (1997: 227).
3. Interestingly, a letter from the Earl of Islay to a Mrs Howard on the subject of primes shows that Mississippi investors were affected by what today would be called "moral hazard", that is, the belief that the State would somehow protect their interests. Writing from Paris on 16 January 1720, he suggested that "the government here will find it is so much their interest to prevent any persons losing by accepting their offer [primes at 1000 livres] that I am of opinion there will be something to be got this way". Cited in Wood (1824: 78).
4. The "bureau d'achat et de rente" became the "bureau de conversions".
5. Between 30 December 1719 and 22 February 1720 the Company purchased 800 million livres net of its shares, leading to a corresponding rise in the note issue.
6. Arrêt of 31 January 1720 (reversing arrêt of 22 January 1720 permitting free movement of specie outside France).
7. Arrêt of 4 February 1720.
8. Arrêt of 18 February 1720. Religious objects were exempted, stimulating a boom in the production and trading of gold and silver crucifixes, etc.
9. Arrêt of 27 February 1720.
10. Arrêt of 27 February 1720.
11. Déclaration of 11 March 1720.
12. Wood (1824: 115).
13. On 27 May, the public held 2.235 billion livres of bank notes while the Bank held 336 million livres in specie (Wood 1824: 122).
14. Cited in Murphy (1997: 250).
15. From early June only one 10 livre note per person could be exchanged for specie, the bank opening twice per week for the conversion of 100 livre notes into smaller denominations (Gleeson 1999: 183).
16. Changes with effect from 30 July, 1 September, 16 September, 1 October and 16 October (Murphy 1997: 283).
17. Arrêt of 1 June 1720.
18. Arrêt of 21 July 1720.
19. Arrêt of 15 August 1720.
20. Arrêt of 15 September 1720.
21. Arrêt of 15 September 1720.
22. Arrêt of 10 October 1720.
23. Arrêt of 3 June 1720.
24. Arrêt of 15 September 1720.
25. Arrêt of 24 October 1720. For background, see Wood (1824: 127).
26. Hutcheson (24 September 1720f: 90, second postscript).

27. Murphy (1986: 153).
28. Hutcheson (14 July 1720d: 65).
29. These estimates are derived from the Company's nominal share capital of £37.8 million. Garber (1990: 51) suggests a peak market capitalisation of £164 million, based on a somewhat lower share price.
30. Cobbett (1806–1820: 656).
31. Hutcheson (10 September 1720a: 79, Preface).
32. Scott (1912: 326).
33. See note 10, chapter 8.
34. Milner (15 April 1720: 17–21, second letter).
35. Anderson (1764: 97, 123).
36. Neal (1990: 101).
37. See Weiller and Mirowski (1990: 1–28). The authors cite Thomas Mortimer in *Every Man his Own Broker* (1761) who states: "India Bonds are the most convenient and profitable security any person can be possessed of, who has any quantity of cash unemployed but which he knows not how soon he may have occasion for …. There is as little trouble with an India Bond as with a Bank Note." (Weiller and Mirowsky 1990: 5). In other words, India Bonds were the equivalent of today's Treasury Bills as a key money market indicator.
38. See Dickson (1967: 191, 470).
39. To the state of the contracts and other obligations by bonds and notes entered into by Colin Campbell, Esq, Anno 1720, in Add. MS 17477 (British Library).
40. Hutcheson (14 April 1720c: 25).
41. *Thomas Harrison, Esq, Appellant, Moses Hart and Isaac Franks, Respondents, the Appellant's Case* (London: 1727) p. 1.
42. The relevant distinction here is between the riskless rate of interest, generally represented by the interest on short-term government debt, and the interest on private sector debt instruments subject to default risk. In the eighteenth century context, however, there was no truly riskless rate since governments did not always service their debt on schedule.
43. See *Bank of England Minutes of the Court of Directors* of 15 August 1720, 27 September 1720, 6 October 1720 (Bank of England Manuscript Collection).
44. See Silverman (2002).
45. Cited in Dickson (1967: 148).
46. See Harris (1994: 610–627).
47. Scott (1912: 427).
48. Scott (1912: 427).
49. Carswell (1993: 140, note).
50. Hutcheson (24 September 1720f: 86).
51. Hutcheson (24 September 1720f: 86).
52. *The London Journal* (5–12 November 1720).
53. Schubert (1988).
54. Wilson (1941: 106).

CHAPTER EIGHT

Crisis Resolution

BY MID-SEPTEMBER 1720, it was becoming increasingly apparent that the South Sea Scheme was unravelling. Attempts to stabilise the share price having failed, the South Sea directors now sought to address two critical problems: a growing shareholder rebellion and a developing liquidity crisis.

As Hutcheson had long foreseen, the eventual collapse of the South Sea share price exposed the massive wealth distribution that had occurred between original shareholders and latecomers who had subscribed at prices up to 1000. There were now clear winners and losers and the latter were in an ugly mood; far from being prepared to fulfil their remaining subscription obligations, they threatened legal action to have their subscriptions withdrawn and lobbied the Company and Parliament for remedial action on their behalf.

The Company tried to address the shareholder rebellion by proposing a drastic retrospective adjustment of subscription terms. A committee of directors recommended to a General Court held on 20 September that the conversion price of South Sea shares for the second conversion should be halved to 400; that the issue price of the last two money subscriptions should be reduced from 1000 to 400 and the calls thereon more widely spaced; and that redeemable stock should be exchanged at par and not 105. This move represented a tacit admission on the part of the directors that the true value of South Sea stock was little more than the £360 figure estimated (on generous assumptions) by Hutcheson. However, by reducing the latecomers' subscription prices the proposal would, according to Hutcheson's calculations, reduce the value of South Sea stock, based on assets per share, to £206[1]; this was hardly an attractive proposition for the original shareholders. Given this conflict of interest between new and old shareholders, it is hardly surprising that the proposed voluntary composition resulted in an increasingly acrimonious dispute among those concerned.

LIQUIDITY CRISIS

Meanwhile the Company had to confront a growing liquidity crisis. It had exhausted its cash resources in a futile attempt to sustain the share price and had to meet short-term obligations, as it later transpired, amounting to £14.6 million (see table 8.1). These consisted of some £7 million owed to the government under the conversion scheme, repayment of the £1 million Exchequer Bills borrowed from the Treasury, bonds outstanding of perhaps £5 million and interest and dividend obligations amounting to £1.4 million.

However, the Company was far from being "hopelessly insolvent" as Carswell has claimed,[2] since it had solid assets of £37.75 million in the form of loans to the government, against which it might set off the debt it owed to the state. It also possessed other (doubtful) assets amounting to around £76 million. The problem, therefore, was not one of negative net worth but rather negative cash flow, which could not be financed through new bond issues given that, during September, South Sea bonds had fallen to a substantial discount on face value. The Company's inability to raise funds could result in a default on its outstanding bonds which, being short-term instruments, would have to be repaid or rolled over during the next twelve months.

TABLE 8.1
Summarised Balance Sheet of the South Sea Company End 1720

Assets[a]	£million
1. Loans to government	37.8
2. Loans against stock and scrip*	11.2
3. Due from money subscribers*	64.5
Total assets	113.5

*doubtful assets
[a] excludes £15.7 million (nominal) of holdings of South Sea Stock.

Liabilities	£million
1. Loans to government	7.2
2. Exchequer Bills borrowed from Treasury	1.0
3. Due on bonds, etc.	5.0
4. Due on interest and dividends	1.4
Total liabilities	14.6
Shareholder funds excluding doubtful assets	23.2

Sources: Dickson (1967: 125, 160–161); Scott (1912: 354–359).

Faced with a looming liquidity crisis, the South Sea Company reluctantly approached the Bank of England for help. The government was also informed of this initiative and at a meeting held on 19 September representatives of the government (including Aislabie), the South Sea Company and the Bank of England reached broad agreement in principle on what amounted to a private sector bail-out of the South Sea Company. There were two key elements in this so-called "Bank Contract", the first involving the Bank's undertaking to underwrite £3 million of South Sea bonds (for which purpose it would itself hold a subscription[3]) and the second obliging the Bank to convert its holdings of government annuities worth nearly £190,000 per annum into South Sea stock at a conversion price (negotiated later) of £400. The purchase of shares at this price by the Bank of England would help to support South Sea stock at a level that the Company's directors evidently felt to be fair value.

After prolonged discussions, and despite considerable pressure from the government, the Bank of England eventually notified the South Sea Company on 9 November that it was withdrawing from the Bank Contract, prompting a further decline in South Sea shares to around 130 in mid-December. The Bank's decision is hardly surprising given that its own attempt to raise £3 million by subscription had failed,[4] that South Sea stock was trading in early November at half the price the Bank was proposing to pay and that there was a developing banking crisis as investors exchanged bankers' notes for cash and bullion. Five well-established banks failed around this time and on 24 September the South Sea Company's own bank, the Sword Blade Company, stopped payments, leading over the next fortnight to a run on the Bank of England itself.

The Bank, as a private institution, had become reluctantly involved in the South Sea Company's problems partly because of pressure from the government but also because it wished to head off what contemporaries referred to as a threat to "Publick Credit" but today would be called a systemic threat to financial stability. In the event, the problem proved to be too big for the Bank to handle and it now fell to the government and Parliament to orchestrate an official bail-out, in much the same way that, in modern times, national authorities have been forced to exercise their lender of last resort role after private sector support initiatives have been exhausted.[5]

Tens of thousands of individuals were directly affected by the bursting of the South Sea Bubble. The number of public creditors involved in the conversion scheme has been put at 30,000 but on top of this there were thousands of money subscribers and countless others who had traded stock in the secondary market. Furthermore, the losses incurred by investors were the result of a debt conversion scheme sponsored by the government and endorsed by Parliament. As the evidence of bribery, corruption and mismanagement began to emerge, the public outcry demanding official remedial action became irresistible.

SOUTH SEA WINNERS AND LOSERS

In considering the resolution of the crisis, it is helpful to categorise those caught up in the South Sea affair as winners, losers and culprits. The winners were clearly those who had acquired South Sea stock early on at favourable prices and whose interests would be damaged by any attempt to adjust the subscription terms of later purchasers. The losers, however, were a more disparate group whose interests were in some respects in conflict with each other, as evidenced by the furious pamphleteering that now ensued.

There were, in fact, five groups of losers or potential losers. First, there were the money subscribers who had made down payments on share purchases at prices up to 1000. Ideally, they would like to withdraw their subscriptions and have their money returned, but in default of that option they hoped to benefit from a retrospective adjustment of subscription prices. In pleading his case, one money subscriber pointed out that around four-fifths of those who had bought partly paid stock had done so because they could not afford the price of the fully paid-up stock. Nor could such subscribers afford to pay the remaining calls on their subscriptions, their assumption all along being "that the stock would rise, and consequently the subscriptions too; and then that they could sell the same to others".[6]

Second, there were those who had bought South Sea stock at high prices in the secondary market. In many cases these were forward transactions and the buyers would have liked to have these contracts declared null and void, thereby excusing eventual payment for what, as it turned out, were wildly overpriced shares. One purchaser expressed a view that was no doubt shared by others who had been duped into paying extravagant prices for stock:

> Whoever bought stock upon time at 1,000 per cent after taking in of the third subscription, did it with some sort of reason; for the South Sea directors ... were certainly presumed men of great honour and honesty; and any man might well argue with himself, that honest men would never pretend to make people pay [1,000 per cent] for stock, unless it was really worth so

much. He was ignorant of the matter himself, but he thought he might depend on the skill and integrity of those men who had received such a great trust from the Parliament, and for that reason he entered into contracts for stock at these high prices.[7]

Third, there were subscribers to the third money subscription who had sold their subscriptions for cash against future delivery of subscription receipts. However, the failure of the South Sea Company to issue subscription receipts for the third and fourth money subscriptions opened up the possibility that these transactions would be nullified thereby requiring the sellers of subscriptions to reimburse the buyers. This was considered by those affected to be grossly unfair, the more so as many of them (so it was claimed) had used the proceeds of subscription sales to reinvest in South Sea stock.[8]

Fourth, there were the public creditors who had converted their holdings of government debt into exorbitantly priced South Sea stock during the second debt conversion. Like the money subscribers, they would have liked to be able to withdraw from their subscriptions but a retrospective price adjustment would be a second best solution for them. Some who had registered their redeemable debts for conversion claimed they had done so without realising that the conversion terms would be determined unilaterally by the Company with no opportunity for withdrawal. Apparently they had entered their names without reading the small print "in certain loose sheets of paper, lying at the South Sea House, on some of which there appeared something printed; but what it was, or whether it was designed for a preface, or a preamble, could not then be read, both by reason of the crowd, and because the sheets were doubled in such manner, that but one half of it appeared ..." The subscribers had not expected "where the public faith was concerned, to meet with the little mean arts of tricking and shuffling, from a Company in whom the legislature had put so much confidence".[9]

Finally, there were those investors, among whom were 138 MPs, who had borrowed from the South Sea Company on the security of stock and subscription receipts. Their interests would be best served by having such loans declared unenforceable but a scaling down of obligations might also protect their interests, although the pool of Company assets available to other shareholders would be thereby diminished.[10]

The culprits to be held responsible for the debt conversion fiasco were, first, the directors of the South Sea Company who had been charged with implementation of the scheme and, second, those members of the government who had corruptly accepted bribes in the form of secret share options. Restoration of public confidence required that in any final resolution of the South Sea crisis these individuals should be held to account.

Parliament, which reassembled on 8 December 1720 after its long recess since June, now had to respond to the public clamour for remedial action. On 20 December, a Committee of the Whole House tried to hold the line by resolving that all subscriptions and contracts with the South Sea Company should be binding unless altered by a General Court of the Company or set aside by due course of law. This did not, however, prevent some public creditors from preparing a class action to have their subscriptions withdrawn. Others were in favour of more direct methods and some months later the Riot Act had to be read to a crowd of South Sea subscribers who had invaded the lobby of the House of Commons.

In the late autumn and winter of 1720–1721, Hutcheson contributed actively to the debate on measures needed to resolve the South Sea crisis. His recurrent theme was that ways had to be found of making the winners give up their ill-deserved gains in order to compensate the losers, if necessary by voiding stock transactions under the Gaming Act. In his view, a relatively few Exchange Alley gamesters, whom he compared to the robbers that frequented Hounslow Heath and Finchley Common, had amassed great fortunes by hood-winking many thousands of innocent investors. The latter, he argued, were typically "middling people", among whom he singled out as most deserving the many women who had converted their holdings of annuities in 1720.[11]

Hutcheson also had the foresight to see at an early stage that Parliament would have to forego the £7 million plus owed to it by the South Sea Company. If payment of the debt were enforced, the money would in effect come out of the pockets of the very people Parliament should be trying to protect. Furthermore, such a concession "would serve as a precedent for others to refund, and will justify the Parliament in obliging the refractory to comply …".[12]

Hutcheson's unrelenting campaign against the South Sea Company naturally made him enemies in high places. And in the autumn of 1720 he intimated that his life had been threatened. He had heard "that I am threatened with great mischiefs on account of my declared enmity to the vile execution of the South Sea scheme; viz. that I shall be sent to the Tower, and expell'd the House of Commons, at the meeting of Parliament, and that, my life is in danger from the resentments of those who think themselves injured by what I have wrote."[13] But he went on to assert proudly that "a coward cannot be thoroughly an honest man; and that he who will be frighted from doing his duty through fear of death does not really deserve to live."[14]

The first attempt to provide relief to the victims of the South Sea collapse was abortive. This was the "engraftment scheme" prepared by Robert Walpole and his financial adviser, Robert Jacomb, which involved a retrospective adjustment of subscription prices coupled with a partial takeover ("engraftment") of the South Sea Company by the Bank of England and the East India Company, thereby offering South Sea shareholders a more diversified portfolio consisting of shares in each of the three companies. Walpole's scheme was approved by Parliament in March 1721 but never implemented because the Bank and the East India Company both decided that it was not in the interests of their shareholders to proceed. Indeed, Hutcheson may have influenced their decision given that his own careful calculations showed that the net asset value per share of these two great companies would be reduced by £14 (Bank of England) and £24 (East India Company) under the takeover proposals.[15]

In early April, Walpole replaced Sunderland as First Lord of the Treasury and at the same time assumed the office of Chancellor of the Exchequer. Walpole, ably assisted by the long-serving Senior Treasury Secretary, William Lowndes, worked on a new rescue package which was eventually embodied in a statute—an Act to Restore the Publick Credit—that received the royal assent on 10 August. The main elements of the rescue plan, the first ever official bail-out of a major private sector enterprise, were as follows:

1. The £7 million owed by the South Sea Company to the government under the conversion scheme was excused, although the £1 million Exchequer Bills borrowed by the Company still had to be repaid.
2. Those who had borrowed from the Company on the security of South Sea shares or subscription receipts had to pay only 10 percent of the amount borrowed (it was later determined that brokers had to pay 20 percent). The pledged securities were forfeited.
3. Further calls on the money subscriptions were waived and subscribers were credited with stock valued at 300 (first subscription) and 400 (the other three subscriptions) in respect of cash already paid down.
4. The holders of government debt who subscribed in the second (August) conversion were credited with additional stock to equate their conversion terms with those of the first (May) conversion.
5. Any stock remaining in the Company's hands was to be distributed rateably among all shareholders.

6. All contracts for the sale of company stock or scrip were to be invalid unless registered by 1 November 1721. All contracts for the sale of securities which the seller did not possess within six days of the bargain were to be void unless performed by Michaelmas 1721.

The last measure had the effect of restricting the ability of investors to "short" stock by selling forward shares they did not currently possess. However, the more general issue involving the enforceability of forward sales of South Sea stock was left to the courts to decide. In the historic case of *Harcourt v. Thomson*, where Thomson, on 18 June 1720, had agreed to sell South Sea stock to Harcourt at a forward price of 920, it was held that the subsequent collapse of the share price did not invalidate the contract. In the words of the Lord Chief Baron of the Court of Exchequer:

> By our laws every man may sell as dear as he can; but it appears that this stock was sold at the usual or common price at the time of making the contract ... therefore I can see no pretence for calling it an unreasonable bargain, unless it be unreasonable to sell things at the market price ...[16]

The key objective underlying the final settlement was not the solvency of the South Sea Company (which was not an issue) but rather the re-allocation of losses and gains arising from investors' roller-coaster ride in South Sea shares. This redistribution involved not only winners and losers in share subscriptions but also the general taxpayer on whose behalf the debts owed by the South Sea Company to the state were to be excused. The package as a whole represented an unprecedented intervention by the state which broke new ground by overriding contractual arrangements entered into by the government, a private sector company, the company's shareholders and those who had borrowed from the company.

In order to achieve the desired redistribution of gains and losses, contracts previously entered into were rewritten in two ways. First, there was an important element of debt forgiveness, both by the state vis à vis the South Sea Company (involving some £7 million) and by the Company via à vis those who had borrowed from it (involving perhaps £10 million). It may be noted that large-scale debt forgiveness has featured in the resolution of modern financial crises, notably in 1989 when massive debts incurred by developing countries, mainly in Latin America, were partially excused.[17]

Second, there was a composition among different classes of shareholder based on a retrospective adjustment of the prices at which they had bought their shares. A voluntary arrangement along these lines had already been proposed by the South Sea Company itself, but now the deal was to be mandated by government and enshrined in statute. It is difficult to find either an earlier historical precedent or a modern parallel for such large-scale contractual reorganisation, although voluntary composition, such as that agreed by members of the ill-fated UK life assurance company, Equitable Life, has been a familiar feature of crisis resolution in modern times.[18]

While the effect of the South Sea settlement was to partially compensate later subscribers at the cost of original shareholders, the losses borne by the former were nevertheless severe, as Dickson has shown.[19] The money subscribers acquired less than £52 nominal of stock for each £100 subscribed, representing an actual loss of 50 percent given that the price of South Sea stock had fallen to below par by the end of 1721. Compared with the amount they would have enjoyed had they not converted, holders of long annuities lost around one-third, holders of short annuities two-thirds and holders of redeemable debt one-half of their former income. Even so, the position of the losers was much better than it would have been in the absence of a settlement, since money subscribers could have lost the full amount of their subscriptions and annuitants could have seen their income reduced to a small fraction of its previous level.

By entrusting an ill-conceived debt conversion scheme to a private company with dubious antecedents run by unscrupulous men, Parliament must be held responsible for the ensuing South Sea debacle. However, the subsequent crisis management did much to redeem Parliament's reputation. By dispensing rough justice to those caught up in the South Sea deluge, the Act to Restore the Publick Credit saved many families from impoverishment, avoided numerous bankruptcies, largely eliminated the need for costly and lengthy litigation and, above all, helped to restore confidence in the domestic money and capital markets. Of course, the fact that no less than 462 members of the House of Commons had been subscribers to South Sea stock gave added impetus to Parliament's endeavours to resolve the crisis.

It should be added that while the statutory settlement excused £7 million of South Sea debt owed to the government, thereby going some way towards resolving the Company's liquidity problems, further measures proved necessary. Faced with the need to redeem its bonds, the South Sea Company sold Exchequer annuities amounting to £200,000 per annum to the Bank of England in October 1722, thereby realizing a capital sum of £4.2 million. This needed cash inflow finally restored stability to the Company's finances which were later further strengthened by receipts of over £2 million from the forfeiture of the estates of those identified as culprits (see below).

SOUTH SEA CULPRITS

The Act to Restore the Publick Credit had settled matters as far as the South Sea winners and losers were concerned but Parliament had also to consider how to identify and deal with the culprits. In early January 1721, the House of Commons resolved to establish a committee of enquiry, selected by secret ballot, to investigate the actions of the South Sea Company in implementation of the debt conversion scheme. Crucially, most of the 13 representatives elected to the committee, including Archibald Hutcheson, were members of what might be called "the awkward squad"—individuals of independence and integrity who would not be influenced by the government's understandable concern not to rock the boat. Meanwhile legislation was enacted towards the end of January preventing South Sea directors from leaving the country, requiring them to draw up inventories of their estates for presentation to Parliament, and excluding them for life from holding directorships in any of the "big three" companies (Bank of England, East India Company and South Sea Company).

The Parliamentary committee of enquiry, known as the Committee of Secrecy (because it met behind closed doors), held daily meetings from mid-January at South Sea House lasting from 9.00 a.m. to 11.00 p.m. Between February and June 1721, the Committee produced seven reports which sought to identify the South Sea Company's malpractices and the recipients of bribes.[20] The Committee's investigations were hampered by a web of lies and deceit concocted by the Company's senior officials, flagrant tampering with key documents and, most damaging of all, the disappearance on 21 January of the Company's Chief Cashier, Robert Knight, who took with him his notorious "Green Book" containing details of bribes and other corrupt transactions.[21] It is clear that Knight's flight to the Austrian Netherlands, where extradition to England was conveniently prevented by law, was arranged with the connivance of the government which had much to lose from the revelations he might make under parliamentary examination.

Despite these difficulties, the Committee of Secrecy was able to discover at the outset that £574,000 of fictitious stock had been "sold" to those who might support the South Sea Company while its Bill was passing through Parliament. Stung by this evidence of corruption within the government, the House of Commons conducted what were in effect trials of those on whom suspicion had fallen, including in particular those key Ministers who had been involved in the implementation of the South Sea Scheme: the Postmaster General (James Craggs), the Chancellor of the Exchequer (Aislabie), the junior Treasury Secretary (Charles Stanhope) and the Prime Minister himself (the Earl of Sunderland). James Craggs committed suicide by taking an overdose of laudanum (part of his estate being subsequently sequestered), Charles Stanhope was narrowly acquitted despite damning evidence against him and Sunderland, although fatally damaged politically, escaped censure thanks partly to Walpole whose vigorous support helped to swing the vote in his favour.

Stanhope's escape is all the more remarkable since he appears to have received by far the biggest bribe. In March 1720 he was credited with £50,000 of fictitious South Sea Stock at the then market price of 250, which he "sold" three months later at a price of 750.[22] He thereby netted an extraordinary profit of £250,000 which was paid to him via a nominee account at the Sword Blade Bank. There was then a clumsy cover-up. A clerk at South Sea House testified to the fact that the name Stanhope had been erased from the Company's cash book with a "white handle penknife" and replaced with the name Stangape, although the name Stanhope was inadvertently left in the index.[23] However, attempts to give fictional names to Lords Castlemain and Londonderry had been unsuccessful, "the paper being wet".

The fury of Parliament and the people was now focussed on Aislabie who became the political scapegoat for the collapse of the South Sea Scheme. Indeed, it was rumoured that a decision had been taken at the highest level to sacrifice Aislabie in order to save Sunderland. According to Arthur Onslow, a backbench MP familiar with all the political gossip, "… It was thought he (Aislabie) was given up at Court by way of composition, to save my Lord Sunderland."[24] Again, it was reported that "Walpole undertakes to screen Sunderland and the German ladies [the King's mistresses] and to let Aislabie and the rest take their chance …".[25]

Events moved rapidly as Aislabie came under fire from all directions. On 21 January 1721 the House of Lords, which had begun to conduct its own investigations into the South Sea affair, "examined the extracts of the brokers' books that had been called for … by which it appeared that large quantities of South Sea stock had been transferred to Mr Aislabie".[26] Two days later, Aislabie resigned his office. Shortly after, the Second Report of the Commons Committee of Secrecy produced further damaging circumstantial evidence relating to Aislabie's share dealings, including the fact that he had burned his account books. On 8 March, the House of

Commons, having considered the Committee's evidence, passed eleven resolutions against Aislabie, before expelling him from the House, committing him to the Tower of London, and freezing his assets.

In a subsequent defence before the House of Lords on 19/20 July, Aislabie provided a detailed rebuttal of the charges which the House of Commons had levelled against him. Several of the charges were spurious and on the really key issue—whether he had received South Sea stock without paying for it—the evidence was strongly suggestive but inconclusive. Much was made of the "headline figure" of £700,000 which had passed through the share dealing account of Edmund Waller, Aislabie's son-in-law who was suspected of acting for his father-in-law. While denying that Waller had been his agent, Aislabie pointed out that "… this sum is not the balance of the account at any point in time, as is generally understood, but the total amount of several sums paid and repaid many times backward and forward, and sometimes great part of it the same day." It was well known, he said, that at the height of the South Sea boom "a great many young gentleman" had transacted on a similar scale, although "it is very plain that £10,000 stock not stirred at all till sold out at the best advantage would have brought more profit, than all the numerous transactions put together".[27] This is consistent with Aislabie's general line of defence which was to reject the allegations against him but at the same time to deny that the allegations would amount to wrongful conduct if proved. So, for instance, he denied that he had purchased South Sea stock in 1719 as an insider, before approval of the South Sea Scheme, but at the same time argued that he would have done nothing wrong if he had; and while insisting that he had not burned his account books in order to avoid Parliament's examination of his transactions, he also claimed to be entitled in law not to produce documents such as these that might incriminate him.

Aislabie was more persuasive when dismissing the idea that he had been involved in the Company's decision to lend money on the security of its stock: he had not himself benefited from such loans "… and if I had had those avaritious views, that are suggested, I must have mistaken my way very much and have been little in the Secret, not to have secured a good share of the public spoils out of these unfavourable loans".[28]

Aislabie's appeal to the House of Lords failed, he was returned to the Tower, and his name was included in the "Directors' Bill" dealing with forfeiture of the estates of the South Sea Directors. However, due partly to the intervention of Walpole, Aislabie, who was possessed of considerable inherited wealth, was eventually stripped of only that part of his estate that had been increased since October 1718, a forfeiture of

£45,000 from net assets of £165,000 finally being agreed and paid in 1723, representing, according to his biographer, a bribe of perhaps £30,000–38,000 and stock exchange gains of £7,000–13,000.[29] Removed from the London political scene, Aislabie was able to enjoy his Studeley Manor estate in Yorkshire where he devoted much of the remaining twenty years of his life to landscape gardening, the results of which were widely admired by contemporaries.

The Directors' Bill received the royal assent on 29 July. Under the terms of this statute, the House of Commons had determined the amounts that were to be allowed to South Sea directors to live on after confiscation of their estates. A flat rate allowance equivalent to one-eighth of net assets had been suggested but in the event each director and senior official was individually assessed according to his perceived culpability. Those not directly implicated in the Company's corrupt practices were allowed £10,000 each (which, of course, hit the wealthiest hardest) but those at the centre of the scandal were allowed lesser sums. Blunt was voted only £1000 out of an estate of £183,000, a figure subsequently raised to £5000, perhaps because he co-operated with the Committee of Secrecy by naming recipients of bribes. The £239,000 estate of the absconding Chief Cashier, Robert Knight, was confiscated in its entirety.

The financial penalties on directors and others eventually yielded some £2.3 million for the benefit of the South Sea Company and its share-holders. The sequestration procedure, unparalleled in parliamentary history, represented very rough justice. The estates of two of the worst offenders, Stanhope and Sunderland, escaped altogether because Walpole and others had provided political protection. The fines imposed on the Craggs estate and Aislabie were based, crudely, on the principle of resti-tution, so that financial gains enjoyed during the Bubble period had to be disgorged. The directors and senior officials of the South Sea Company were, on the other hand, subject to variable fines linked to their alleged involvement in corporate malpractices.

Within a year of the collapse of the Bubble, Parliament had restored calm by redistributing gains and losses among South Sea shareholders and by punishing at least some of the guilty. Recalling the events of 1720 in his defence before the House of Lords, Aislabie no doubt expressed the feelings of many:

> This unhappy affair, my lords, began at a time when the passion and avaricious desires of mankind were grown up to a madness and a distemper, and one cannot without pity look back upon the rage and folly of the year.[30]

NOTES

1. See Hutcheson (30 November 1720i: 130–132).
2. Carswell (1993: 202).
3. The terms of this Bank subscription were (a) a 15 percent down payment, (b) a 3 percent premium allowed on the full amount subscribed and (c) interest on the deposit and all future calls at 5 percent per annum. The effective interest rate was therefore approximately 8 percent, although Dickson suggests it was 25 percent—very improbable given that East India bonds were then yielding around 5 percent. See South Sea Company Court Minutes for 22 September 1720, Bank of England Court Minutes of 22 September 1720 and Dickson (1967: 164–165).
4. The Bank of England subscription, which closed on 15 October, yielded only £342,180. Of this amount, £300,000 was lent to the South Sea Company on the security of £360,000 of South Sea Bonds.
5. For the Bank of England's preference for private sector bail-outs of failing financial institutions, see Dale (1995).
6. Goodalle (1721: 13).
7. Anon (1721c: 2).
8. There was a vigorous pamphlet campaign on this issue. See, for instance, *The Case of the Contracts for the Third and Fourth Subscriptions to the South Sea Company Considered, in a Letter to a Member of Parliament* (Anon, 1720b), *A Full Confutation of the Subscribers Pretensions to Receipts for the First Payment, Made Upon the Third and Fourth Subscriptions: Wherein the True Case of the Sellers of Those Subscriptions is Examined and Answerd, In a Letter to a Noble L–d* (Anon, 1720d), *The Nature of Contracts Consider'd: As They Relate to the Third and Fourth Subscriptions Taken In by the South Sea Company: In a Letter to a Friend, With a Postscript Concerning the Meeting at Salters-Hall the 18th Instant; By a Tradesman of the City* (Anon, 1720g) and *A True State of the Contracts Relating to the Third Money Subscription Taken by the South Sea Company* (Defoe, 1721).
9. Anon (1721e: 3).
10. In a typical loan from a goldsmith-banker, the loan would be fixed at around 50 percent of the market value of South Sea shares deposited as security. A collateral top-up clause might be triggered when the excess value of the collateral or "margin" fell below 15–25 percent. A "defeazance" allowed the lender to sell the pledged stock if the borrower defaulted or if a margin call was missed. For details of one such agreement, see *Thomas Harrison, Appellant, Moses Hart and Isaac Franks, Respondents, the Appellant's Case* (London: 1727).
11. Hutcheson (7 January 1720j: 3).
12. Hutcheson (30 November 1720i: 138).
13. Hutcheson (20–30 October 1720h: 111).
14. Hutcheson (20–30 October 1720h: 111).
15. Hutcheson (7 January 1720j: 5–8).

16. Anon (1724).
17. The so-called Brady Plan launched in 1989 allowed heavily indebted countries to convert their bank borrowings into bonds of lower nominal value.
18. Equitable Life Assurance Society (2001).
19. Dickson (1967: 183–186).
20. See Anon (1721d). A slightly adapted version of these reports is reproduced in Cobbett (1806–1820: 711–827).
21. Following Knight's disappearance, the Court of Directors resolved that "the Committee of the Treasury seal up the lock of the door of the Dark Room in which the Iron Chest is kept and also the locks of the Secretoir in the Little Treasury Room called Mr Knight's Little Room". Minutes of Court Meeting held 23 January 1721.
22. Cobbett (1806–1820: 722).
23. Cobbett (1806–1820: 839).
24. Cited in Dickson (1967: 173).
25. Cited in Darwin (1950: 313).
26. *Historical Register* 6 (1721) 46.
27. Aislabie (1721: 5–6).
28. Aislabie (1721: 20).
29. Darwin (1950: 67).
30. Cobbett (1806–1820: 886).

Lessons from the South Sea Bubble*

How, THEN, SHOULD we interpret the dramatic events of 1720? Was the South Sea Bubble an isolated episode of interest now only to financial historians and students of the evolution of stock markets? Or is there a message here for modern finance theorists, stock market investors and policy makers? And if there is a lesson to be learned from the rise and fall of the South Sea Company, is it that investors, then as now, are prone to bouts of irrational speculative mania, or that at a time of rapid financial innovation even rational investors have difficulty in determining the fundamental value of financial assets?

ASSET BUBBLES

As a preliminary to further discussion of these key issues, it is necessary to refer briefly to the burgeoning economic literature on asset bubbles, which are said to occur whenever there is systematic deviation of market prices from fundamental values. Although bubbles may be classified in a number of ways,[1] the important distinction for present purposes is between "rational" and "irrational" bubbles.

A rational bubble is characterised by the continuing rise in the price of an asset that is generated by the belief on the part of investors that this price rise will persist, thereby allowing the overvalued asset to be sold at a higher price at some point in the future. Although investors understand that the bubble will eventually burst, they continue to hold the asset in question so long as they expect to be compensated for the risk of a price collapse. Because the probability of a price collapse increases as the bubble grows larger, investors may need to be compensated by ever higher returns, giving rise to an accelerating rise in prices that culminates in the bursting of the bubble. Empirical support for this kind of phenomenon may be found, for instance, in survey evidence showing that, just

---

* A more formal approach to the analysis presented in this chapter is to be found in Dale, Johnson and Tang (2004, in press).

before the 1987 US stock market collapse, the great majority of both private and institutional investors believed the market was overvalued but nevertheless chose not to liquidate their holdings.[2]

Irrational bubbles, on the other hand, arise where the relationship between asset prices and fundamental values breaks down because investors have totally unrealistic expectations about a company's future profitability and therefore dividend-paying capacity. Such episodes, where investor behaviour is driven by irrationally optimistic expectations, may be described as "fads", the dot.com bubble possibly being a case in point.[3]

The distinction between irrational and rational bubbles is not without its problems. After all, those who are late entrants to a "rational" speculative bubble and are caught in the crash presumably misjudged the probability of the bubble continuing. At what point such misjudgements cease to be rational is an open question. Similarly, participants in an "irrational" bubble may be genuinely convinced, however mistakenly, that market valuations are realistic. At what point misconceptions about underlying values become irrational is again a matter of subjective judgement.

Modern historians of the South Sea affair have arrived at very different conclusions about the nature of the bubble that occurred in 1720. Neal uses statistical analysis in an attempt to categorise various phases of the South Sea Bubble according to the rational/irrational distinction. He concludes that: (1) the first phase (early February to mid-May) represented "an upward shift in fundamentals caused by a financial innovation to be implemented on an unprecedented scale";[4] (2) the second phase (mid-May to late June) was a rational bubble driven by shrewd foreign speculators alerted to price-rigging by South Sea directors; (3) the third pre-collapse phase (late June to late August) was in reality not part of the bubble at all but rather a technical convergence of the forward and spot prices during the period when the transfer books were closed; (4) the subsequent collapse was caused by an unwinding of speculative positions in response to a credit squeeze; and (5) in the final stage price fluctuations reflected uncertainties about the reorganisation schemes being proposed. Neal's overall assessment is that the South Sea Bubble "appears to be a tale less about the perpetual folly of mankind and more about the continual difficulties of the adjustments of financial markets to an array of innovations".[5]

A group of American economists use a similar methodology to test whether or not there was a bubble in the shares of the Royal African Company during the South Sea Bubble. They claim that their results, although inconclusive, are consistent with investor rationality, and "call into question the latest arguments by Chancellor (1999) that the South Sea Bubble was the result of mania and speculative excesses".[6] Also using formal statistical analysis, a recent study by Temin and Voth examines own-account trading in South Sea stock and subscriptions by Hoare's bank. Based on the documentation underlying Hoare's highly profitable transactions (profits of over £19,000 on turnover of £140,000 during 1720), the authors argue that Hoare's was aware that South Sea stock was overvalued and that a bubble was in progress. According to this interpretation, Hoare's invested rationally (rather than luckily) in the confident belief that it would be able to sell out before the crash, which indeed it did.[7]

Other commentators have used a narrative rather than a statistical approach to interpreting events during the bubble year. Scott, in his classic treatment of the subject, distinguishes between the "secret" history of the South Sea Company and the "apparent" history.[8] He argues that until the end of May 1720, South Sea investors were ignorant of the various malpractices, including price-rigging, by the South Sea directors. Based on the "apparent" conduct of the company's affairs, the share price of 400 reached towards the end of May was, in his view, "not excessive", with an estimated asset backing per share of 60 percent and goodwill of 40 percent.[9] However, while Scott's view seems to be that on the whole investors acted "optimistically but rationally" he does not provide a convincing explanation for the final run-up in the share price beyond May, other than through general references to market manipulation and (a concession to the manic view of investor behaviour) "a spirit of wild speculation which had now been aroused".[10]

Garber, in his more general study of historic bubbles, argues that the South Sea episode "is readily understandable as a case of speculators working on the basis of the best economic analysis available [sic] and pushing prices along by their changing view of market fundamentals".[11] Based on market prices prevailing at the end of August 1720, he arrives at a market capitalisation for the South Sea Company of £164 million, some £60 million in excess of its total net assets and around five times tangible net assets. He then concludes that intangible assets, represented by the potential for commercial expansion associated with the South Sea Company's accumulated "fund of credit", justified such a market valuation. In other words, on Garber's interpretation, there was no bubble at all.

The main weaknesses of Garber's study are that: (1) his assertion that speculators were working on the basis of "the best economic analysis

Plate 10 Share speculation in the Rue Quincampoix, and caricature of Law converting coins into paper money. From Het Groote Tofereel der Dwaasheid, Amsterdam, 1720. Copyright Guildhall Library.

available" is clearly refuted by Hutcheson's calculations; (2) he uses a market capitalisation for the South Sea Company that is nearly 20 percent off its peak; and (3) supposed popular perceptions about the prospects for commercial expansion seem to be contradicted by his acceptance that the South Sea trade was known to be dead and that "only the [Company's] holdings of government debt are important to the economic story".[12] It is worth adding that nowhere in the contemporary literature on the South Sea Company can one find specific references to plans for commercial expansion, beyond the possible revival of the South Sea trade.

Those commentators and historians who seek to explain the South Sea Bubble in terms of speculative mania tend to rely on telling anecdotes and quotations[13] together with contemporary descriptions of investor behaviour. Among them, Kindleberger, who characterises the South Sea episode as a prime example of irrationality in financial markets, complains that "the dismissal of conventional explanations of historical events with the remark that they violate the assumptions of economic analysis [i.e., rationality] is infuriating .... It is time economics accept reality."[14]

Carswell leaves open the question how the promoters of the South Sea project, still more investors, could have "believed their airy structures would not, in the absence of real assets or even prospects, collapse in ruins ...".[15] Dickson suggests that the early eighteenth century economic and social environment "bred an appetite for gain" that "could and did become uncontrolled", even affecting the judgement of those experienced in business.[16] Finally, Chancellor asks the question whether an investor who bought South Sea stock at £1000 was behaving rationally. His answer is an unequivocal no, on the grounds that (1) there was sufficient public information to suggest that the share price was severely overvalued; (2) late entrants to the bubble faced a poor ratio of risk to reward; and (3) the "fundamentals" of the South Sea Company did not change during 1720 in a way that could justify extreme share price volatility.[17]

There are, then, several different approaches to interpreting the South Sea affair, including formal statistical testing of bubble theory, narrative history combined with personal judgement, and reliance on contemporary quotations to provide insights into the mindset of South Sea investors. Such approaches have yielded varied conclusions ranging from no bubble at one extreme (Garber) to irrational mania at the other (Kindleberger et al.), while some hold to an intermediate position, Neal favouring a rational bubble and Scott a largely rational explanation based on his distinction between financial appearances and reality.

New Evidence

None of the interpretations of the South Sea Bubble to date have, however, taken proper account of two key pieces of evidence: first the cogent writings of Hutcheson and, second, the price performance of South Sea shares in relation to subscription receipts. The analysis offered here attempts both to fill this gap and to provide a rather different explanation of what was motivating investors in the spring and early summer of 1720.

The first point to be emphasised is that investors in early eighteenth century England did have access to sound valuation techniques, as described in chapter 2. One author, writing in 1720, refers to the established method of valuation based on a comparison of a share's dividend yield with the return on alternative investment opportunities:

> The main principle, on which the whole science of stock-jobbing is based, viz. that the benefit of a dividend (considered as a motive for the buying or keeping of stock) is always to be estimated according to the rate it bears to the price of the stock, because the purchaser is supposed to compare that rate with the profits he might make of money, if otherwise employed.[18]

It was on the basis of established valuation techniques that a leading figure of the day, Archibald Hutcheson, MP, whose views on financial matters were widely respected, circulated carefully calculated valuations of the South Sea Company as described in previous chapters. Hutcheson's writings, which were not seriously challenged, demonstrated the growing divergence between fundamental values and market prices during the spring and early summer of 1720.

Of course, Hutcheson's meticulous calculations would not have been easily accessed or understood by the general investing public and in an attempt to reach a wider readership he leaked advance summaries of his South Sea valuations to the press.[19] He also tried to encapsulate his conception of the South Sea scam in a simple fable which even unsophisticated investors would be able to understand (see appendix I to this chapter). It is this drastically "dumbed down" version of his work that has come down to us through those few historians, beginning with Adam Anderson, who have given Hutcheson some credit for anticipating events.[20]

The real significance of Hutcheson's writings, however, lies not in the influence his views may or may not have had on contemporary opinion. Rather it is the fact that Hutcheson, far from developing new share valuation techniques, was merely applying with great rigour and care, valuation principles that were already well known to the early eighteenth century financial community. If others had valued South Sea shares on the same basis they could hardly have avoided the conclusion that by the mid-summer of 1720 the stock had become wildly overpriced.

It appears that in 1720 investors simply abandoned established valuation methods in the belief that South Sea stock would be issued at ever higher prices and that anyone who invested in such issues was assured of large capital gains. There is an obvious parallel here with the valuation of dot.com companies in 1999/2000 when traditional valuations based on cash flow, price earnings ratios and dividend yield were discarded in favour of market share and the sheer volume of internet traffic generated by web sites.[21] Indeed the normally cautious Bank for International Settlements gave warning of the unsustainably high level of US stocks in 1999/2000 when commenting that valuations had ceased to reflect companies' track records and that, in the case of high tech initial public offerings, there were frequently "no earnings to show, and their assumed earnings growth rates relied on new and untested valuation concepts".[22]

It is also important to stress that the South Sea Company, in contrast to the Mississippi Company, was relatively easy to evaluate, since the bulk of its assets consisted of loans to the government earning a specific and known rate of interest. Indeed, while the South Sea trade was dead, it could be valued essentially as an annuity holding company or a bond, subject to a call option after seven years (when the government was entitled to begin to repay its debt at face value). Bubble theory suggests that such assets, with known terminal values and cash flows, cannot be the subject of rational bubbles since investors face the certainty of capital loss when the "bond" is repaid.[23] The same point was made forcefully by James Milner writing in April 1720:

> But our Mississippi here is no more than so many millions, with a fund of interest at four and five percent ... and for no more continuance than seven years. Must it not be amazing, then, to see the madness of the people in being drawn into a stock, which has but seven years continuance, and which every man may see through.[24]

Some theorists also emphasise the crucial role of fund managers and other financial intermediaries in the development of financial market bubbles. Allen and Gale, for instance, seek to explain asset price bubbles in terms of credit expansion and risk transfers involving investment agents who thereby acquire an incentive to invest in risky assets.[25] From a rather different perspective, Persaud focuses on "momentum" investing by institutional investors who follow the herd in order to safeguard their relative performance.[26] Such explanations cannot, however, be applied to the South Sea period when institutional investment barely featured and investors bought for their own account.

More puzzling still, bubble theory suggests that a rational bubble is only possible if the assets concerned are subject to a fixed or inelastic short-run supply since the market will be unable to absorb an ever increasing supply of stock at a price higher than the fundamental value.[27] Yet a key feature of the South Sea Bubble was the huge increase in the supply of stock associated with successive money subscriptions at ever higher prices; indeed, the higher the price, the bigger the permissible increase in supply. Investors must surely have understood that the higher they bid up the price the greater the volume of new shares that would come onto the market, because of the well-publicised connection between the Company's issuable capital and the conversion price at which it was able to exchange its own stock for government debt (pp. 79–80).

Paradoxically, the successive money subscriptions, while appearing to further mystify the South Sea conundrum, may provide an important clue as to what really happened. Subscription receipts could be transferred through a simple legal assignment and the receipts therefore continued to be actively traded while the South Sea company's transfer books were closed.[28] Even when receipts were not immediately given out by the Company (as in the case of the third and fourth subscriptions) transactions could be conducted on the basis that receipts would be provided when available (see below). Furthermore, Freke's *Prices of Stocks* provides a continuous price series for subscription receipts from 14 May 1720, one month after the first money subscription. (Castaing, on the other hand, does not provide subscription price data until 28 May.)

Whereas some other partly paid shares (e.g., Royal African Company "New" shares issued in 1720[29]) were not entitled to declared dividends until fully paid, the first three South Sea money subscriptions, but not the fourth, were explicitly included in the 10 percent mid-summer stock dividend of 1720.[30] Furthermore, all subscriptions were to be credited with the cash dividends extravagantly promised by the Company in September 1720.[31] The first three partly paid subscriptions were, accordingly, on all fours with fully paid registered shares except for the phasing of the subscription payments. Therefore, by applying an appropriate discount rate, it is possible to express the theoretical value of a subscription receipt in terms of its fully paid share equivalent. On the other hand, it is necessary to add 10 percent to the market value of the fourth money subscription in order to compare it with the cum-dividend stock price and the market prices of the other subscription receipts which reflected their entitlement to the 10 percent mid-summer stock dividend. The schedule of payments for each of the four money subscriptions, taken on 14 April, 29 April, 17 June and 24 August, is given in table 9.1.

The pricing of subscriptions is complicated by the fact that the

TABLE 9.1
Schedule of Payments for South Sea Money Subscriptions (£)

First subscription		Second subscription[a]		Third subscription		Fourth subscription	
14 April 1720	60	29 April 1720	40	16 June 1720	100	24 August 1720	200
14 June	30	14 September	40	2 January 1721	100	24 February 1721	200
14 August	30	14 January 1721	40	2 July	100	24 August	200
14 October	30	14 May	40	2 January 1722	100	24 February 1722	200
14 December	30	14 September	40	2 July	100	24 August	200
14 February 1721	30	14 December	40	2 January 1723	100		
14 April	30	14 March 1722	40	2 July	100		
14 June	30	14 June	40	2 January 1724	100		
14 August	30	14 September	40	2 July	100		
		14 December	40	2 January 1725	100		
Total	£300		£400		£1000		£1000

Source: Dickson (1967: 125).

[a] This is the revised schedule for the second subscription. The intervals between the later calls were adjusted slightly towards the end of July.

receipts were not delivered out by the Company immediately, or at all in the case of the third and fourth subscriptions. Receipts for the first two money subscriptions appear to have been issued about two months after the subscription dates and the expectation at the time was that receipts for the third and fourth subscriptions would be issued within a similar time frame. The secondary market in subscriptions accordingly consisted of two types of contract: transactions "for money" where buyers paid cash up front in anticipation of receiving receipts when they became available; and contracts for time where the buyers deferred payment until the receipts were received. Sometimes it is unclear to which type of contract quoted prices relate, although from August 1720 Freke quotes two sets of prices for the third subscription, one being "for money" and the other (implicitly) for time, the settlement date in this case being indeterminate.

Sales of subscriptions for money exposed the buyer to substantial risk: there was uncertainty as to when precisely the Company would deliver out receipts; there was the possibility that such receipts might not be delivered out at all (as happened in the case of the third and fourth money subscriptions); and, most important, there was the risk that the counterparty might fail to deliver to the buyer receipts given out by the company. To cover this last possibility some sellers, "not well enough known in the world to be trusted for the delivery of the receipts ... prevailed with some friend to be answerable for the receipts".[32]

Given the above risks, it is not surprising that subscription receipts "for money" sold at a substantial discount relative to receipts sold for time, reflecting the buyer's exposure to settlement risk as well as the interest foregone on money paid down. Accordingly, where prices for both types of contract are quoted by Freke, it seems more appropriate to take the time contracts, subject to an appropriate discount rate to arrive at a spot price equivalent.

The question, then, is what discount rate should be used to calculate a present value equivalent for subscription receipt prices, and also for stock prices during the two month period when the South Sea Company's books were closed and contracts were therefore "for the opening of the books". The following indicators suggest that an interest rate of around 5 percent would be appropriate:

1. The yield on the East India Company bonds, the benchmark short-term interest rate, averaged 5 percent during both the second and third quarters of 1720.

2. From the spring of 1720 both the South Sea Company and the Bank of England lent money freely on the security of their stock, initially at 5 percent and then at 4 percent. The Royal African Company similarly lent at 4 percent on its stock from late July.

3. The South Sea Company from mid-August allowed subscribers to the first and second subscriptions to prepay their remaining calls with the benefit of a 4 percent per annum discount.

4. Although the rates at which individuals borrowed varied enormously, at least some investors were able to borrow from goldsmith-bankers at rates as low as 5 percent in the summer of 1720.

5. Even during September, when the Bubble had burst, the Bank of England was making business loans at 5 percent and discounting bills of exchange at the same rate.[33]

Using a 5 percent discount rate, it is possible to test the rationality of South Sea Company investors by comparing the market price of two substitutable instruments: South Sea Stock and South Sea subscription receipts. Table 9.2 shows for each of the four money subscriptions: (1) the issue price; (2) the present value equivalent of the new issue price; (3) the stock price on the day prior to the new issue; (4) the stock price one week after the new issue; (5) the market price of subscription receipts one week after the new issue; and (6) the price quoted in (5) after adding in the present value of unpaid calls. Since stock and subscription receipts represent equivalent claims on South Sea assets and dividends, the figures in columns (4) and (6) should equate, if investors are behaving rationally.

From table 9.2 it is possible to extract three key variables: first, the premium or discount on each subscription issue price relative to the stock price (applying a present value adjustment to the former); second, the market premium on each new issue relative to the issue price; and third, the market premium of each new subscription relative to the stock price. However, data are missing for the first two subscriptions in columns (5) and (6) because Freke did not begin to publish subscription prices until mid-May (and Castaing later still). Nonetheless, the gap can be filled because Defoe, writing in 1721, tells us that the market prices of the first two subscriptions rose initially to a premium of 10–12 percent over the issue price.[34]

From table 9.3 a clear pattern emerges but it is a very curious one. First, following the successful first subscription which was issued at "fair value" relative to the stock price, subsequent issues were priced at substantial

TABLE 9.2
Stock and Subscription Prices

	(1) New issue price (£)	(2) PV equivalent (£)	(3) Stock price at issue (£)	(4) Stock price one week after issue (£)	(5) Subscription price one week after issue (£)	(6) PV equivalent of (5) (£)
1st subscription 14 April	300	291	294	344	[66]	[297]
2nd subscription 29 April	400	372	339	338	[44]	[376]
3rd subscription 16 June	1000	894	737	763	250	1093
4th subscription 24 August	1000	951	820	812	307	1056
	(1100)[a]	(1046)[a]			307	(1163)[a]

[a] After 10 percent price adjustment.

TABLE 9.3
Stock Versus Subscription Prices

	(1) *PV issue price relative to stock price (%)*	(2) *Market premium relative to issue price (%)*	(3) *PV market premium/ discount relative to stock price (%)*
1st subscription	−1.0	10–12	−13.7
2nd subscription	9.7	10–12	11.2
3rd subscription	21.3	150	43.3
4th subscription	16.0 (27.6)[a]	53.5	28.8 (43.2)[a]

[a] After 10 percent price adjustment.

premiums over the stock price. Second, subscription prices in each case went to a premium over the issue price, one paradox being that the severely "overpriced" third subscription went to by far the largest premium. Finally, while the first subscription sold at a discount relative to the stock price, the third and fourth subscriptions show major upward deviations from the stock price.

A more precise picture of relative valuations of stock and subscription receipts can be obtained by charting the data over the period mid-May to the end of September. This period is selected because Freke's data on subscription prices do not begin until 14 May while from the end of September prices are distorted by the South Sea Company's proposals for relief based on a retrospective adjustment of subscription prices.

Figure 9.1 shows that, as the South Sea stock price fell during August/September, the prices of the third and fourth subscriptions, in particular, held up relatively well, the result being a widening divergence between the price series. Put another way, the discount rate that would equate the present value of the subscriptions with the stock price rose markedly, as shown in figure 9.2.

It might be supposed that by applying higher, and rising, discount rates rather than the 5 percent assumed for the whole period, the various price series could be brought more closely into line. However, we have shown that benchmark interest rates such as East India Bond yields, remained at 5 percent throughout the summer and early autumn of 1720. As far as personal borrowing rates are concerned, the only examples we have of very high interest charges relate to short-term loans of two months or so. On the other hand, the discount rate that would have to be applied to the

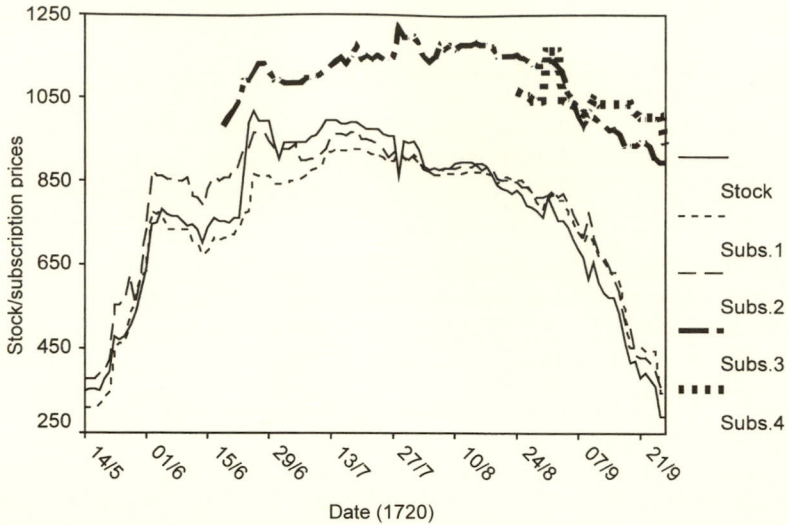

Figure 9.1 Subscription prices relative to stock price. Price series 14 May to 27 September 1720.

third and fourth subscriptions to bring their prices into line with stock price would, towards the end of September, have to be in excess of 100 percent over 1–3 years. Given the level of market interest rates, it is implausible to suggest that such an astronomic discount rate would be appropriate.

Most importantly, varying the discount rate on unpaid calls has little

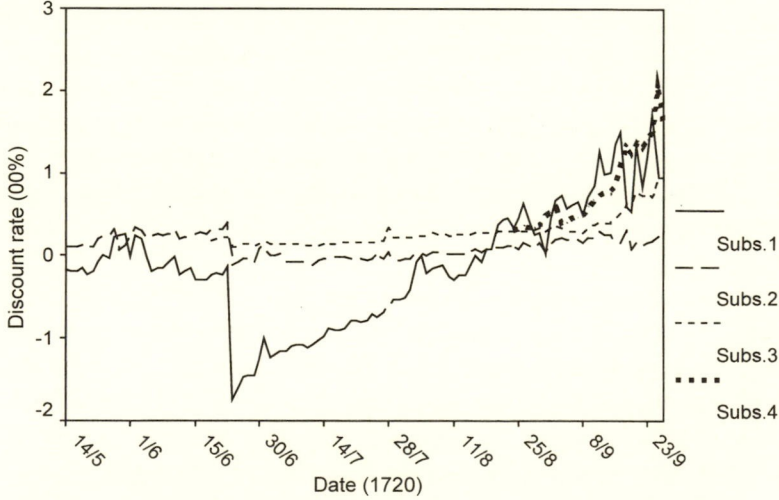

Figure 9.2 Discount rate to equate South Sea stock and subscription prices (1720).

effect on the pricing anomaly between different subscriptions. As figure 9.2 clearly shows, only markedly different discount rates applied simultaneously to each subscription can bring their market values into line with each other. In particular, the second and fourth subscriptions have a similar average life or duration of around 12–18 months; irrespective of the discount rate used, there is a massive disparity in their relative market prices.

There are, therefore, three features of the data that call for explanation. First, why were subscription prices generally priced so extravagantly relative to stock? Second, why did the price of subscriptions, especially the third and fourth, diverge increasingly from the stock price towards the end of the period? And finally, why were the third and fourth subscriptions valued far above the first and second subscriptions? In considering these questions, it is important to understand that investors were free to engage in arbitrage-type transactions.[35] Those who felt that South Sea shares were overvalued were able to short the stock by selling in the forward market (as Blunt appears to have done in the summer of 1720[36]); those who believed that the subscriptions were overvalued relative to stock could sell subscriptions and buy stock (as some investors in the third subscription, in particular, appear to have done[37]); and those who felt that one subscription issue was overpriced relative to another could readily switch between different issues.

On the first question—the extravagant pricing of subscriptions relative to stock—a partial explanation may be that subscriptions were priced as if they were one-way call options on stock. Legally, subscribers were contractually bound to meet all scheduled calls on their subscriptions even if the stock price collapsed, leaving them exposed to losses in excess of the price paid. However, it was improbable that the South Sea Company would take thousands of investors through the courts to enforce contractual calls; arguably, the worst that could happen to subscribers who failed to meet calls would be the cancellation of their subscriptions and their related entitlement to stock. Against this, it should be recalled (p. 145) that Parliament, when it first intervened in the South Sea crisis, was insistent that all subscribers' contractual obligations should be met.[38]

On the second question—the increasing divergence between stock and subscription prices—one important contributory factor could have been distress selling of shares. We know that many investors borrowed heavily on the security of South Sea stock. On the other hand, borrowing on the security of subscription receipts seems to have been largely confined to loans from the South Sea Company for the specific purpose of funding scheduled call payments. In fact, subscription receipts, unlike stock, did not represent "bankable" security since they would become worthless if calls were not paid. Given that borrowing against security was concentrated on South Sea stock, it is probable that distress selling of pledged shares by lenders helps to explain the divergence between the price of stock and subscription receipts during September.

Finally, how can one account for the very different valuations placed on subscriptions? This is, perhaps, the most puzzling discrepancy of all, since investors were attaching wildly different valuations to directly substitutable instruments representing the same claims to assets and dividends.[38] It seems that investors were convinced that each new money subscription would yield substantial "stagging" profits irrespective of the pricing of each issue relative to the stock price. It is also apparent that the company quickly became aware of investors' infatuation with new issues after the first money subscription and thereafter exploited market sentiment by ratcheting up the pricing of each subsequent subscription.

Accordingly the first money subscription was priced cautiously at what might be described as fair value relative to the stock price. The second subscription was priced 10 percent above fair value but nevertheless went to a premium in the secondary market. The third subscription was priced 21 percent above fair value but in short order soared to a premium of 150 percent over the issue price. And, finally, the fourth and final money subscription was priced nearly 28 percent above fair value (adjusting for the fact that this subscription, unlike the others, was not entitled to the 10 percent mid-summer stock dividend) and rose to a premium of over 40 percent in the secondary market, despite the fact that, by that time, the Bubble was beginning to deflate. Significantly, successive money subscriptions also rose to progressively higher market prices relative to the stock price (column (3), table 9.3).

A study of the day-to-day relationship between South Sea stock and subscription receipts using co-integration analysis confirms these core findings; formal statistical investigation shows that there was no relationship between the daily prices of South Sea stock and the prices of the third and fourth subscriptions. Evidently there was a complete breakdown in the pricing mechanism that one would expect, within a rational framework, to establish a long-run equilibrium between these substitutable instruments.[39]

In summary, there is overwhelming evidence to the effect that the South Sea boom represented an irrational bubble. It is clear from Hutcheson's writings that, during the spring and summer of 1720, the price of South Sea stock rose far above its readily determinable fundamental value. It is also clear that subscription receipts generally traded at prices well above, and sometimes far above, the equivalent stock price. And, finally it has been shown that different issues of subscription receipts traded at prices that were dramatically out of line with each other. The only conclusion to be drawn from these valuation anomalies is that, during the Bubble year, the behaviour of South Sea investors became manic and irrational in a way that is difficult if not impossible to reconcile with modern finance theory.

APPENDIX I: HUTCHESON'S SOUTH SEA PARABLE

I shall now give the Reader a short Parallel, which he may easily carry in his Mind, without the Help of Figures; and tho' it does not exactly come up to it, I think it has a very near Resemblance to the South Sea Scheme, as it has been executed. A having 100 l. in Stock, altho' pretty much in Debt, represents it, on account of his beneficial Trade, to be worth 300 l. B, relying on the Wisdom and Integrity of A, prays to be admitted a Partner at that Price, and brings 300 l. into the Stock. On further Consideration, A finds out, that this 100 l. was really worth 500 l. and thereupon C, at his humble Suit, is admitted on those Terms. In a little Time after, A discovers this 100 l. to be worth 1100 l. and thereupon D, more earnest than either of the former Partners, is admitted at that Price, and the Capital is then completed to the Sum of 2000 l. If the Partnership had proceeded no further than A and B, A had got, and B had lost 100 l.; if it had stopt at C, then A had got, and C had lost 200 l. and B had been just where he was, without either Gain or Loss; but D coming into the Scrape, pays for all: For ' tis evident, That 2000 l. divided equally amongst Four Partners, affords to each of them only 500 l. By this, A gains 400 l. and B. 200 l. and C neither gains nor loses; but D loses 600 l. Indeed, if A can shew, that this 2000 l. Capital is really worth 4400 l. there is no Harm done to D, and B and C are highly obliged to him. But if this 2000 l. be worth only 2000 l. and the Benefit of the Trade scarce sufficient to answer the Debt of A before the Partnership, it must be acknowledged, that poor D has had hard measure. It had surely been much fairer Dealing in A, to have brought in all the said Partners equally to the making of his Fortune, and to have set his Stock at the Price of 500 l. The Capital would have then been 1600 l. by which he would have gained 300 l. to himself, and the others had lost only 100 l. a-piece.

Source: Hutcheson (14 July 1720d: 64).

APPENDIX II: TECHNICAL NOTE ON STOCK AND SUBSCRIPTION PRICE DATA

1. John Freke's price-list, called *Freke's Prices of Stock etc.*, ran from 1714 to 1722. The list was published twice per week, each issue covering three days' trading (Wednesday to Friday and Saturday to Tuesday), there being no trading on Sundays. It has been suggested by Larry Neal[40] that Freke's prices were less reliable than those of John Castaing's *Course of the Exchange* which began publication in 1697 and eventually became the official stock exchange price list. The grounds for this allegation are not clear but we have preferred to use Freke's data for the Bubble period, April 1720 to September 1720, because it is more comprehensive; for instance, subscription prices are quoted for periods not covered by Castaing, and for the third and fourth subscriptions, a distinction is made by Freke but not by Castaing, between "for money" and forward subscription prices (see text). The most complete series of Freke's prices are to be found in the British Library but issue no. 96, covering data for 21, 23 and 24 May 1720 is missing.

    Freke was known to be a supporter of the South Sea Scheme but this does not invalidate his prices. He was, after all, running a data business and he would have been well aware of the need to maintain a reputation for accuracy—particularly as he was in direct competition with Castaing. Parsons, who uses Freke in his study of the behaviour of London stock prices, compares Freke's prices with a third source[41] based mainly on quotations in the *Daily Courant*. He finds "reasonable similarity between the two price series".[42]

2. Stocks traded every day except on Sundays, and those days when the company's books were closed to process dividend payments.

3. Freke's data set for subscription prices begins only on 14 May, that is, one month after the date of the first subscription. Subscription prices continue to be available during the rest of 1720 but they cease to be meaningful towards the end of September because from 20 September onwards the South Sea Company was proposing remedial action that would involve retrospective adjustments of the prices at which the third and fourth subscriptions had been issued. Therefore the data set used for the purposes of our analysis is mid-May to the end of September 1720.

4. The South Sea transfer books were closed from 23 June 1720 until 22 August to allow processing of the mid-summer dividend. During

this period quoted stock prices are "for the opening of the books", that is, they are forward prices. To calculate a spot price or present value equivalent a 5 percent per annum discount rate has been applied to the quoted prices.

5. After the books were closed on 23 June, Castaing generally quoted South Sea prices ex-dividend whereas Freke's prices are cum-dividend and therefore approximately 10 percent higher than Castaing's prices. For purposes of comparison with prices prior to closure of the books, the cum-dividend price is the more appropriate since the 10 percent mid-summer stock dividend amounted in effect to a bonus share or capitalisation issue which should not of itself have affected the stock price.

6. The mid-summer 10 percent stock dividend was payable to investors in the first, second and third subscriptions but not the fourth. Therefore a 10 percent upward adjustment is made to quoted prices for the fourth subscription in order to put these on a comparable basis to the first three subscriptions and to the stock price.

7. Freke collected his prices both in the morning and until 3.00 p.m. in the afternoon, sometimes recording as many as three daily prices, both of stock and subscription receipts. Where multiple daily prices are quoted they are averaged.

8. The interpretation of subscription prices is complicated by the fact that transactions in subscriptions receipts, where the receipts had not yet been delivered out by the company, were in effect forward transactions, the (indeterminate) settlement date being the date on which delivery of the receipts was made to the buyer. There were two kinds of forward transactions for subscription receipts, namely: (a) a forward/forward contract where both payment for and delivery of receipts were deferred until the receipts were given out; and (b) a spot/forward contract where payment was made up front against the expectation of receiving the receipts in due course. The latter type of transaction (designated by Freke as "for money") was risky, amounting in effect to an unsecured loan to the seller of receipts, and it also involved loss of interest to the buyer on the money deposited. Accordingly, the spot/forward ("for money") quoted prices are significantly lower than the regular forward/forward prices quoted by Freke. The following choices and adjustments have been made in relation to the subscription price data:

    i. Where Freke gives separate prices for regular and "for money" transactions (as in the case of the third and fourth subscriptions), we use the former on the grounds that settlement risk distorts the latter.

ii. Where no separate prices are given for these two types of transaction, we assume that the prices quoted relate to forward/forward transactions rather than spot/forward. This is consistent with Freke's terminology.

iii. In order to calculate a present value or spot price equivalent for subscription receipts, we apply a 5 percent per annum discount rate to the quoted forward price. For this purpose an assumption has to be made about the expected maturity of the forward transaction, that is, on what date the subscription receipts were expected to be delivered out by the company. Since we know that receipts for the first subscription were given out between six weeks and two months after the issue date,[43] and market expectations would presumably be based on this experience, we assume a two month interval between the issue date of each subscription and the expected delivery of the corresponding receipts.

9. Each subscription price is converted into a (fully paid) stock price equivalent by adding to the quoted price, discounted as per 8 above, the present value of all unpaid calls, using a discount rate of 5 percent per annum. This allows comparison between the stock prices and subscription prices and between subscription prices themselves.

10. For tables 9.2 and 9.3 we use prices for the first and second subscriptions based on Defoe, since Freke's prices for subscriptions do not begin until 14 May. Defoe tells us that the market prices of the first two subscriptions rose initially to a premium of 10–12 percent over the issue price.[44] Prices in these tables relate to transactions one week after the issue date because neither Freke nor Castaing report prices for the days immediately following the third subscription, when trading may have been erratic.

11. Note from the above that a 5 percent discount rate is applied to (a) the forward stock price during the closing of the books, (b) the forward price for subscriptions, and (c) the unpaid calls on subscriptions to arrive at a present value market price. Where the discount rate is varied to equate the subscription price to the stock price (figure 9.2), the discount rate adjustment applies uniformly to (a), (b) and (c).

NOTES

1. For a readable review of bubble theory and evidence, see Hassett (2002).
2. Shiller (2000: 90).
3. Shiller (2000: chapters 8 and 9).
4. Neal (1990: 111).
5. Neal (1990: 90).
6. Carlos et al. (2002: 61–87).
7. Temin and Voth (2004).
8. Scott (1912: 303 ff.).
9. Scott (1912: 313).
10. Scott (1912: 319).
11. Garber (1990: 52).
12. Garber (1990: 48).
13. The following quotations have been cited as evidence of irrational investor behaviour:
    (i) John Martin, banker, who subscribed to £500 worth of South Sea stock in June 1720 with the comment "When the rest of the world are mad, we must imitate them in some measure". Cited in Carswell (1993: 163).
    (ii) William King, Archbishop of Dublin, wrote in May 1720: "I am of the opinion that most that go into the matter (South Sea stock) are well aware it will not [succeed], but hope to sell before the price fall". Cited in Scott (1912: 424).
    (iii) Richard Cantillon wrote as investment adviser to lady Mary Herbert, 29 April, 1720: "People are madder than ever to run into the [South Sea] stock and don't so much as to pretend to go in to remain in the stock but to sell out again to profit ... there appears but a melancholy prospect for those who shall stay in the last". Cited in Murphy (1986: 165).
    (iv) An anonymous pamphleteer wrote in early 1720 "The additional rise of this stock above the true capital will be only imaginary; one added to one, by any rule of vulgar arithmetic, will never make three and a half, consequently, all the fictitious value must be a loss to some persons or other, first or last ... the only way to prevent it to oneself must be to sell out betimes, and so let the Devil take the hindmost." Cited in Carswell (1993: 99).
    (v) The Duchess of Marlborough, on selling her stock in late May, wrote to a friend: "Every mortal that has common sense or that knows anything of figures sees that 'tis not possible by all the arts and tricks upon earth to carry £400,000,000 of paper credit with £15,000,000 of specie. This makes me think that this project must burst in a while and fall to nothing". Cited in Chancellor (1999: 80).
14. Kindleberger (1996: xiii).
15. Carswell (1993: 241).
16. Dickson (1967: 156).
17. Chancellor (1999: 94).
18. Anon (1720h).
19. See, for instance, *The Weekly Journal/Saturday Post* (2 April 1720).
20. See Anderson (1764: 123) and, for example, Melville (1921: 113).

21. See generally Cassidy (2002: chapter 14).
22. Bank of International Settlements, *Annual Report 1999/2000*, p. 107. The BIS showed that in the second half of 1999 the price-earnings ratio of US stocks exceeded two times its historic average while the dividend yield was less than one-third of its historic average. Given similar excesses in other markets around the world, the BIS concluded that "the historically high valuations of major stock markets clearly pose risks of a sharp market-wide correction". In 1999/2000, as in 1720, level headed analysis based on traditional valuation methods pointed to the inevitable bursting of the stock market bubble.
23. Brock (1982).
24. Milner (15 April 1720: 17–18, second letter).
25. Allen and Gale (2000: 236–255).
26. Persaud (2000).
27. Tirole (1985: 1499–1528).
28. The preambles to the subscriptions included the following statement: "... that the cashier ... shall give a receipt or receipts under his hand for the first payment to be paid down as aforesaid upon and for every subscription and that the receipts for all future payments shall be written upon the same paper and that the rights and property of such subscriptions shall be and be deemed to be assignable by indorsement on the said receipts." See *Preambles to Subscriptions*, House of Lords Public Record Office, Parchment Series, Box 157.
29. Carlos et al. (2002: 68).
30. A General Court held on 21 April 1720 resolved that "all such further additions as shall be made to the capital stock of this company before mid-summer next, either by subscription or otherwise shall be entitled to the [10 percent stock] dividend". An advertisement to this effect appeared in the *Daily Courant* of 23 April 1720. The fourth subscription, made on 24 August was, of course, beyond the mid-summer cut-off date although at an emergency meeting of the General Court held on 29 September it was proposed that, in order to relieve the burden on later subscribers, the fourth subscription should be included in the 10 percent mid-summer stock dividend.
31. Cobbett 1806–1820: 666–667).
32. Defoe (1721: 14). In effect the buyer of subscription receipts "for money" was making an unsecured loan to the seller for an indeterminate period.
33. See, for example, Bank of England Minutes of 22 September 1720, *Bank of England Minutes of the Court of Directors* (Bank of England Manuscript Collection).
34. Defoe (1721: 10).
35. Strictly, financial arbitrage involves the simultaneous purchase of an asset against the sale of the same or equivalent asset from zero initial wealth to create a riskless profit from price discrepancies. See, for example, Varian (1987: 55–72). Arbitrage may be ineffective in eliminating price anomalies for a number of reasons, including the presence of transaction costs, settlement lags, settlement risk and limitations on borrowing for arbitrage purposes. See Schleifer and Vishny (1997: 35–55). Given capital market

imperfections during the Bubble period some price discrepancies are to be expected, but the argument here is that the magnitude of these anomalies defies conventional explanations based on arbitrage constraints.

Finally, it might be argued that since we do not have volume figures for trading in South Sea stock or subscription receipts, quoted daily prices might not give a true indication of market values. However, contemporary anecdotal accounts suggest that secondary market activity was heavy, as does the fact that just one individual (Edmund Waller, Aislabie's son in law) could generate a turnover of £700,000 in his South Sea trading account (see chapter 8).

36. See Toland (1726: 432–433).

37. See, for instance, Anon (1720b: 13).

38. Some might argue that subscriptions were in effect options because if the stock price turned out to be less than the future calls, subscribers might be able to walk away from their payment obligation and simply forfeit their stock ownership. At the height of the boom the embedded option is not so important for the first and second subscriptions because they were heavily "in the money" (e.g. £210 to pay on the first subscription when the stock price was £800 or more) and it was therefore improbable that subscribers would have wanted to walk away from their obligation. In contrast, the third and fourth subscriptions were "near the money" at the height of the boom (with remaining payments of £900 and £800, respectively), making it quite probable that subscribers would have wanted to default on future payments. In other words, the embedded option feature was more valuable in the case of the third and fourth subscriptions. However, this interpretation is inconsistent with the pricing of the first (and, to a lesser extent, the second) subscription which for much of the summer traded at a discount relative to stock (see figure 9.1). If subscriptions were viewed as options by the investing public, they would certainly have traded at a premium relative to stock, in recognition of their more limited downside risk. The implication is that subscribers were far from confident that they could simply walk away from their outstanding payment obligations.

This conclusion is further underlined by the fact that subscribers had borrowed nearly £2.25 million from the South Sea Company on the security of subscription receipts at an average rate of £300 advanced for each receipt pledged. (Cobbett, 1806–1820: 738). These borrowings were well in excess of the amounts paid up on the pledged subscriptions, meaning that the subscribers concerned would still owe the Company money if they tried to walk away from their obligations. See Dale et al. (2004).

39. See Dale et al. (2004).

40. Neal (1988: 101).

41. Rogers (1902).

42. Parsons (1974: 67).

43. Receipts had to be given out by the time of the first call on 14 June (since the company was prepared to advance the money due on the security of the receipts), but we know from the South Sea Company's Court minutes that the form of these receipts had not been finalised as of 2 June 1720.

44. Defoe (1721: 10).

CHAPTER TEN

Conclusion

DESPITE ITS STATUS as the most spectacular episode in English financial history the South Sea Bubble had little lasting impact on the British economy. Indeed, economic activity was largely unaffected:[1] industrial output, so far as it can be measured, showed no discernible downturn; overseas trade dipped only very slightly in 1720–1721; and there is no reason to believe that agriculture, the largest sector of the economy, would have been impacted. The resolution of the crisis also ensured that there were no mass bankruptcies,[2] although it is perhaps significant that, according to the bills of mortality, the number of suicides in London jumped by 40 percent in 1721.

Furthermore, the Bubble Act appears to have had little influence on the development of joint stock companies. As one commentator has stated:

> The legal ambiguity of the [Bubble Act], together with a weak enforcement mechanism ... and a widespread disregard of it by businessmen made it practically a dead letter.[3]

Nor was there a major setback to the longer-term development of London's securities market. The Act to Restore the Public Credit of 1721 included provisions against the short selling of stock although in its original form, as passed by the House of Commons, the Bill would have gone much further by altogether prohibiting "the infamous practice of stock-jobbing".[4] The following decade witnessed a continuing debate on the allegedly damaging effects of stock market speculation and in 1734 Parliament finally enacted legislation, known as Barnard's Act, which voided all option contracts, prohibited contracts for differences and reaffirmed the ban on short sales by declaring void all contracts for the sale of stock which the seller was not actually possessed of or entitled to at the time the contract was entered into. However, investors continued to enter into such contracts, even though they could no longer be enforced in the courts, on the basis that "their sense of honour, and the disgrace and loss of future credit, which attend a breach of contract, are the principles by which the business is supported."[5]

In short, from the standpoint of Britain's economic and financial development, the story of the South Sea Bubble may be dismissed as a historical curiosity that hardly deserves the serious attention of financial analysts, economic historians and, still less, business professionals.

However, the events of 1720 do have deep and lasting significance in so far as they offer insights into investor behaviour, not just during the Bubble year, but in today's financial markets. The 1990s global stock market boom and subsequent collapse, and especially the bubble in dot.com and technology stocks, has intensified the debate among financial economists and policy makers about the respective roles of rationality and irrationality in stock market valuations and investment decisions. If we can gain some understanding of investors' motivation during the extreme events of 1720, we may better appreciate the underlying causes of other extreme stock market occurrences, including investors' infatuation with dot.com and technology shares during the late 1990s.

There are, indeed, close parallels between the South Sea Bubble and the dot.com/technology bubble of recent years. In both cases, traditional valuation techniques were abandoned during the boom phase as stock prices reached levels that could be justified only by some new economic paradigm that would transform the prospects for economic growth, productivity and corporate profitability.

In Congressional testimony delivered in July 2000, Alan Greenspan, Chairman of the US Federal Reserve Board, stated that the extravagant stock market capitalisations of the late 1990s "arguably engendered an outsized increase in opportunities for avarice" and that "an infectious greed seemed to grip much of our business community".[6] He went on to suggest that there had been "a once-in-a-generation frenzy of speculation that is now over".[7] Much the same language was used by Hutcheson to describe the London market's mood during 1720 in the wake of the great Mississippi speculation; "... the late frenzy which has reigned amongst us, [being] a pestilential infection from our neighbour nation".[8]

Furthermore, the bursting of both bubbles was accompanied by revelations of financial malpractice. The litany of abuses included the misuse of stock options, insider trading by top management, a breakdown of corporate governance that produced rogue chief executive officers and financial officers (Blunt and Knight in the case of the South Sea Company), the absence of reliable accounts, wildly optimistic earnings and dividend projections and preferential allocations of new stock issues to favoured clients. It was even suggested in 1720 that Exchange Alley stock-jobbers had been bought by the South Sea interest and were no longer acting impartially on behalf of their investment clients,[9] echoing today's concern with conflicts of interest among the investment banking and broking communities.

Clearly both stock market episodes are tales of corporate greed and financial skullduggery but the fundamental question that this study seeks to address is whether the South Sea Bubble provides an example of irrational investor behaviour that may be viewed as a direct lineal forbear of today's stock market turbulence. The argument presented here is that the behaviour of investors during 1720 must indeed be characterised as irrational. Two new pieces of evidence have been offered to support this conclusion.

First the writings of Archibald Hutcheson demonstrated clearly and rigorously that market valuations of the South Sea Company were deviating increasingly from fundamental values during the spring and summer of the Bubble year to the point where, as he foresaw, a crash became inevitable. Hutcheson is the voice of rationality that highlights the loss of reason among the investing public. He made few friends and many enemies by pointing out the fatal flaws in implementation of the South Sea Scheme and his remarkable insights have been too often neglected by modern economic historians, although the first historian of the South Sea Bubble, Adam Anderson, gave him credit for helping to trigger the eventual turn-round in investor sentiment.

Hutcheson's writings are of crucial importance, not necessarily because of their influence on contemporary investors, but because they demonstrate the extent to which established valuation techniques, well known to the London financial community, had been abandoned in the South Sea stampede. In summary, Hutcheson provides important evidence that absolute valuations of the South Sea Company departed from accepted valuation criteria to an extreme degree that amounted to irrationality.

The second piece of evidence is provided by subscription prices which have not previously been analysed. This data demonstrates that relative market valuations as between both stock and subscriptions receipts and between different subscription issues became distorted in a way that defies rational justification. The later subscriptions sold at a substantial valuation premium against South Sea stock; successive subscriptions sold at ever larger premiums; and, at any given point in time, the prices of subscriptions were dramatically out of line with each other. This despite the fact that investors were free to engage in arbitrage transactions, whether by selling subscriptions to buy stock, or by selling one class of subscription receipts to buy another.

In short, at the height of the South Sea boom, investors appear to have lost their ability to price South Sea shares and subscription receipts either in relative or absolute terms. South Sea stock was absurdly overvalued, despite the fact that the Company was known to be little more than an annuity holding enterprise. The later subscriptions, on a straightforward present value basis, were absurdly overvalued relative to South Sea stock. And, most tellingly, subscription receipts were trading at prices that were absurdly out of alignment with each other. If all this does not provide overwhelming evidence of irrationality on the part of investors, it is difficult to know what would.

There is one important clue as to the true motivation of investors at this time. The four South Sea money subscriptions were issued by the Company at successively higher prices relative to the stock and yet the price which each issue sold for in the market represented successively higher premiums on the issue price. Investors were evidently "stagging" each partly paid issue in the confident expectation of being able to sell out at a profit before further calls were made, almost regardless of the issue price set by the Company. The implication is that investors "trusted" the Company to set the terms of each new issue, and to manage subsequent issues, in a way that would guarantee profits to subscribers.

That there was a popular perception that the South Sea Company would guarantee the success of each new issue, and thereby ensure profits to speculators, is supported by two other circumstances. First, South Sea directors claimed at the time that they were under constant pressure from the investing public to make new issues of stock,[10] suggesting that the speculative focus was on stagging each new issue rather than on buying fully paid stock or subscription receipts in the secondary market, even though the latter might be cheaper. Second, as described in chapter 6, annuitants agreed to convert their holdings of government debt on terms to be decided unilaterally by the South Sea Company, presumably in the belief that the Company could be trusted to look after their interests and ensure advantageous terms.

Of course, once investors' trust was shattered by revelations of corporate malpractice, the disillusionment that set in accentuated the flight from equities and the ensuing stock market crash. In much the same way, the investing public's over-reliance on bullish investment analysts and wildly optimistic corporate earnings projections at the height of the

1990s dot.com boom led to a savage retreat from stocks when corporate malpractices and Wall Street scams were uncovered.

Although the two stock market episodes are nearly three centuries apart, the observations of Archibald Hutcheson and Alan Greenspan on the breakdown of trust are remarkably similar. Hutcheson focussed his comments after the collapse of the South Sea Bubble on the damage done to "... the general trust and confidence in dealings betwixt man and man without which it is impossible to carry on the trade and commerce of every nation."[11] Alan Greenspan gave similar emphasis to the restoration of trust in the aftermath of the dot.com bubble:

> Our market system depends critically on trust—trust in the word of our colleagues and trust in the word of those with whom we do business. Falsification and fraud are highly destructive of free market capitalism and, more broadly, to the underpinning of our society.[12]

Finally, it is worth noting that the management of the South Sea Scheme bore an uncanny resemblance to the government's earlier lottery loans. Lotteries returned the money that ticket buyers paid in, partly through the guaranteed minimum return or "dividend" and partly through the allocation of winners' prizes. In the same way, the South Sea Company issued new shares with a view to returning the cash proceeds to subscribers by way of dividends rather than for the purpose of funding business investment. Furthermore, it will be recalled that the hugely popular "Two Million Adventure" lottery devised by Blunt in 1711 offered five successive lottery draws, each yielding a higher maximum prize than the last. The longer participants stayed in the game the more they stood to gain. South Sea investors similarly appear to have believed that each successive subscription issue offered the prospect of higher capital gains, as if they were trading lottery tickets in different draws, the latest always having the highest value.

This analogy with lotteries perhaps becomes more persuasive when one considers that Blunt, according to the Secret History, always insisted that the Company's money should be lent, not to "traders and other such fair dealers" but rather to "those who frequented the Alley and to Ladies and young Gentlemen, who came from the other end of Town [the West End], with a spirit of gaming" since these "were the most likely to advance the price of the stock".[13]

Interestingly, in seeking to explain the boom in internet stocks in 1999/2000, Alan Greenspan also invoked the lottery analogy in a rather different context:

There is something else going on here, though, which is a fascinating thing to watch. It is, for want of a better term, the 'lottery principle'. What lottery managers have known for centuries is that you could get somebody to pay for a one-in-a-million shot more than the value of that chance. In other words people pay more for a claim on a very big pay-off, and that's where the profits from lotteries have always come from. So there is a lottery premium built into the prices of internet stocks.[14]

Given the obvious parallels between the South Sea Bubble and more recent stock market events, the key conclusion of this study—that investor behaviour was demonstrably irrational in 1720—has a direct bearing on today's financial markets and the continuing debate on investor rationality. Some may argue that it would be a mistake to draw general conclusions from a single stock market episode and that financial markets have become more rational over time in response to improvements in disclosure, corporate governance and investor protection legislation as well as greater investor understanding of risk and diversification.[15] On the other hand, the story of the South Sea Bubble recounted here shows clearly that, with all the admitted deficiencies in the securities trading environment of 1720, investors still ignored the information and recognised valuation methods that were readily available to them.

Paradoxically, the most recent interpretations of the South Sea Bubble have tended to downplay or deny irrationality, emphasising instead the difficulties of stock valuation during a period of rapid financial innovation. These revisionist histories have, in an important sense, unlearned the lessons of the past and obscured the message of Adam Anderson's original history of the Bubble written nearly 250 years ago. Anderson justified his description of "the unaccountable frenzy in stocks and projects of this year 1720" on the grounds that memory of such events would serve "as a warning to after ages".[16] The present study claims no more than to have reaffirmed Anderson's cautionary conclusion that from time to time markets can go mad.

Sceptics may ask if, at the end of the day, it matters very much whether the South Bubble was irrational or not. After all, as indicated earlier, the Bubble was short-lived and had little discernible impact on economic activity. It should be stressed, however, that irrationality may, in different circumstances, inflict serious economic damage. Extended stock market bubbles of the kind experienced by Japan in the 1980s and by the United States in the late 1990s can result in systematic mispricing of assets over several years, leading to a misallocation of resources, excess business capacity and severe dislocation when the bubble eventually deflates. If financial markets are susceptible to periodic bouts of irrational investor behaviour, it is important that investors themselves, business decision makers and, above all, economic policy makers, are aware of this so that they can take protective, if not preventive, action. In this important sense, the extraordinary scenes to be observed in Exchange Alley during 1720 have a message for us today.

NOTES

1. For a discussion of the economic impact of the Bubble, see Hoppit (2002: 141–165).
2. See Hoppitt (1986: 39–58). It is worth noting, however, that since bankrupts were imprisoned, which would have the effect of reducing their capacity to pay, bankruptcy proceedings tended to be used primarily as a threat to induce payment by those who were judged able to pay, rather than as an enforcement measure against those who could not. See Neal and Quinn (2001: 21–22).
3. Harris (1994: 623).
4. See Banner (1998: 81–82).
5. Anon (1816: 15).
6. Greenspan (2002: 4).
7. Greenspan (2002: 5).
8. Hutcheson (1723: 11).
9. *The London Journal* (18 March 1721) claimed that stock brokers had become agents of the South Sea Company: "Their office is an office of trust .... They are obliged to discharge their duty impartially between man and man .... Now it is well known that they broke their trust to the publick; that they ceased to be common and indifferent officers in the Alley; and yet retaining the name and pretence of their office ... they became only spies and liars for the Directors [of the South Sea Company] and their managers and sellers for them only."
10. See Blunt (1732: 39–41) and Dickson (1967: 127).
11. Hutcheson (1723: 17).
12. Greenspan (2002: 4).
13. Toland (1726: 446).
14. Cited in Cassidy (2002: 202).
15. See, for instance, Smith (2001).
16. Anderson (1764: 123).

Glossary

Contracts for time: contracts for forward delivery

Exchange Alley (or Change Alley) street adjacent to the Royal Exchange which became the central location for securities trading

Exchequer Bill: a printed "promise to pay" issued by the Exchequer, bearing interest; such Bills were allowed to circulate like currency but only for a limited period before being paid off and cancelled

The Funds: the market for government debt obligations

Floating debt: short-term government debt for which no specific parliamentary, or other, provision had been made for repayment

Lottery loans: loans to the government repaid in the form of lottery prizes; the prizes, although expressed as a lump sum, were paid out as interest over a fixed period

Long annuities: government annuities for terms of years expiring between 1792 and 1807

Redeemable debt: debt that could be redeemed at the option of the government (cf. irredeemable debt, e.g., fixed term annuities)

Refusals: call options

Royal Exchange: grandiose building at the centre of London's financial district, housing the City's money, ship-broking and commodity markets

Short annuities: government annuities for a term of years expiring 1742

Scrip: partly paid shares/subscription receipts

Subscription: general term covering both the conversion of government debt into South Sea stock and the purchase for cash of newly issued South Sea shares in the primary market on a partly paid basis ("money subscription")

Subscription receipts: signed receipts issued against partly paid new shares; being transferable through a simple legal assignment the receipts could be actively traded on a secondary market

Tallies: receipts issued against sums lent short-term to the Exchequer, charged on anticipated tax revenues

Unfunded debt: see Floating debt

POLITICAL

Glorious Revolution: in 1688, William of Orange displaced James II as King of England at the invitation of the English Parliament, becoming William III; this peaceful changeover became known as the Bloodless or Glorious Revolution

Jacobite: supporter of the Stuart claimant to the thrones of England and Scotland

Pretender: James Stuart, exiled claimant to the English and Scottish thrones

Restoration: the restoration of the English monarchy under Charles II in 1660, following the protectorship or Commonwealth of Oliver Cromwell

Tories: One of the two mainstream political parties in England, associated with the landed interest, the Church of England and support for the royal prerogative

Whigs: political party opposed to the Tories, associated with religious dissent, the moneyed interest or merchant class and support for a constitutional monarchy

Bibliography

Aislabie, John (1721) *Mr Aislabie's Second Speech on his Defense in the House of Lords, on Thursday July 20, 1721* (London).

Allen, Franklin and Gale, Douglas (2000) Bubbles and Crises. *Economic Journal* 110: 236–255.

Anderson, Adam (1764) *An Historical and Chronological Deduction of the Origin of Commerce, From the Earliest Accounts*, Vol. III (London).

Anon (n.d.) *The Case between the Proprietors of Newspapers and the Coffee-Men of London and Westminster Fairly Stated* (London).

Anon (n.d.) *The Case of the Coffee House Men* (London).

Anon (1667) *News from the Coffee House* (London).

Anon (1720a) *An Argument to Shew the Disadvantage That Would Accrue to the Publick, From Obliging the South Sea Company to Fix What Capital Stock They Will Give for the Annuities* (London).

Anon (1720b) *The Case of the Contracts for the Third and Fourth Subscriptions to the South Sea Company Considered, in a Letter to a Member of Parliament* (London).

Anon (1720c) *A Farther Examination and Explanation of the South Sea Company's Scheme. Shewing, That It Is Not the Interest of the South-Sea Company to Offer the Annuitants Such Terms as May Induce Them to Come In; And That the Proposal of the Bank is More Likely to be Accepted by the Annuitants, and the Publick Not Disappointed* (London: 8 March).

Anon (1720d) *A Full Confutation of the Subscribers Pretensions to Receipts for the First Payment, Made Upon the Third and Fourth Subscriptions: Wherein the True Case of the Sellers of Those Subscriptions is Examined and Answerd, In a Letter to a Noble L–d* (London: 1 February).

Anon (1720e) *A Full and Impartial Account of The Company of the Mississippi: Otherwise Call'd the French East-India Company, Projected and Settled by Mr Law : With an Account of the Establishment of the Bank of Paris by the Said Mr Law: To Which Are Added a Description of the Country of Mississipi and a Relation of the First Discovery of It; In Two Letters From a Gentleman to his Friend, in French and English* (London: Printed for R. Francklin and four others).

Anon (1720f) *An Impartial Enquiry into the Value of South Sea Stock. With Some Thoughts of the Occasion of the Present Decay of Trade and Credit: And Some Means Proposed for Restoring the Same*. In a letter to Sir Richard Steele, knt. (London).

Anon (1720g) *The Nature of Contracts Consider'd: As They Relate to the Third and Fourth Subscriptions Taken In by the South Sea Company: In a Letter to a Friend, With a Postscript Concerning the Meeting at Salters-Hall the 18th Instant; By a Tradesman of the City* (London).

Anon (1720h) *Remarks on the Celebrated Calculations of the Value of South Sea Stock, in the Flying Post of the 9th of April 1720 ... In Order to Remove the*

Aspersions Thereby Cast on the Present Contract with the Company (London).

Anon (1720i) *Remarks upon Several Pamphlets Writ in Opposition to the South Sea Scheme: Particularly an Examination and Explanation of the South Sea Scheme etc and a Further Examination and Explanation etc* (London).

Anon (1721a) *The Case of the Right Honourable John Aislabie Esq* (London).

Anon (1721b) *Letter to Mr Law Upon his Arrival in Great Britain* (London: 11 November).

Anon (1721c) *A Reply to a Modest Paper, Call'd, Reasons for Making Void Fraudulent and Usurious Contracts* (London).

Anon (1721d) *The Reports of the Committee of Secrecy to the Honourable House of Commons Relating to the Late South Sea Directors* (London).

Anon (1721e) *A State of the Case Between the South Sea Company and the Proprietors of the Redeemable Debts* (London).

Anon (1724) *A Report of a Case Argued and Adjudged in the Court of Exchequer and Affirmed in the House of Lords, Relating to a Contract About South Sea Stock, Term. Sanct. Mich. Anno IX, Georgii Regis, inter Harcourt & Thomson* (London).

Anon (1729) *The Case between the Proprietors of Newspapers and the Subscribing Coffee Men Fairly Stated* (London).

Anon (1816) *The System of Stock-Jobbing Explained* (London).

Ashton, John (1898) *History of Gambling in England* (London: Duckworth & Co).

B., A. (1720) *An Impartial Enquiry Into the Value of South Sea Stock, With Some Thoughts of the Occasion of the Present Decay of Trade and Credit: And Some Means Proposed for Restoring the Same*. In a letter to Sir Richard Steele, knt. (London). Introductory letter signed A.B.

Balen, Malcolm (2002) *A Very English Deceit, the Secret History of the South Sea Bubble and the First Great Financial Scandal* (London: Fourth Estate).

Bank of England (1720) *Bank of England Minutes of 22 September 1720 of the Court of Directors* (Bank of England Manuscript Collection).

Bank of International Settlements (1999–2000) *Bank of International Settlements Annual Report 1999–2000*.

Banner, Stuart (1998) *Anglo-American Securities Regulation, Cultural and Political Roots 1690–1860* (Cambridge: Cambridge University Press).

Bateson, F. W. (Ed.) (1951) *Epistle to Several Persons, Alexander Pope*, Vol. III, part 2 (London).

Bernstein, Peter L. (1996) *Against the Gods, the Remarkable Story of Risk* (New York: John Wiley).

Black, Jeremy (1987) *English Press in the 18th Century* (Philadelphia, PA: University of Pennsylvania Press).

Blunt, Sir John (1732) *A True State of the South Sea Scheme, As It was First Form'd etc With the Several Alterations Made In It Before the Act of Parliament Pass'd. And an Examination of the Conduct of the Directors in the Execution of That Act. With an Enquiry Into Some of the Causes of the Losses Which Have Ensued. As Also an Abstract of Several Clauses of the Acts of Parliament, Made Against Those Directors, and the Grounds of Them; With Some Remarks on the Whole* (London); the first edition was published in 1722. Attributed to Sir John Blunt.

Boys, Thomas (1825) *The South Sea Bubble, and the Numerous Fraudulent Projects to Which it Gave Rise in 1720, Historically Detailed as a Beacon to the Unwary Against Modern Schemes Equally Visionary and Nefarious* (London: Ibotson and Palmer).

Brewer, John (1989) *The Sinews of Power: War, Money and the English State, 1688–1783* (New York: Knopf).

Brock, William (1982) *Speculative Hyperinflations in Maximising Models*. Working paper, University of Wisconsin, Madison, NJ.

Carlos, Ann, Moyen, Nathalie and Hill, Jonathan (2002) Royal African Company Share Prices During the South Sea Bubble. *Explorations in Economic History* 39: 61–87.

Carruthers, Bruce (1996) *City of Capital* (Princeton, NJ: Princeton University Press).

Carswell, John (1993) *The South Sea Bubble*, revised edition (Dover: Alan Sutton).

Cassidy, John (2002) *dot.con* (London: Allen Lane/Penguin Press; New York: Harper Collins).

Castaing, John (1720) *The Course of the Exchange* (London).

Chancellor, Edward (1999) *Devil Take the Hindmost, A History of Financial Speculation* (London: Macmillan).

Chandler, G. (1964) *Four Centuries of Banking, as Illustrated by the Bankers, Customers and Staff Associated with the Constituent Banks of Martins Bank Limited*, Vol. 1 (London: Batsford).

Clapham, Sir John H. (1944) *The Bank of England, A History* (Cambridge: Cambridge University Press).

Clark, Geoffrey (1999) *Betting on Lives; The Culture of Life Insurance in England, 1695–1775* (Manchester: Manchester University Press).

Cobbett, William (1806–1820) *Parliamentary History of England* (London: T. C. Hansard).

Collier, Jeremy (1713) *An Essay Upon Gaming in a Dialogue Between Callimachus and Dolomedes* (London).

Cowles, Virginia (1960) *The Great Swindle: The Story of the South Sea Bubble* (London: Collins).

Cruickshanks, Eveline, Handley, Stuart, Hayton, D. W. (Eds.) (2002) *The History of Parliament: The House of Commons 1690–1715*, Vol. IV (Cambridge: Cambridge University Press).

Dale, Richard (1995) Bank Crises Management: the Case of the United Kingdom. *Journal of International Banking Law* 8: 326–333.

Dale, Richard, Johnson, John J. and Tang, L. (2004) *Financial Markets Can Go Mad: Evidence of Irrational Behaviour During the South Sea Bubble* (In press).

Darwin, Kenneth (1950) John Aislabie (1670–1742) A Study in Augustan Politics and Hanoverian Finance. *Yorkshire Archaeological Journal* 262–324.

Daston, Lorraine (1988) *Classical Probability in the Enlightenment* (Princeton, NJ: Princeton University Press).

Defoe, Daniel (1869) *Defoe's Uncollected Works*. William Lee (Ed.) (reprinted 1968).

———— (1719) *Anatomy of Exchange Alley or a System of Stock-Jobbing* (London); reprinted in Francis (1849).

_____ (1721) *A True State of the Contracts Relating to the Third Money Subscription Taken by the South Sea Company* (London).

De la Vega, Joseph (1688). *Confusion de Confusiones*. A modern translation is to be found in Fridson (1996: 147–211).

Dickson, P. G. M. (1967) *The Financial Revolution in England: A Study in the Development of Public Credit 1688–1756* (London: Macmillan; New York: St Martin's Press).

Emmett, Ross B. (2000) *Great Bubbles: Reactions to the South Sea Bubble, the Mississippi Scheme and the Tulip Mania Affair*, 3 volumes (London: Pickering and Chatto).

Equitable Life Assurance Society (September 2001) *Background to the Proposed Compromise* (London).

Erleigh, Viscount (1933) *The South Sea Bubble* (London: Peter Davies).

Ewald Jr, William Bragg (1956) *Newsmen of Queen Anne* (Oxford: Basil Blackwell).

Faure, Edgar (1978) *La Banqueroute de Law 17 juillet 1720* (Paris: Gallimard).

Francis, John (1849) *Chronicles and Characters of the Stock Exchange* (London: Willoughby & Co).

Freke, John (1720) *Freke's Prices of Stocks, etc.* (London).

Fridson, Martin S. (Ed.) (1996) *Extraordinary Popular Delusions and the Madness of Crowds and Confusion de Confusiones* (New York: John Wiley).

Garber, Peter M. (Spring 1990) Famous First Bubbles. *Journal of Economic Perspectives* 4: 35–54.

Giraud, M. (1966) Histoire de la Louisiane francaise. *L'Epoque de John Law 1717–1720*, Vol. 3 (Paris).

Gleeson, Janet (1999) *The Moneymaker* (London: Bantam Books).

Goodalle, Thomas (1721) *Everyone's Interest in the South Sea Examined, and by Rules of Justice and Equity Settled, to their Reciprocal and Mutual Advantage* (London).

Gordon, Thomas (1724) *An Essay in Stock-jobbing* (London).

Gower, L. C. B. (April 1952) A South Sea Heresy. *Law Quarterly Review* 68: 214–225.

Gray, W. (1721) *The Memoirs, Life and Character of the Great Mr Law and his Brother at Paris* (London).

Greenspan, Alan (2002) *Testimony Before the Committee on Banking, Housing and Urban Affairs* (US Senate, 16 July) p. 4.

Hanson, Laurence William (1936) *Government and the Press 1695–1763* (Oxford: Oxford University Press).

Harris, Michael (1938) *London Newspapers in the Age of Walpole, a Study of the Origins of the Modern English Press* (Madison, NJ: Fairleigh Dickinson University Press).

Harris, Ron (1994) The Bubble Act: Its Passage and its Effects on Business Organisation. *The Journal of Economic History* 54(3): 610–627.

Harrison, Paul (2001) Rational Equity Valuation at the Time of the South Sea Bubble. *History of Political Economy* 33(2): 269–281.

Harsin, Paul (1928) *Les Doctrines Monétaires et Financières en France du xvi au xviii Siecle* (Paris: Librairie Felix Alcan).

Hassett, Kevin (2002) *Bubbleology: The New Science of Stock Market Winners and Losers* (New York: Crown Business).

Heckscher, Eli F. (1930–1931) A Note on South Sea Finance. *Journal of Economic and Business History* 321–328.

Historical Register (1721) Vol. 6.

Hoare's Bank: A Record, 1673–1955 (London: Collins, 1955).

Hoppit, Julian (1986) Financial Crises in Eighteenth Century England. *Economic History Review* XXXIX(1): 39–58.

_____ (2002) The Myths of the South Sea Bubble. *Transactions of the Royal Historical Society* 12: 141–165.

Hough, Richard (1995) *Captain James Cook* (London: Hodder & Stoughton).

Houghton, John (1692 and 1694) *Collection for Improvement of Husbandry and Trade* (London).

Hunter, Paul (1990) *Before Novels: the Cultural Contexts of Eighteenth Century English Fiction* (New York, London: Norton).

Hutcheson, Archibald (1720a) *Collection of Calculations and Remarks Relating to the South Sea Scheme and Stock, Which Have Been Already Published With an Addition of Some Others, Which Have Not Been Made Publick 'Till Now* (London).

_____ (1720b) *Some Calculations Relating to the Proposals Made by the South-Sea Company and the Bank of England, to the House of Commons; Shewing The Loss to the New Subscribers, at the Several Rates in the Said Computations Mentioned; and the Gain Which Will Thereby Accrue to the Proprietors of the Old South Sea Stock* (London: 31 March).

_____ (1720c) *Some Seasonable Considerations for Those, Who Are Desirous, by Subscription, or Purchase to Become Proprietors of South-Sea Stock with Remarks on the Surprizing Method of Valuing South-Sea Stock, Publish'd in the Flying Post of Saturday, April 9th 1720* (London: 21 April).

_____ (1720d) *Several Calculations and Remarks Relating to the South Sea Scheme and the Value of that Stock* (London: 14 July).

_____ (1720e) *A Supplement to the Aforegoing Calculations and Remarks* (London: 28 August).

_____ (1720f) *An Estimate of the Value of South-Sea Stock with Some Remarks Relating Thereto* (London: 24 September).

_____ (1720g) *An Additional Supplement to the Aforegoing Calculations and Remarks Stating the Value of South-Sea Stock According to the Alterations Which Have Been Lately Made in the Scheme of that Company* (London: 14 October).

_____ (1720h) *To the Author of the Calculations in the White-Hall Evening Post* (London: 20–30 October).

_____ (1720i) *An Appendix to Mr Hutcheson's Calculations and Remarks Relating to the South-Sea Company* (London: 30 November).

Four Treatises relating to the South Sea Scheme and Stock published since 30 November 1720: viz. 7 January, 6 February, 1 March 1720 and 4 April 1721 and a fifth added dated 13 May 1721:

Hutcheson, Archibald (1720j) *Some Computations Relating to the Proposed Transferring of Eighteen Millions of the Funds of the South Sea Company to* the Bank, and East India Company Shewing How the Same Will Come Out on Two Different Suppositions, to the Old Proprietors of Bank and India, and to the New Proprietors of the Ingrafted Stock (London: 7 January).

_____ (1720k) *A Computation of the Value of South Sea Stock on the Foot of the Scheme as it Now Subsists* (London: 6 February).

_____ (1720l) *Some Computations and Remarks Relating to the Money Subscribers and the Proprietors of the Publick Debts. And a Letter Relating Thereto to the Sub-Governor, Deputy-Governor, and Directors of the South Sea Company* (London: 1 March).

_____ (1721a) *Some Further Computations Relating to South Sea Stock with a Proposal Made Therefrom, To Be Laid before the House of Commons at the Meeting of the Parliament* (London: 4 April).

_____ (1721b) *A Proposal for the Relief of the New Proprietors in the South Sea Company. And a State of the Value of the Reduced South-Sea Capital, According to the Said Proposal* (London: 13 May).

_____ (1720m) *A Letter to the Author of the Calculations in the Whitehall Evening Post, Relating to South Sea Stock Shewing the Mistakes in the Said Calculations and These Being Rectified What the Present Value of South Sea Stock Is* (London).

_____ (1723) *Some Paragraphs of Mr Hutcheson's Treatises on The South-Sea Subject: Which Relate to the Relief of the Unhappy Traders in South Sea Stock and to Publick Credit. And the Reason of his Reprinting Them at this Time. To Which is Added, a Near Estimate of the Value of South Sea Stock, if the Bill Now Order'd to be Brought In, Pass Into a Law* (London).

Hyde, Harford Montgomery (1969) *John Law; the History of an Honest Adventurer* (London: W. H. Allen).

Johnson, Samuel (1755) *A Dictionary of the English Language* (London: J and P Knapton).

Kindleberger, Charles P. (1996) *Manias, Panics, and Crashes: A History of Financial Crises*, 3rd edition (New York: John Wiley).

Lillywhite, Bryant (1963) *London Coffee Houses* (London: George Allen & Unwin).

Mackay, Charles (1996) *Extraordinary Popular Delusions and the Madness of Crowds, 1841*. In Martin S. Fridson (Ed.) (New York: John Wiley).

McCusker, John (1986) The Business Press in England before 1775. *The Library*, Sixth Series VIII(3): 205–231.

McFarland Davis, Andrew (1887) An Historical Study of Law's System. *The Quarterly Journal of Economics* I(3): 289–318.

Melville, Lewis (1921) *The South Sea Bubble* (London: Daniel O'Connor).

Milner, James (1720) *Three letters Relating to the South Sea Company and the Bank, the First Written in March 1719/20, the Second in April 1720, the Third in September 1720 Now First Publish'd, by James Milner Esq* (London).

Minutes of the Court of Directors of the South Sea Company (British Library).

Morgan, E. Victor and Thomas, W. A. (1962) *The Stock Exchange, its History and Functions* (London: Elek Books).

Mortimer, Thomas (1762) *Every Man his Own Broker or a Guide to Exchange Alley*, 2nd edition (London).

Murphy, Antoin E. (1986) *Richard Cantillon: Entrepreneur and Economist* (Oxford: Clarendon Press).

_____ (1997) *John Law Economic Theorist and Policy Maker* (Oxford: Clarendon Press).

Neal, Larry (1988) The Rise of a Financial Press: London and Amsterdam, 1681–1810. *Journal of Business History* 30(2): 163–178.

_____ (1990) *The Rise of Financial Capitalism, International Capital Markets in the Age of Reason* (Cambridge: Cambridge University Press).

_____ (2000) The Money Pitt: Lord Londonderry and the South Sea Bubble; or How to Manage Risk in an Emerging Market. *Enterprise and Society* 1: 659–674.

Neal, Larry and Quinn, Stephen (2001) Networks of Information, Markets, and Institutions in the Rise of London as a Financial Centre, 1660–1720. *Financial History Review* 8(1): 21–22.

Parsons, Brian (1974) *The Behaviour of Prices on the London Stock Market in the Early Eighteenth Century*, PhD (Chicago: University of Chicago).

Persaud, Avinash (2000) *Sending the Herd off the Cliff Edge* (Institute of International Finance: December).

Plumb, J. H. (1956) *Sir Robert Walpole, The Making of a Statesman* (London: Cresset Press).

Pope, Alexander in F. W. Bateson (Ed.) (1951) *Epistle to Several Persons, Alexander Pope*, Vol. III, part 2 (London).

Preambles to Subscriptions. House of Lords Public Record Office, Parchment Series, Box 157.

Robinson, E. F. (1893) *The Early History of Coffee Houses in England* (London: Kegan Paul & Co).

Rogers, Therold (1902) *A History of Agriculture and Prices in England* (Oxford: Clarendon Press).

Roseveare, Henry (1991) *The Financial Revolution 1660–1760* (London: Longman).

Schleifer, Andrei and Vishny, Robert W. (1997) The Limits of Arbitrage. *Journal of Finance* 62(1): 35–55.

Schubert, Eric Stephen (1988) Innovations, Debts and Bubbles: International Integration of Financial Markets in Western Europe, 1688–1720. *Journal of Economic History* XLVIII(2).

Scott, William Robert (1912) *The Constitution and Finance of English, Scottish and Irish Joint Stock Companies to 1720*, Vol. 3 (Cambridge: Cambridge University Press).

Sedgwick, Romney (1970) *The History of Parliament: The House of Commons 1715–1754*, Vol. II (London: HMSO).

Shiller, Robert J. (2000) *Irrational Exuberance* (Princeton, NJ: Princeton University Press).

Silverman, Gary (2002) Fears grow over capital market freeze. *Financial Times* 17 February.

Smith, B. Mark (2001) *Towards Rational Exuberance: The Evolution of the Modern Stock Market* (New York: Farrar, Straus and Giroux).

South Sea Company Minutes of the Court of Directors (British Library).

Sperling, J. G. (1962) *The South Sea Company, An Historical Essay and Bibliographical Finding List* (Cambridge, MA).

Steele, Sir Richard (under alias Sir John Edgar) (1720) *The Theatre* (London).

To the State of the Contracts and Other Obligations by Bonds and Notes Entered Into by Colin Campbell, Esq, Anno 1720. In Add. MS 17477 (British Library) notes drawn up in 1748-9 by Adam Anderson for submission to Charles Erskine.

Temin, Peter and Voth, Hans-Joachim (2004) Riding the South Sea Bubble. Discussion paper 4221 (London: Centre for Economic Policy Research).

Thomas Harrison, Appellant, Moses Hart and Isaac Franks, Respondents, the Appellant's Case (1727) (London).

Tirole, Jean (1985) Asset Bubbles and Overlapping Generations. *Econometra* 53(6): 1499–1528.

Toland, John (1726) The Secret History of the South Sea Scheme. *A Collection of Several Pieces of Mr John Toland, Now First Publish'd From his Original Manuscripts; With Some Memoirs of his Life and Writings* (London). Later published under *The Miscellaneous Works of Mr John Toland* by Mr Pierre Des Maizeaux (1747).

Trenchard, John (1720a) *A Comparison Between the Proposals of the Bank and the South Sea Company. Wherein it is Shewn, That the Proposals of the First are Much More Advantageous to the Publick, Then Those of the Latter* (London).

_____ (1720b) *An Examination and Explanation of the South Sea Company's Scheme for Taking in the Public Debts. Shewing, That it is Not Encouraging to Those Who Shall Become Proprietors of the Engrafted Stock, to Join With the Present Proprietors of the Company, at Any Advanced Price. And That it is Against the Interest of Those Proprietors Who Shall Remain with Their Stock Till They are Paid Off by the Government, That the Company Should Make Annually Greater Dividends Than Their Profits Will Warrant. With Some National Considerations and Useful Observations* (London).

Varian, H. R. (1987) The Arbitrage Principle in Financial Economics. *Economic Perspective* 1(2): 55–72.

Weiller, Kenneth and Mirowski, Philip (1990) Rates of Interest in 18th Century England. *Explorations in Economic History* 27: 1–28.

Wilson, Charles (1941) *Anglo Dutch Commerce & Finance in the 18th Century* (Cambridge: Cambridge University Press).

Wood, John Philip (1791) *Sketch of the Life Projects of John Law of Lauriston, Comptroller General of the Finances in France* (London).

_____ (1824) *Memoirs of the Life of John Law of Lauriston Including a Detailed Account of the Rise, Progress and Termination of the Mississippi System* (London).

CONTEMPORARY JOURNALS

The Daily Courant

The Daily Post

Evening Post

The Flying Post

The London Gazette

The London Journal

The Observer

The Post Boy

The Postman

The Tatler

The Theatre

The Weekly Journal (John Applebee)

The Weekly Journal or Saturday's Post (Nathanial Mist)

Whitehall Evening Post

Index